Jersey Norman French

A Linguistic Study of an Obsolescent Dialect

D1615148

Publications of the Philological Society, 34

Jersey Norman French

A Linguistic Study
of an
Obsolescent Dialect

Mari C. Jones

Publications of the Philological Society, 34

Oxford UK & Boston USA

Copyright © The Philological Society 2001

ISBN 0–631–23169–2

First published 2001

Blackwell Publishers
108 Cowley Road, Oxford, OX4 1JF, UK

and
350 Main Street,
Malden, MA 02148, USA.

British Library Cataloguing in Publication Data
A catalogue record for this publication is available from the British Library

Library of Congress Cataloging-in-Publication Data
Applied for

Typeset by Joshua Associates Ltd., Oxford
Printed in Great Britain by
MPG Books Ltd, Bodmin, Cornwall

I Mam a Dad

CONTENTS

ACKNOWLEDGEMENTS

Writing this book has been made possible by the generosity of many people. First and foremost, I would like to thank the fifty informants who provided the data on which this work is based. Their willingness to spend time being interviewed and recorded made the fieldwork a truly enjoyable experience. Special thanks must go to Anthony Scott Warren, Jean le Maistre, François le Maistre, Ralph and Jayne Nichols, Angela Le Pavoux and, in particular, Dr Frank Le Maistre.

I would also like to express my gratitude to Professor Nancy Dorian and Professor April McMahon for their invaluable advice during the period in which the book was written and for their constructive comments on a previous draft, and to Dr Keith Brown, Secretary for Publications of the Philological Society, for his help with the preparation of the manuscript. The work was written with the aid of research leave funded by the Arts and Humanities Research Board.

Finally, on a personal note, I would like to thank my parents, Philip and Eirwen Jones, for their constant support and encouragement and to dedicate this book to them.

LIST OF FIGURES

LIST OF MAPS

LIST OF TABLES

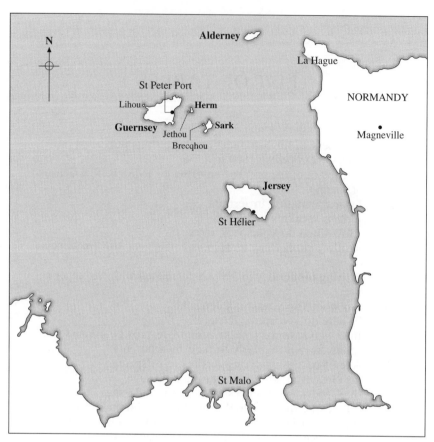

Map 1 The Channel Islands

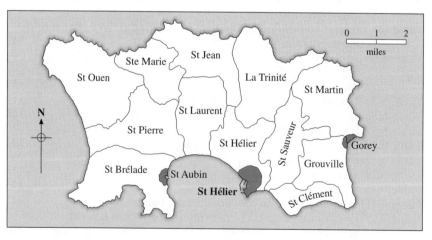

Map 2 The twelve parishes of Jersey

1

INTRODUCTION

Fewer languages will exist in the third millennium than in the second. According to current estimates, some six thousand different vernaculars are now spoken in the world and, of these, about half will probably die out during the next hundred years (Krauss 1992). As Crystal (1999) points out, this means that, on average, the world loses one speech variety every fortnight.

Language death is neither a recent nor an uncommon phenomenon. Hittite and Etruscan are well-known examples of varieties which became extinct in prehistory and which have left precious little trace. Dorian (1981: 1–2) also describes how, during the twentieth century, dying languages were attested and documented all over the world. However, it is only since the early 1970s that the field of language death has become established as a separate sub-discipline of linguistic study, and much of the thanks for this must go to Dorian herself.

It would be wrong, however, to assume that the field of language death is concerned with dead languages. Languages only die with the disappearance of their last native speaker and, at this point, they are little more than curiosities – they cannot develop and, in most cases, have no function.[1] Within linguistics, language death is the study of varieties which are typically undergoing both reduction in terms of their speaker numbers and territorial contraction. In its strictest conceptual sense, it is the end point of the process of linguistic obsolescence, characterized by Bauman (1980) as a situation where:

(i)   an age gradient of speakers terminates in the adult population
(ii) the language is not taught to children in the home
(iii) the number of speakers declines very rapidly
(iv) the entire (speaking) population is bilingual and English is preferred in essentially all situations
(v)   the language is inflexible, it no longer adapts to new situations
(vi) there is no literacy.[2] (cited in Dauenhauer and Dauenhauer 1998: 59)

Obsolescent languages are not inherently different in nature from so-called 'healthy' ones – two varieties may undergo similar types of linguistic change but while such change is, in one case, associated with obsolescence, in the other there are no such connotations. Take, for example, the phenomenon of borrowing. In English, this is neither stigmatized nor an indication of obsolescence while, for varieties such as Scots Gaelic (Abalain 1989: 103) or Breton (Dressler 1991: 102–3), it is considered a sure sign of attrition. In fact, the types of linguistic change recorded in dying and 'healthy' varieties differ very little and it is the sheer quantity of these changes, rather than their precise nature, together with the rate at which they occur and the sociopolitical situation of the variety in question, which make them indicative of language obsolescence. It should also be emphasized that the term 'language death' is not prescriptive – indeed, it is impossible to foretell the fate of any variety with great accuracy. Languages may survive with very few speakers,[3] and, as seen in Haiti, strong entrenchment can often compensate for a lack of prestige (Cobarrubias 1983: 55). It is also possible that, with a change in the sociopolitical context, revitalization may occur. Moreover, the existence of mixed languages such as Copper Island Aleut (Vakhtin 1998) and Ma'a (Thomason and Kaufman 1988: 223–8) indicates that to speak of 'living' versus 'dying' languages may often be to over-simplify the situation.

The complexity of issues involved in the decline of a variety within its native speech community has meant that, as Grenoble and Whaley point out, most comparative work on threatened languages tends to focus on the points they have in common rather than on the characteristics that separate them (1998: 22).[4] Indeed, several linguists, including Grenoble and Whaley themselves, have attempted to establish a typology or classification of language-death situations.

The most frequently cited of these classifications is that described by Campbell and Muntzel (1989: 182–6), who mention four possible scenarios:

(i) *sudden death*, where there is language loss due to the sudden death, or massacre, of most of a variety's speakers, such as in the case of Tasmanian.

(ii) *radical death*, where loss is similarly rapid and is usually due to severe political repression, often with genocide, with the result that speakers stop using the language out of self-defence. This was seen, for example, in El Salvador in the early 1980s, when many people stopped speaking their native languages in order to avoid being identified as Indians, and thus killed.

(iii) *gradual death*, where a language is lost in a contact situation, with the dominant language gradually ousting the subordinate – often minority – variety. The scenario typically involves intermediate stages of bilingualism, an age-governed proficiency continuum, where young speakers tend to be least proficient in the dying language and older speakers most proficient, and the existence of one or more generations of semi-speakers (Dorian 1981: 107).

(iv) *bottom-to-top death*, where a language is lost in intimate contexts and remains exclusively in ceremonial usage. This category is rarer and is illustrated by Campbell's own fieldwork in South America, where he found four men who were able to recite several prayers in South-eastern Tzeltal, which speakers of other Tzeltal dialects were unable to translate as they no longer used this form of ritual language.[5]

The case of Jèrriais, the Norman dialect spoken on the Island of Jersey, is of interest to the field of language obsolescence since it does not 'fit' any of the four categories outlined above. Although the variety has been suffering a decline in speaker numbers since the nineteenth century, the progression towards obsolescence has taken less time than in most case studies found in the literature, which frequently describe varieties treading a slow, albeit steady, path towards extinction, as Campbell and Muntzel's term 'gradual death' implies. Unlike most dying varieties, which may have a large number of older-generation speakers and fewer in each subsequent generation so that, to all intents and purposes, they gradually peter out, with Jèrriais no such marked age-continuum is present: native speakers are relatively easily locatable amongst Jersey-born inhabitants over the age of sixty but speakers under this age are thinner on the ground and very few native speakers are to be found under the age of forty. In other words, intergenerational transmission of Jèrriais has ceased completely and comparatively abruptly.

As seen above, Campbell and Muntzel give the names 'sudden death' and 'radical death' to more rapid types of linguistic extinction. These are both triggered by catastrophic events in a variety's sociopolitical context and involve either the death or massacre of the native speech community, or at least fear of the latter. Although the linguistic situation of Jèrriais conforms to neither of the above scenarios, one easily identifiable catastrophic event did undeniably loom large in its history, namely the Second World War (Bunting 1996). In 1940, realizing that it would be impossible to defend the Channel Islands effectively against the German army, the British government decided to demilitarize. The Islands were subsequently invaded and were occupied by Germany until 1945. At the time of demilitarization, Islanders were given the opportunity of being evacuated to the mainland, an offer which, on Jersey, was taken up by some 10,000 people (out of a population of some 51,000), and included many women and children. The evacuees did not return to Jersey until the end of the war. The evacuations therefore meant that many of Jersey's then children and teenagers spent five years in Great Britain and, as a corollary of this, were forced, during this time, to have almost exclusive recourse to the language with which their native tongue was in competition. Unlike Campbell and Muntzel's 'radical death' (1989: 183), the severe political repression experienced by the Islanders who lived under German Occupation did not encourage them to stop speaking Jèrriais – if anything, it became a strong motivation for them to use it – but the result of these events brought about a marked change in circumstances after the German surrender in 1945. Although the Second World War did not literally result in the death of a significant number of the Jèrriais speech community, then, the German Occupation of the Island during this period did lead to the elimination of many of its members from Jersey for the best part of five years, and meant that a considerable proportion of the Island's children were denied the opportunity to grow up in a Jèrriais-speaking environment, and hence the potential to speak Jèrriais as their first language. Those who had been evacuated as infants or young children had grown up with English as their native tongue and few of these ever became truly bilingual in Jèrriais. Moreover, despite the fact that speakers of Jèrriais were able to renew their acquaintance with their native tongue on returning to Jersey after the war, many older children and younger adults had either forgotten their Jèrriais or preferred not to use it, seeing English as a more fashionable, progressive variety, the language of social advancement and the key that unlocked the world outside the Island, whereas Jèrriais effectively locked its speakers into Jersey. Many parents considered proficiency in English to be far more beneficial to their offspring and thus made little attempt to teach them the native dialect. Dorian (1998: 3) mentions that it is common for a variety to become so exclusively related to a low-prestige people that its potential speakers prefer to distance themselves consciously from it and speak another language. This seems to have been true of Jèrriais-speaking parents at that time, who sought to provide their children with a different identity (or, at least, a means to escape their identity). Therefore, although the widespread Anglicization of the Island from the nineteenth century onwards meant that Jèrriais had certainly taken its first steps on the path to obsolescence before the outbreak of the Second World War, the unprecedented population movement which was brought about by the war in the space of half a decade had repercussions for both the Islanders' ability in, and their attitudes towards, Jèrriais, and this greatly precipitated the process of obsolescence.

On Jersey, therefore, there exists a situation whereby language obsolescence began gradually but seems to have been speeded up by a catastrophic event which greatly accelerated speaker reduction both physically, by taking many Islanders away from Jersey during the war, and also psychologically, by holding up English as the symbol of the outside world. As such, the circumstances seem to represent a mixture of both gradual and radical death, although, unlike in El Salvador, the language death following the catastrophic event was instigated indirectly rather than directly by the perpetrators of the political repression.[6]

Language death is found in all language families and on all continents. Indeed, Hill suggests that 'at least half the languages in the world have disappeared in the last 500 years' (1978: 69). Many of these varieties have vanished with little or no trace, taking with them valuable information about linguistic change. Although the work of Spence has provided detailed information on the phonology of Jèrriais (see, for example, Spence 1957a, 1957b, 1985, 1987, 1988) and that of Brasseur has attempted to situate the different varieties of Norman with respect to one another (Brasseur 1978a,

1978b), other than this, to date much of the academic writing on Jèrriais consists of occasional articles, such as Mason (1980), where Jèrriais is studied as a comparison with mainland Norman, rather than in its own right. A wealth of writing by dialect enthusiasts also exists but, as these individuals have generally received no linguistic training, such work tends to be largely comprised of general discussions on the state of the dialect (see, for example, Le Maistre 1947, 1981) or on a particularity of the lexis (see, for example, Le Feuvre 1979).

By undertaking a detailed examination of Jèrriais, this book presents a case study of an obsolescent variety whose sociolinguistic history differs from the more common 'gradual death' pattern but which, unless effective revitalization measures are implemented within the very near future, will nevertheless be to all intents and purposes dead in thirty so so years. As obsolescence is a sociolinguistic process rather than an exclusively linguistic one (Hoenigswald 1989: 353; Dressler 1981: 5), the study will attempt to give equal prominence to the external setting, speech behaviour and structural consequences of the process, described by Sasse (1992a: 19) as the interacting factors that come into play in a situation of this kind. As such, the work is of importance to the field of language obsolescence by offering a case study which differs from the more common 'gradual death' scenario and also helps answer Schmidt's appeal for more empirical evidence to be gained about terminal language stages (1985: 5).

The second and third chapters provide essential background information for readers unfamiliar with Jèrriais. Chapter 2 gives an account of the sociohistorical setting against which Jèrriais has developed. It also explains why the Channel Island varieties of Norman show the effect of prolonged contact with English, the language that is currently playing an instrumental role in their demise, rather than with mainland varieties of Norman, from which the Channel Island varieties differ significantly.

Chapter 3 gives a brief description of the phonology of Jèrriais, outlining its differences from standard French and illustrating the most salient ways in which it diverges from the other Channel Island varieties and from Mainland Norman. It also discusses the extensive regionally determined internal variation which is to be found within the dialect.

Chapters 4 and 5 examine the 'external' situation of Jèrriais. Chapter 4 draws a sociolinguistic profile of the speech community, based on data gathered by means of a survey undertaken in July 1996 of a sample of fifty native speakers of Jèrriais. Although, as will be seen in chapter 2, the 1989 Census of Jersey was able to establish the *number* of Jèrriais speakers for the first time, it did not provide any information on the *nature* of the speech community. Chapter 4, therefore, represents the first attempt of its kind to remedy this situation. The methodology and sampling technique used for the fieldwork are also presented in this chapter.

Chapter 5 documents the language planning that is currently being undertaken as part of the campaign to revitalize Jèrriais. As well as examining the major driving forces and institutions behind the movement, it discusses recent examples of corpus planning and focuses on issues such as the embryonic standardization of Jèrriais and its implications for the future of the dialect.

Chapters 6 and 7 focus on the 'internal' situation of Jèrriais by examining linguistic developments attested in the contemporary dialect. They draw extensively on original data collected via tape-recorded interviews and lexical questionnaires. In both cases, the sample consists of the same informants as in chapter 4.

Chapter 6 examines linguistic developments at two levels. In the first instance, there is an analysis of the change taking place in the morphosyntax and lexis of Jèrriais, which has resulted in a situation whereby contemporary Jèrriais often differs significantly from traditional descriptions of the dialect. While it is demonstrated that some of these developments are undoubtedly due to contact with English, it becomes clear that others are more ambiguous in terms of their motivation. The second type of development discussed is phonological in nature and serves to illustrate the unpredictable nature of obsolescent varieties. Despite the fact that the Jèrriais setting seems to be ripe for the occurrence of a form of koinéization between the highly localized sub-dialects, analysis of the corpus revealed far more resistance to such levelling than had been anticipated.

Chapter 7 is intended to complement chapter 6 by extending the discussion of the lexis undertaken in that chapter to encompass the concept of lexical erosion. Terminology from ten common speech domains is examined in order to determine the relative vitality of different terms in everyday usage.

Chapter 8 is an attempt to complete the linguistic picture by considering the possible influence of Jèrriais on local varieties of French and English spoken on the Island, as well as possible recent influences of standard French on Jèrriais. Constraints of time and resources precluded as extensive or systematic a study of these varieties as that undertaken for Jèrriais in chapters 6 and 7. However, the analysis of Jersey English was undertaken on the basis of original data gathered from notes and observations made during field trips to Jersey between 1996 and 2000. The data used to examine the influence of standard French on Jèrriais are taken from the same recordings as those analysed in chapter 6 and represent 'intrusive' features that appeared so often in the speech of informants as to warrant further comment. The discussion of the influence of Jèrriais on the French of Jersey is based not on original data but, rather, on a reanalysis of data collected by Hublart (1979). All three types of influence examined in this chapter would make interesting subjects of study in their own right, and it is hoped to extend this analysis in the near future.

2

THE SOCIOHISTORICAL SETTING

Lying off the coast of Normandy in the Bay of St Malo, the Channel Islands form part of a small archipelago in the English Channel. Despite their status as dependencies of the British Crown, the Islands are actually situated geographically closer to France than to the United Kingdom (see map 1). With an area of 45 square miles, Jersey, the southernmost island of the archipelago, is also the largest (measuring 10.8 miles by 6.8 miles) and most populous island[1] and, together with two rocky reefs, known locally as the Minquiers and the Ecrehous, it forms its own bailiwick. The other islands, in descending order of size, are Guernsey, Alderney, Sark, Herm and Jethou. These form the bailiwick of Guernsey.

As will be demonstrated, its proximity to France has influenced Jersey's history from the earliest times right through to the present day. Archaeological evidence suggests that people have lived on the Island for some 80,000 years. Human occupation probably took place during the last Ice Age, when the Island was joined to the French mainland, and, in Roman times, the Channel Islands formed part of the province of Gaul, when Jersey was known as Andium.[2] During the Gallo-Roman period, the indigenous language of the Islands at that time – probably Gaulish – was, as on the mainland, gradually replaced by Vulgar Latin, the variety which, after centuries of evolution, has given rise to modern Jèrriais.

Despite Jersey's Gallo-Roman linguistic heritage, its modern name is of Norse origin.[3] The ending -ey, meaning 'island', is also seen in the names of two other members of the archipelago, Guernsey and Alderney, and, although the precise meaning of the first syllable is unclear, suggestions range from the Norwegian personal name Geirr, perhaps denoting a pirate who may once have seized the Island, to the Frisian word gers, which would make Jersey 'the grassy isle'.

The Norsemen were to influence Jersey far more than in terms of its toponymy. During the ninth century, their raids on the French coasts led to the French king, Charles the Simple, purchasing peace with Rollo, the Viking chief, in the Treaty of Saint-Clair-sur-Epte in 911. The land yielded under the treaty became known as the Normans' Land, or Normandy, to which the Channel Islands were annexed by Rollo's son, William Longsword, in 933.

As the Channel Islands formed part of the duchy of Normandy, Jerseymen may well have been part of William I's victorious army at the battle of Hastings in 1066. Although this victory meant that, during the next century and a half, the realms of England and Normandy were often held by the same ruler,[4] it was to the latter that the Channel Islands looked in terms of their administration, culture and language. Indeed, the twelfth-century poet Wace, author of the *Roman de Brut* and *Roman de Rou*, heralded as two of the most important works of medieval French literature, was a Jerseyman:

> Jo di et dirai que je suis
> Wace, de l'isle de Gersui.[5,6]
> *Roman de Rou*, l. 5322

After the death of Richard the Lionheart, a dispute over the rightful successor to the joint kingdoms left the door open for King Philippe Auguste of France to invade Normandy against King John of England and, in 1204, Normandy became part of the kingdom of France.

Despite their strong ties with Normandy, the Channel Islands were not subjugated to French rule in 1204 and, when King John's son, Henry III, formally renounced his claim on mainland Normandy in the Treaty of Paris (1252), no mention was made of them. The Channel Islands now officially formed part of the kingdom of England. However, there was no concomitant Anglicization: indeed, Jersey was allowed to remain part of the diocese of Coutances and no attempt was made to introduce English law to the Island. Although its political allegiance had changed, Jersey continued to have strong links with France – its main industry during medieval times, fishing, would undoubtedly have brought the Islanders into contact with the fishermen of the Cotentin, and the coins they used were struck at the French mint at Tours.

The fact that the Channel Islanders did not speak English was of no great consequence during the medieval period due to the fact that, at that time, official documents were written in Latin. Moreover, ever since 1066, Norman French had been the language of polite society, schools, courts and the law in England and, in the towns, even a few of the poorer people had some knowledge of both languages. However, within a century and a half, the situation had begun to change, and a major role in this was played by two significant events. First, the Hundred Years War against France encouraged the feeling in England that it was unpatriotic to speak the language of the enemy and, secondly, the decimation of the English population which occurred during the Black Death gave rise to a serious shortage of labour. This in turn increased the economic importance of the labouring classes and with it the importance of the English language that they spoke (Baugh and Cable 1993: 139). Within a relatively short space of time, Norman French gradually ceased to be spoken in England. English gained respectability as a literary medium with the writings of Chaucer and its dominance was assured with the advent of the printing press a century later.[7]

England, therefore, became increasingly English-speaking, with Norman French used less and less and Latin reserved for the church. The Extente of

1528, a survey of Jersey written in English (the only previous one so far discovered is dated 1331 and is written in Latin), indicated that the visiting officials had trouble with Jersey names. Henceforth, the languages of Jersey and England would be mutually unintelligible.

The fifteenth century was a period of social and political change for Jersey. It saw its rights and privileges reaffirmed under monarchs such as Henry IV and Edward IV but in 1461, during the War of the Roses, the Island was seized by a French force under Jean Carbonnel and was held for seven years. This was but one in a series of French invasions of Jersey, and even though, encouraged by the church, Edward IV and Louis XI agreed that the Channel Islands should remain neutral if their countries were at war – a period of neutrality which was to last officially for more than 200 years, until it was annulled by William III in 1689 – the threat from France was not entirely removed. In 1549, a French expedition was launched against the Islands. Although it was routed both in Guernsey and Jersey, the French held Sark for nine years and, during this time, were a constant menace to the other Channel Islands.

The fifteenth century also saw changes on the religious front. In 1496, Henry VII obtained a bull from Pope Alexander Borgia transferring the Channel Islands from the diocese of Coutances to that of Salisbury.[8] Despite the fact that, in practice, the bishops of Coutances continued to serve and to administer the Islands, the Act of Uniformity of 1549 put an end to all Latin religious services and decreed that Cranmer's First Prayer Book be used all over the kingdom. The fact that a French translation of the Prayer Book was issued for use in the churches of Calais, Guisnes, Jersey and Guernsey in April 1550 is proof that, at this time, Jersey was still strongly francophone.[9] There is, however, evidence that, during the fifteenth century, knowledge of English was on the increase among the upper echelons of Jersey society. For example, Syvret and Stevens (1998: 59) note that Thomas Le Hardy, Seigneur of Mélèches, and Philippe de Carteret, Seigneur of St Ouen,[10] both had English wives.

English appears to have played a part in the daily life of Jersey since at least the fifteenth century. The Channel Islands enjoyed profitable trading links with English, Welsh and Irish ports as well as those of France, the link with Southampton being especially important, and, from Elizabethan times, the fishing and knitting industries both played a significant role in the Island's prosperity. An English garrison had been established in Mont Orgueil Castle (Gorey) to defend Jersey against the French since the Middle Ages, but numbers of English soldiers were relatively small. However, the conquest of the Island by Cromwell's troops in 1651 brought large numbers of English soldiers to Jersey, and the revocation of neutrality between France and England in 1689 also heralded the arrival of large military units at both Mont Orgueil and St Hélier (cf. De Guérin 1905). The troops had a clear effect on the language of the vicinity, bringing the tradespeople and inhabitants of St Hélier into regular contact with English, and their influence was to remain constant for many decades. Indeed, at the time of the Battle of Jersey (1781), the Island was garrisoned by 1,000 regular soldiers and 3,000 militiamen.

The combined influence of visiting traders, the garrisons and the increasing possibility of working in London left its mark on the Island linguistically. In the second edition of his *Account of the Island of Jersey* (1734), Philippe Falle made the following comments:

> Albeit French be our ordinary language, there are few gentlemen, merchants or considerable inhabitants, but speak English tolerably. The better to attain it, they are sent young to England. And among the inferior sort who have not the like means of going abroad, many make a shift to get a good smattering of it in the Island itself. More especially in the town of St Hélier, what with this, what with the confluence of the officers and soldiers of the garrison, one hears well-nigh as much English spoken as French. And accordingly the weekly prayers in the Town Church, are one day in French, and another in English. (1734: 125–6)

Syvret and Stevens also note that, during this period, English and French versions of Christian names were interchangeable, stating that Mr James Amice Lemprière, a member of Jersey's first Chamber of Commerce (1768), might well have been referred to as Jacques Amyas (1998: 193). However, despite the gradual encroachment of English, evidence that French still predominated on Jersey may be seen from the fact that, in 1709, alongside *The Groans of the Inhabitants of Jersey*, a political pamphlet attacking the States (the Island's main legislative body) and other officials, which was published anonymously in London, there appeared a French version for use on the Island. Furthermore, before 1800, the six journals regularly published on Jersey were all written in French.[11] The presence of French on the Island can only have been reinforced by the arrival of thousands of French aristocrats during the French Revolution. Their numbers were swollen in 1792 when 1,800 priests who had refused to take an oath of loyalty to the new Constitution also sought to make their home on Jersey after being expelled from France.[12,13]

The linguistic situation at the beginning of the nineteenth century is captured by two travel writers. The first of these, John Stead, wrote in his *A Picture of Jersey* (1809) that, in St Hélier, most young people could write both English and French and that Jèrriais was 'daily falling into disuse and discredit, and doubtless in a few years hence English will be the only prevailing language' (Seren-Rosso 1990: 37). Although it is likely that bilingualism was on the increase in St Hélier, at least, his remarks on Jèrriais seem to present an overly pessimistic picture and certainly do not tally with Henry Inglis's assessment of the situation in 1830s, namely: 'The universal language is still a barbarous dialect' (1844: 72). Inglis describes a Jersey where Jèrriais was still very much the common tongue – even among the gentry – and where knowledge of standard French and English was still quite limited:

> French, though the language of the court proceedings, and of the legislature, is not in common use even among the upper ranks; nay, the use of it, is even looked upon as affectation; and although the English language be sufficiently comprehended for the purposes of intercourse, and is most usually spoken in the best mixed society, it is certainly not understood by many, in its purity. (1844: 72)

However, the signs of Anglicization were also plain to see:

> Children are now universally taught English; and amongst the young, there is an evident preference of English. The constant intercourse of the tradespeople with the English residents; and the considerable sprinkling of English residents in Jersey society, have also their effect. (1844: 73)

Moreover, the political environment of the eighteenth and early nineteenth centuries, a period which saw the battle of Jersey against the French and further threat of attack during the Napoleonic wars, must surely have produced an atmosphere conducive to the learning of English. Indeed, the early nineteenth century is held by many as the start of the Anglicization 'proper' of the Channel Islands: 'C'est à partir de cette epoque, après 1815, que la langue anglaise commence à se répandre et à être couramment parlée dans les îles, ce qui n'avait pas été le cas jusque-là' (Guillot 1975: 47).[14] This can be seen all too clearly by comparing the numbers of English and French journals published on the Island at the beginning and end of the century (table 2.1).

The main reasons behind this progressive, and increasingly rapid, Anglicization were numerous. In 1824, two rival companies established weekly paddle steamer services transporting both passengers and goods between Southampton, Portsmouth and Jersey and, in 1831, this was supplemented by a service from London. The introduction of the paddle steamers, together with the fleet of mailboats which also carried passengers, meant that

Table 2.1 Numbers of English and French journals published on Jersey from before 1800 to 1978

Journals	Before 1800	1800–25	1825–50	1850–75	1875–1900	1900–25	1925–50	1950–78	Total
French	6	4	7	7	2	1	0	0	27
English	0	6	15	16	5	4	7	3	56

Source: after Hublart 1979: 38

thousands of British people now came to visit Jersey.[15] Indeed, by 1840, there were said to be 15,000 English residents, forming almost a separate colony within the Island's society (Uttley 1966: 174). As the total resident population of Jersey at that time was 47,544, this means that English-born people formed 31.54 per cent of all the Island's residents. That these incomers were numerous, and did not learn Jèrriais – or French – may be seen from events such as the Methodists' decision to build a chapel for their English-speaking members in 1827 and the fact that ten weekly English-language papers were published on the Island at that time (Syvret and Stevens 1998: 242–3). In the early nineteenth century, some 2,000 men from England and Ireland came to work in the fisheries at Grouville Bay and these were followed, in 1847, by 800 English labourers engaged to help build St Catherine's breakwater. Trade links with Britain were also strengthened during this period.

By the last quarter of the nineteenth century, many wealthy English families were settling on Jersey, attracted by its climate, low taxation and good educational facilities. Moreover, newspaper advertisements show that the tourist trade had grown to such an extent that many hotels had sprung up and it was common for Islanders to supplement their income by taking in lodgers: in 1882, 29,263 visitors came to Jersey and, by 1891, this number had increased to 42,803. The incursion of English was almost certainly felt more in the town parishes than in rural ones but, although it may have precipitated a certain degree of bilingualism in urban areas, it by no means wiped out Jèrriais, which continued to be spoken by most of the indigenous population, as can be seen from the fact that, in the early 1870s, the banners proclaiming the enlargement of the harbour in St Hélier were written in Jèrriais. However, the English way of life was gaining ground inexorably: in 1834, the States abolished Jersey's centuries-old currency – the *livre tournois*, the *sou* and the *liard* – and adopted the English system of pounds, shillings and pence, and the small independent Jersey banks started to be taken over by large English companies. Other signs of the Anglicization of the Island during this period can be seen from, first, the fact that, from its foundation in 1833, the minutes of the Royal Jersey Agricultural and Horticultural Society were published in English, a highly significant decision in view of the importance of agriculture on Jersey, and, secondly, that, in 1841, 63 per cent of children in St Hélier were recorded as having English first names. In 1858, Jersey and Guernsey were connected to the British telegraphy system (Uttley 1966: 181), and in 1919, the old Jersey liquid measures were abandoned in favour of the English ones. Anglicization was also prevalent in the domain of education: in 1852, Victoria College was opened on the model of the English public school. Its lessons were conducted exclusively through the medium of English and many teachers forbade their charges to speak Jèrriais. Use of English was not, however, restricted to one educational establishment. In 1862, Anstead and Latham tell us that 'In all the parishes in the various Islands there are schools for the education of the children of the farmers and small proprietors. In these, instruction is given in French and English' (1865: 553).

By the end of the nineteenth century, there is evidence that the indigenous Jersey-folk had realized that the increasing Anglicization posed a potential threat to Jèrriais:

> The Old language still lives and we certainly will not give it its death blow
> – for we respect its grey hairs too highly. If we desire to preserve our old
> patois, we must not neglect French, which is the language of our
> Churches, of our legislature, and of our Law-Courts, in short, the
> language of our civilization. Let it become still more the language of
> education, and that not only in our elementary schools but also in our
> Colleges. Let us give as much attention to French as we do to English. Let
> it not be to us a dead language. And while we are proud of belonging to
> the British Crown, let us never forget that we are pre-eminently Norman.
> We ask in conclusion, is it not an advantage, at a time when everything is
> becoming Anglicized, to be able to understand Wace and the Trouveres;
> to think at once with Shakespeare and with Corneille; to meditate with
> Milton and with Racine, and to dream with Byron and with Lamartine.
> (Le Gros 1883: 25)

> Les temps changent; la navigation à vapeur, après avoir été une source de
> prospérité pour l'archipel, pourrait bien aussi déterminer sa ruine. Ces îles
> sont désormais trop près de Londres; l'élément anglais s'y implante
> rapidement, et trop de voix intéressées jasent sur ce petit monde.[16]
> (N. N. 1849: 962)

According to Fleury, however:

> Les Anglais, maîtres de cette île depuis plus de huit cents ans, font des
> efforts inouïs pour l'angliciser. Le monde officiel, le monde commercial
> sont de plus en plus anglais, mais la population indigène a conservé
> l'idiome natal et parle le patois normand.[17] (1886: 1)

Certainly, the fact that Jèrriais was still spoken widely througout the Island at this time was recorded by Victor Hugo in *L'archipel de la Manche*:

> L'Archipel de la Manche parle le français, avec quelques variantes,
> comme on voit paroisse qui se prononce *paresse*. On a 'un mâ à la
> gambe qui n'est pas commua'. – Comment vous portez-vous? – Petite-
> ment. Moyennement. Tout à l'aisi. C'est à dire mal, pas mal, bien. Être
> triste, c'est 'avoir les esprits bas'. Sentir mauvais, c'est avoir 'un mauvais
> sent'; causer du dégât, c'est 'faire du ménage'; balayer sa chambre, laver
> sa vaiselle, etc., c'est 'picher son fait'; le baquet, souvent plein d'immon-
> dices, c'est 'le bouquet'. On n'est pas ivre, on est 'bragi'; on n'est pas
> mouillé, on est 'mucre'. Être hypocondriaque, c'est avoir 'des fixes'. Une

fille est une 'hardelle', un tablier est un 'devantier', une nappe est un 'doublier'; une robe est un 'dress', une poche est une 'pouque', un tiroir est un 'haleur', un chou est une 'caboche', une armoire est une 'presse', un cercueil est un 'coffre à mort', les êtrennes sont des 'irivières', la chaussé est 'la cauchie', un masque est un 'visagier', les pilules sont des 'boulets'. Bientôt, c'est 'bien dupartant'. . . . *Noble* est un des mots les plus usités dans ce français local. Toute chose réussie est un 'noble train'. Une cuisinière rapporte du marché 'un noble quartier de veau'. Un canard bien nourri est 'un noble pirot'. Une oie bien grasse est 'un noble picot'. La langue judiciaire et légale à, elle aussi, un arrière-goût normand. Un dossier de procès, une requête, un projet de loi sont 'logés au greffe'. Un père qui marie sa fille ne lui doit rien tant qu'elle est 'couverte d'un mari'.[18] (1883: 55–6)

However, in spite of such remarks, that the tide was slowly turning in favour of English may be illustrated by an examination of its changing fortunes in the States (Hublart 1979: 33–4). On 16 February 1893, a bill calling for English to be used in debates was defeated by 26 votes to 6. An amendment was subsequently passed in which the States recorded that they wished to reaffirm their loyalty to the crown, but they also stated that they considered French 'comme un héritage trop précieux pour être désavoué ou modifié'.[19] Only seven years later, on 2 February 1900, a bill to make English optional in the same debates was carried by 26 votes to 15 and, significantly, when the same amendment was proposed as in 1893, it was rejected by 26 votes to 17. In 1928, the Income Tax Law became the first piece of legislation to be drafted entirely in English, and use of English in this domain increased during the 1930s.[20] In 1946, the States approved the view put forward by some of its members, who were appearing before a Privy Council committee, that English should be the recognized language of the States, with French henceforth reserved for formal and official occasions (Le Hérissier n.d.: 149), and in 1966, English also replaced French as the language in which the official record of States proceedings was kept (Bois 1976). Today, French is used only for opening prayers, oral voting and other ceremonial usage and, apart from the occasional exception, all new pieces of legislation are drafted in English.

The changing fortunes of English in the States is a reflection of its progression in the Island as a whole during the first half of the twentieth century. At the turn of the century, French was still used for all proceedings of the Royal Courts, whether written or spoken, except in a case where the parties did not know each other, when English was allowed. However, by the 1930s, it was rare for a trial to be held officially in French. The first person to deliver his judgement in English was Lieutenant-Bailiff Le Quesne in 1950, and in 1963, a law was passed authorizing English as the language of the record, although the formal record of instruction by the Royal Court that

Orders in Council and other texts be entered in the records of Jersey was still expressed in French until June 1972 (Price 1984: 214).

French has also been replaced by English in other domains. In 1947, Le Maistre wrote that French Wesleyanism (introduced to the Island in the late eighteenth century) had initially served as a force to hinder the Anglicization of Jersey and that 'not so long ago' there had been almost equal numbers of French and English services every Sunday, but that, at the time of writing, very few services were still conducted in French (1947: 9). It is plain that such services were becoming less and less common from the fact that when French services were held they needed to be advertised beforehand. At the time of writing, no regular religious services are held in any language other than English, apart from the Roman Catholic masses at the Church of St Thomas, Val Plaisant, St Hélier, which are provided primarily for French visitors and residents. The Island's last French-language newspaper, *Les Chroniques de Jersey*, ceased publication at the end of 1959.

From the strong foothold that it had established in the nineteenth century, the advance of English, therefore, progressed steadily in the twentieth. Contact with the British mainland also increased further, with a daily air service being established in 1933, carrying nearly 20,000 passengers in its first year, and the appearance of radios, television (1962) and cinemas bringing even the inhabitants of rural parishes into regular contact with English (Lemprière 1974: 214–16).

The defining event of the twentieth century for the Channel Islands was, undoubtedly, the Second World War. As mentioned in the introduction, mass evacuation from the Channel Islands in anticipation of the German Occupation had serious repercussions for Jèrriais. Moreover, the change in attitude towards the dialect that occurred during the post-war period meant that, by the 1960s, the intergenerational chain of transmission was beginning to break. This chapter has illustrated that the sociopolitical situation on Jersey prior to the war makes it extremely likely that Anglicization would have advanced in any case, but the events of the Second World War certainly put wind in its sails.

Jersey's recovery after the five-year Occupation was greatly aided by the expansion of its tourist industry, which, during the 1950s and 1960s, was the mainstay of the Island's economy, generating over half Jersey's national income in 1960. Although, by the late twentieth century, the revenue generated by this industry represented only about one quarter of the Island's income, numbers of tourists remained high: according to Syret and Stevens, 1990 saw 1,507,000 tourists in Jersey, with 80 per cent of these coming from mainland Britain (1998: 286).[21] Such a huge annual influx of even temporary residents can only serve to increase the Island's Anglicization.

Anglicization has also been furthered by immigration from mainland Britain. According to the 1996 Census, out of a population of 85,150, only 44,886, or just over half the current residents of Jersey, were born on the

Island, with 29,342 and 2,238 inhabitants born in the United Kingdom and the Republic of Ireland respectively (table 2.2). Thus, more than one third of Jersey's current resident population are natives of an English-speaking country. The linguistic consequences of this are clear.

Recent immigration has been partly in the shape of wealthy individuals, seeking to take advantage of Jersey's low rate of taxation, but also, since the 1970s, thousands of people have come to the Island to work in the finance industry, which is now Jersey's biggest single generator of income and which, as well as attracting workers from mainland Britain, has served to strengthen ties between Jersey and London.[22] Moreover, in the 1960s, the huge population boom (mainly due to immigration) made it necessary to 'import' technical staff to work in Jersey's civil service, health service and other public services. Even though the States have since taken a number of measures to regulate immigration, it is still possible for residents of the United Kingdom to settle in Jersey on a temporary basis.

The second half of the twentieth century, therefore, saw English progressively ousting French and Jèrriais from all domains. There was a watershed in 1976, when French finally stopped being used in parish notices in St Ouen (the parish that continued its use longest in this capacity) due to the appointment of a *greffier* ('parish clerk') who only knew English. In the legal domain, the one area that has succeeded in resisting penetration from English has been conveyancing.[23] Other official documents such as the *liste des contribuables au rât* ('the list of tax payers') may sport French titles but are otherwise drafted in English.

Jèrriais has suffered a marked decline in use as an everyday means of communication on Jersey. The 1989 Census, which was the first to include a question on Jèrriais, put speaker numbers at 5,720 out of a population of 82,809 (6.9 per cent).[24] The dialect does, however, persist in the mouths of many Jersey-folk in two guises. As will be discussed in section 8.3., the

Table 2.2 Birthplace of the population of Jersey (March 1996 Census of Jersey)

Birthplace	Number
Jersey	44,886
Elsewhere in the UK (including other Channel Islands)	29,342
Republic of Ireland	2,238
France	924
Portugal	4,580
Other EU member states	942
Elsewhere	2,238
Total	85,150

Norman substrate has left its mark on the variety of English spoken on Jersey, giving it a highly distinctive and immediately recognizable character, and the dialect's influence is still to be seen in the names of places and people. Many of the Island's surnames have succumbed to Anglicization: Le Feuvre is now pronounced 'Le Fever' and Hublart cites the examples of Le Breuilly (now pronounced 'Brailey'), Luce (now pronounced 'Loose') and Le Hégarat (now pronounced 'Garett') (1979: 46), but the Jersey telephone directory is still full of Rondels, Poingdestres, De Gruchys and Le Boutilliers, to name but a few. Numerous place names have also been Anglicized: La Rue d'Haut has become Queen Street and La Banque has become Conway Street (Le Feuvre 1983: 48), although others still live on in French: Mont Cochon, Bel Royal, La Hougue Bie, Le Mont Rossignol, La Rue du Clos Fallu; and some are even to be found in Jèrriais: La Rue Ès Picots, La Rue du Câtel. If Jèrriais does become extinct in the near future, the Island's toponymy and patronymics and, ironically, its distinctive variety of English may well prove to be the last indicators of its linguistic heritage.

3

THE JÈRRIAIS DIALECT

3.1. INTRODUCTION

The aim of this chapter is to provide a detailed picture of Jèrriais. This will be achieved by examining its relationship with other varieties of Norman and the considerable geographically based internal variation that exists within Jersey. The chapter also debates what has become rather a thorny issue on the Island in recent times, namely whether Jèrriais should be considered a language or a dialect.

3.2. RELATIONSHIP WITH OTHER VARIETIES OF NORMAN

In his work *Des caractères et de l'extension du patois normand* (1883), Charles Joret sought to, first, define the features which characterized the Norman dialect and, secondly, determine their geographical extension. Though his study, conducted via correspondence, examined only eight phonological features, these may be taken as a useful starting point from which to consider the varieties spoken in the Channel Islands:

(i) Whereas in Central French,[1] the diphthong [ej], which derived from Latin tonic free ē and ĭ, further differentiated to [ɔj] and eventually to [wa] (CREDERE > St. Fr. *croire* [kRwaR]) ('to believe'), in Norman, there was no such differentiation but instead a reduction to an e sound, hence [krɛr] in Mainland Norman (MN), [kreð] in Jersey (J), [kRɛR] in Sark (S) and [krer] in Guernsey (G) (examples taken from Brasseur 1978a: 56–7).

(ii) Before [a], Latin [k] palatalized to [ʃ] in Central French, but no such development occurred in Norman. Hence, Latin CAMISIA > St. Fr. *chemise* [ʃəmiz] ('shirt'), MN [kmẽz], J [kmẽz], S [kmẽz], G [kmẽz], [kmẽs] (Brasseur 1978a: 52–3).

(iii) In a syllable closed by [r], [a] is maintained in standard French but becomes [ɛ] in Norman. Hence Latin SARC(U)LARE > St. Fr. *sarcler* [saRkle], MN [sɛRkji] (although [sarkji] is also possible), J [sɛrkjɛ], S [sɛRkʎɛ], G [serkjaj] (Brasseur 1978a: 58–60).

(iv) Before a front vowel, [i, e, ɛ], Latin [k] palatalized to [s] in Central French but to [ʃ] in Norman. Hence Latin CENTUM > St. Fr. *cent* [sɑ̃] ('a hundred'), MN [ʃɑ̃], J [ʃɑ̃], S [ʃɑ̃t], G [ʃɑ̃] (Brasseur 1978a: 53).

(v) Vocalization of preconsonantal [l] led to standard French reflexes of Latin plural forms in -ELLOS being realized as [ɛaws] (a triphthong

which was subsequently levelled to [o]). Hence Latin AGNELLOS >
St. Fr. *agneau* [aɲo] ('lambs') (Old French *agnels*). Although this
development did not affect the singular, which remained with an *-el*
suffix < Latin -ELLUM (OFr. *agnel*; 'lamb') in many words, a new
analogical singular was created on the basis of the new plural form. In
standard French, therefore, the singular–plural opposition [ɛl]–[o] was
neutralized (Modern French has [aɲo]–[aɲo]). However, in Norman,
no new analogical singular evolved and the singular *-el* suffix was
retained. Hence MN [aɲe], J [aɲe], G [aɲe] ('lamb').

(vi) Before a yod, Latin ŏ became diphthongized to [wɛ] and combined
with the yod to form a triphthong. This was then levelled to the
secondary diphthong [yj] and became [ɥi] in standard French, for
example NOCTEM > St. Fr. *nuit* [nɥi] ('night'). However, in Norman,
the [yi] diphthong underwent a different development, sometimes
reducing to [y] as in Latin ACUC(U)LA > MN [edʒyl], J [adʒyl], S
[adʒyl], G [edʒyl], or to [ji]/[i], with the stress on the second element,
hence Latin SUDIA > St. Fr. *suie* [sɥi], MN [si], J [si], S [sje], a form
which Brasseur suggests may have occurred via the secondary diphthongization of [i] (1978b: 301–21), G [si].

(vii) Norman has two forms of the definite article: *l(e)* and *la* (as in
standard French) as opposed to their reduction to one form as in
Picard (Dauby 1979: 29; Dickès 1992: 41) (MN *le/la*; J *l(é)/la*; S *l(e)/
la*; G *lé/la*).

(viii) Although it did not feature on his original questionnaire, at a later stage
in his enquiry Joret also examined the development of Latin ĕ before a
palatal element. This originally diphthongized to [je], which then
combined with the yod to form a triphthong [jEj].[2] In standard
French, this triphthong subsequently levelled to [i], hence Latin
LECTUM > *lit* [li] ('bed') cf. MN [li]. However, in the dialects of the
Channel Islands, traces of this triphthong remain: J [λɛ], S [λɛt], G [jɛt].

It is plain, therefore, that the varieties spoken in the Channel Islands all
contain what Joret considered to be the defining features of Norman.
Although Auregnais, the Norman dialect of Alderney, became extinct
before any systematic analysis of the variety had been undertaken,[3] in
fact, the surviving dialects of the Channel Islands share many other features
with Mainland Norman, as is demonstrated in Brasseur (1978a), where
nineteen phonetic features common to all four varieties are isolated and
discussed.[4] Spence points out that Jèrriais still contains a number of
phonetic features which were mentioned by sixteenth- and seventeenth-
century writers and grammarians as being characteristic of the Norman
dialect (1993: 45) and Hublart also lists features that distinguish Jèrriais
from standard French in the medieval, early modern and modern periods
(1979: 66–80).

Despite having identified features which were representative of the Norman dialect, Joret concluded that there was no homogeneous Norman linguistic area since the boundary lines of the features in question did not coincide (Collas 1934: 217). Indeed, only feature (i) was actually to be found over the whole *domaine normand* ('Norman domain'), namely along the valley of the Béthune, some twenty miles west of the eastern frontier of Normandy and continuing along the river Epte to the Seine (Joret 1883: 150). However, not even this feature proved an ideal match as it extended beyond the *domaine* to the south (Joret 1883: 110). Another reason preventing the territory from forming a homogeneous linguistic area was the fact that the development of Latin tonic free ē and ĭ, and the forms of the definite article, differed so radically between the east and west. In the case of the former, in what Joret termed the *région picarde* ('Picard region') the resulting [ej] diphthong differentiated to [ɔj] as in standard French, but it remained as [ej] in what he called the *région normande* ('Norman region') and subsequently reduced to [e] or [ɛ]. In the case of the definite article, the *région picarde* had only one form for the singular: *l'tien Wallet* ('Wallet's dog'), *l'vak à Huret* ('Huret's cow'); but the *région normande* had two, a masculine and a feminine, as in standard French ('le chien de Wallet', 'la vache d'Huret') (Dickès 1992: 41; Dauby 1979: 29).

By studying the boundary lines of the different isoglosses, Joret concluded that – for different reasons – a part of eastern Normandy and the whole of southern Normandy lay outside the 'truly Norman' zone, which he identified as being limited to the Channel Islands, the northern half of the département ('administrative division') of La Manche, Calvados, the northern corner of Eure and the western half of Seine-Inférieure.

Joret realized that the isoglosses marking the southern limits of, respectively, the non-palatalization of [k] after [a] and the development of [k] to [ʃ] after a front vowel were geographically very close, and he was the first to identify their importance as separating the 'truly Norman' varieties from the others.[5] He did point out, however, that although both isoglosses involved modification of the same consonant ([k]) they did not coincide: the [k] after front vowel isogloss being a little more to the north. Joret also noted that some places, such as the valley of the Drouanne, showed the 'Norman' development of [k] after [a] but the Central French development of [k] after a front vowel (1883: 126–7),[6] although he did suggest that the latter might have been a more recent development, due to the influence of standard French. It was further observed that, in southern Normandy, the isoglosses did not coincide with the political frontier of the province (1883: 144) and Joret even suggested that, in medieval times, the location of the isogloss might have been different – for example, he notes that the town known today as Chambray was still called Cambray in 1390 (1883: 140).

The Ligne Joret has become an important isogloss in the study of French dialectology. In the 1960s, it was researched extensively by Lechanteur (1968:

189–90), who made a few modifications to Joret's outline. Lechanteur noted that, despite its clarity in the east and west of Normandy, the line became less distinct in the centre of the region, where the influence of standard French was more prominent (1968: 188–90). The Channel Islands are, once again, identified as lying in the heart of the Norman zone (1968: 189).

In his recent work on the dialects of Normandy, Lepelley identifies the development of [k]/[g] + [a] and [k] + front vowel as the defining 'broad' features of 'le domaine du Nord-Ouest' ('the north-west domain') (1999: 58–61). He also describes the development of Germanic [w] (and certain, late-introduced words of Latin beginning with the letter *v*, which become assimilated to [w]) to [v] in northern Normandy as another linguistic feature that coincides with the Ligne Joret (1999: 61) – although Joret himself made no mention of it – citing as examples Germanic *wer-wulf* ('werewolf'), which becomes *varou* in Mainland Norman, *vârou* in Guernésiais (the Norman dialect of Guernsey) and *varou/vathou* or *ouathou/ouéthou* in Jèrriais, but *loup-garou* in standard French, and also the French surname *Gautier*, which becomes *Vautier* to the north of the Ligne Joret. Lepelley suggests that this bundle of isoglosses may designate the limit of Saxon influence after their arrival in Neustria in the fourth or fifth century (1999: 61). In his discussions of the origins of the Ligne Joret, Lechanteur (1968: 194–5) also admits the plausibility of a Germanic substrate. However, he suggests that this is only one of several possible explanations.

Among the morphosyntactic features shared by the insular and mainland varieties of Norman but not by standard French, it is possible to cite:

(a) the preservation of a morphological singular–plural opposition in nouns and adjectives deriving from Latin words ending in -ELLUM/-ELLOS (see feature (v) above).

(b) the use of *ès* (derived from *en les*) instead of *aux* to render the meaning *à les* (lit. 'to the').

(c) the indefinite pronoun *nou*, a form which Lepelley believes to have derived from *l'on*, with the initial lateral becoming a nasal and the vowel denasalizing (1999: 88). On Guernsey, this form has entirely supplanted the first person plural pronoun *jé*.

(d) the existence of a gender-based distinction between the third person singular indirect pronouns, which are *li* in the masculine and *lyi* [lji] in the feminine, as opposed to invariable [lɥi] in standard French.

(e) the use of *le sien de, à, qui* instead of the standard French demonstrative form *celui de, à, qui*. Lepelley suggests that this form might originate from the possessive construction (1999: 89–90).

(f) a contraction in the end of the root and the ending of the second person singular of the present indicative, hence *sav'ous?* for standard French *savez-vous?* ('do you know?').

(g) in the past historic, the endings of the first conjugation (< Latin -ARE verbs) being brought in line with those of the other conjugations, hence J *je donnis* ('I gave') and so forth (cf. St. Fr. *je donnai*).

(h) use of the pronoun *jé* as a first person plural as well as for the first person singular.

(i) the frequent anteposition of adjectives of colour, hence *la verte salle* ('the green room').

(j) in the Channel Islands (although not in Mainland Norman), the use of the verb *faire* pronominally in the present and past historic in interpolated clauses, hence *s'fait-il* ('he said'). On Guernsey, this has been reduced to [sti] (Lepelley 1999: 92).

It should not be forgotten, however, that standard French has exerted an influence on Insular as well as Mainland Norman for many centuries, with the result that certain forms characteristic of Norman have disappeared from Jèrriais. A case in point would be the palatalization of [k] before [a], for, despite widespread retention of velar [k] in Jèrriais terms such as [ka] ('cat') < Latin CATTUM and [vak] ('cow') < Latin VACCA, even this most Norman of features has been supplanted on the Island in the case of terms such as *chambre* ('bedroom') < Latin CAMERA, *châudgiéthe* ('boiler') < Latin CALDARIA (Spence 1957a: 82), for which borrowings from standard French are now used. Lechanteur has evoked homonymic clash to account for the replacement of long-since disappeared [kãte] ('to sing') by *chanter* [ʃãte], citing the form [kãute] (*caunter*, 'to lean over') as the culprit (since [kãuʃɔu] < *caunchoun* ('song') still exists in Mainland Norman) (1968: 191). However, this phenomenon cannot account for all instances of substitution. Spence also notes how, in some cases, the Norman and borrowed forms may exist side by side. Sometimes these will be no more than simple variants (J *g'veux–j'veux*; 'hair') < Latin CAPILLOS) but the forms may also be differentiated semantically, hence J *chandelle* ('candle') and *candelle* ('icicle') < Latin CANDELA) (1957a: 82). In the last example, the borrowing has ousted the indigenous Norman form for the 'basic' meaning of the word but the Norman form has been retained with a metaphorical meaning. Clearly, such borrowings are more common in Mainland than in Insular Norman due to the greater degree of contact between the former and standard French.

Although standard French may exert less of an influence on Insular than on Mainland varieties of Norman, the dialects of the Channel Islands are, nevertheless, in contact with a similarly powerful presence in the shape of standard English, which is the dominant language on all the Islands. Indeed, the Channel Island dialects share a number of features not found in Mainland Norman which reveal this contact. Spence notes (1984: 347) that anglicisms are widespread in many areas of the lexis (cf. section 6.4.2.1.) – not least in the domain of technical vocabulary. Moreover, he suggests that English interference may be behind the frequent replacement of the secondary palatalization of [k] and [g] before front vowels, so common on the mainland, by 'English type' [tʃ] and [dʒ] affricates – although it is pointed out that Lechanteur (1948: 121) also found [tʃ] regularly in Mainland Norman. The consistency with which diphthongs such as [ej] and [o:w] have replaced lengthened close vowels and the use of alveolar rather than dental [t] and [d] are also seen to reflect English influence. Liddicoat (1990: 200) also claims that, on Jersey, the Norman French phoneme [r] is being replaced by the English alveolar continuant [ɹ], although on the basis of the data I collected I would disagree with this.

Brasseur (1977: 100–1) even goes as far as claiming that the Channel Islands have their own variety of regional French (*français régional*). He cites as evidence the following terms, together with a list of English borrowings, all of which are said to be common to the three Islands of Jersey, Guernsey and Sark, but which are apparently unknown in Mainland Norman:

- *terrerie* ('pottery'; *poterie* in standard French)
- *quart devant douze* ('a quarter to twelve'; *midi moins le quart* in standard French)
- *corset d'oeuvre* ('a Guernsey'; no real equivalent exists in standard French other than *pullover tricoté la main à Guernesey* 'a pullover hand-knitted in Guernsey')
- *veue* ('light'; *lumière/éclairage* in standard French)
- *pas d'autre* ('no longer'; *plus, plus maintenant* [with negative meaning] in standard French).

In spite of Brasseur's claim, I would, however, be reluctant to to apply the term *français régional* to the Jèrriais context. This will be examined further in section 8.2.3. and in the conclusion.

Despite the large number of features that they undoubtedly share it would, however, be mistaken to consider the varieties spoken in the Norman zone – or even on the Channel Islands – as homogeneous. Even though Serquiais (the Norman dialect of Sark) developed from the variety of Jèrriais spoken in St Ouen after Sark was colonized from Jersey in the sixteenth century (Spence 1993: 53), there is no longer any striking resemblance between these two varieties (Brasseur 1978b: 302) and, although it is claimed that the inhabitants of Sark (the Serquiais) understand the Jèrriais of St Ouen, speakers of Jèrriais do not understand Serquiais very well (Brasseur 1977: 100). Furthermore, neither the Serquiais nor the inhabitants of Guernsey (the Guernésiais) can readily understand one another, although some degree of mutual comprehension is possible between Jèrriais and Guernésiais – albeit limited and, in my experience, often varying from one speaker to the next.[7] Brasseur claims that, of all the varieties of Insular Norman, the most difficult for a speaker of Mainland Norman to understand is the Guernésiais of Torteval parish, in the south-west of Guernsey (1977: 100).

Brasseur has calculated that, of the four extant varieties of Norman, it is

Serquiais which diverges most from standard French (1978b: 302). His survey highlighted forty-three differences between these two varieties compared to thirty-seven between Mainland Norman and standard French, thirty-six between Guernésiais and standard French and thirty-four between Jèrriais and standard French. Clearly, these scores would differ slightly according to the precise varieties of Jèrriais, Guernésiais and Mainland Norman that were examined, for, as will be illustrated below in the case of Jèrriais (section 3.3.), there exist considerable regional differences within these dialects.[8] However, if nothing else, the scores do serve as an indication of, at least, the more innovative nature of Serquiais and the greater proximity that exists between Jèrriais and standard French than between standard French and any other variety of Norman. This being said, the differences between the varieties themselves remain so salient that it is impossible to suggest that any one variety of Norman has any particular affinity with another. Brasseur states that there are four instances where Serquiais displays a feature similar to the dialect of Magneville (as opposed to Jèrriais and Guernésiais, which share those particular features with standard French), three instances where Serquiais shares the same development as Guernésiais (as opposed to Jèrriais and the dialect of Magneville), and three instances where it shares the same development as Jèrriais (as opposed to Guernésiais and the dialect of Magneville) (1978b: 302–3).[9]

To sum up, the varieties spoken on the Channel Islands are characterized by their diversity. Linguistically speaking, they resemble and yet also differ from Mainland Norman, and their future is likely to reflect this duality increasingly in that the Channel Island varieties are in daily contact with English whereas the mainland dialects are in daily contact with standard French. However, as mentioned above, the Channel Island varieties do not merely differ between themselves but also display considerable internal variation.[10] The following section examines the regional variation of Jèrriais.

3.3. REGIONAL VARIATION IN JÈRRIAIS

Although Jersey measures, at its maximum, only 10.8 miles by 6.8, Jèrriais shows considerable internal variation. The sub-dialects or, as they are called locally, *parlers* spoken on the Island are usually divided into two main groups – east and west – with the eastern varieties differing most from standard French, mainly because of secondary developments in the vowel system (Spence 1993: 20). Map 3 indicates the location of the sub-dialects that are to be found within these two main divisions.

Within western Jèrriais, the *parlers* of Les Landes, L'Étacq and La Moie are highly distinctive, whilst within eastern Jèrriais, those of Lé Faldouët and La Rocque are worthy of separate consideration. The *parler* of Lé Mont Mado, also worthy of note, spans the northern periphery of both areas.

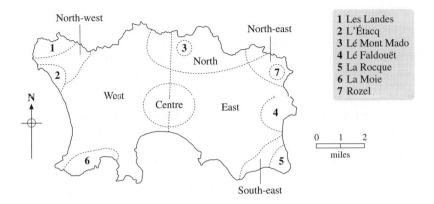

Map 3 Jersey's 'linguistic pockets'

Although this internal variation has never been based on any administrative or other territorial boundaries within Jersey, many of the Islanders feel it to be intrinsically linked with parish boundaries, as the following poem illustrates. Although it is not, therefore, strictly correct to refer to the sub-dialects of Jèrriais by the name of parishes – for instance, using the example of the word *deux* ('two'), Le Maistre (1966: 161) illustrates how, in fact, a variety of forms can be found within a single parish – this practice is so well established on the Island that it has been followed in this study in order to avoid confusion.

Lé Jerriais

J'avons entendu des Angllais
Se moquir du bouan vier Jèrriais:
De trouver à r'dire est lus mode,
De c'mander partout est lus code;
S'i' n'se trouvent pon bein ov nous,
Faut lus dire allouoz-en siez vous;
Mais empliyons mux notre pllume,
Et frappons sus une autre encllume.

We have heard the English
Make fun of good old Jèrriais:
They always find things to say again
and again; Their rule is to order
everyone around. If they don't like it
here with us, We should tell them to
go back home; But let's make better
use of our pen, And talk about
something else.

Les Jèrriais sont tous d'un baté,
Et devraient aimer lus râté;
Car il est vraiment respectablle,
Fort ancien et fort vénérablle:
Sans aver tous le même pâler,
Je pouvons fort bein deviser
Entre nous sus aucune affaire,
Et d'une faichon assez cllaire.

The Jèrriais are all alike, And they
should appreciate their heritage;
Because it is very respectable, Very
ancient and very venerable: Even
without speaking the same *parler*, We
can easily talk To each other about
anything, In quite a clear way.

Les gens de l'Est ont un accent
Du chein du Vouest bein différent:

In the east, the folk have a different
accent From those in the west: In the

Dans le Vouest nou frume la bouoche,
Et la vouaix semblle être pus douoche;
Dans l'Est i'montrent pus les dents,
Et autrement sont différents;
Ch'est au point que j'avons oui dire,
Mais j'pensons que ch'était pour rire,
Qu'un marchi n'pouvait s'faire aut'fais,
D' St.-Ouennais à St.-Martinais:
S'il était question de mariage,
Fille et garçon s'entendraient, j'gage:
Ès cheins qui voudraient en douter,
Je lus requemande d'êprouver.

west they close their mouths, And
their voice seems softer; In the east
they show their teeth more, And are
different in other ways; So much so
that we have heard it said, But I think
it may have been for fun, That in
times gone by a transaction couldn't be
made, Between someone from St
Ouen and St Martin: If it were a
question of marriage, I bet that a girl
and a boy would understand each
other: To those who doubt what I say,
I advise them to try it.

À St.-Martin i'disent *véze*,
Faisant d'l'*r* un *z* comme en *péze*:
Nouz y lève les pids en *haaut*,
Et nouz y bet daut' chose que d'll'*iaaue*:
Les autres pâraisses vaisines
De chu pâler-là sont couôsines;
I' vont à la pêque en *batquaaux*,
Et à terre i' cachent des *chvaaux*;
Mais ous puorrez mux le comprendre
En allant sus les llieux l'entendre.

In St Martin they say *véze*, making
the *r* into a *z* as in *péze*:[11] We lift our
feet up high there,[12] And drink more
than water: The other neighbouring
parishes Are cousins of that *parler*;
They go to fish in boats, And ride
horses on the land; But you can
understand them better By going to
listen to them on their home ground.

Les St.-Ouennais vont au *Puléc*
Ramasser des trainées de *vréc*,
Et aussi bein à Ste.-Marie
Nouz en fait autant, je parie.

The St Ouennais go to Lé Puléc[13]
To collect sled-fulls of seaweed,
And I bet they do the same thing
In Ste Marie.

L'St.-Bréladais pâle d'la *Touo*,
Atou du geon cauffe le *fouo*,
Appèle les vlicots des *coques*,
Est tout environnè de roques.

In St Brélade's they speak about the
Tower,[14] And warm the stove with
gorse, They call periwinkles whelks,
And everything is surrounded by
rocks.

A *St.-Louthains* et à *St.-Pierre*
Nou prend d'temps en temps un ptit *vèrre*;
Nouz y pâle le Jèrriais pllat,
Et nous dit *Coin Vathin, vethe-guia*;
L'*r* entre voyelles se change
En *th*, est-che pon êtrange?
D'autre côté à St-Martin
Ch'est un *z* que nou l'fait devnin:
Nouz y touanne à la grande *quethue*,
Nouz y fait servir tour et cue,
Dans qui nous met le cidre doux,
Dont nous peut bere sans ête souls;
Mais nou n'en est pas pus à s'n aise,

In St Laurent and St Pierre They
like to have a little glass of something
every now and again;[15] They
speak a 'flat' Jèrriais, And say *Coin
Vathin, vethe-guia*; Between vowels,
r becomes *th*, isn't it strange? On the
other side of the Island, in St
Martin, They turn it into a *z*: They
use the big plough And the circular
granite cider trough, In which they
put sweet cider, That you can drink
without getting drunk; But you're not
more at ease there, Because it gives

Car i' donne la guernesiaise;
Je n'cherche pas à faire affront,
J'espere que tous le creront.

you diarrhoea; I'm not seeking to
cause offence, I hope that everyone
will believe me.

Che n' est pas là toute l'histouaire
Du Jèrriais, comme ou pouvez craire;
Je n'ai que touchi le sujet,
Et qui sans doute sera l'objet
D'une êtude de main de maitre,
Et n'tergera pas à paraitre.

That's not the whole story About
Jèrriais, as you may believe; I've only
touched on the subject, Which will
undoubtedly be the object Of a study
by some learnèd person, And will not
be too long in appearing.

Philippe Langlois,
in *La Nouvelle Année,* 1875

(The spelling of this poem has been left as in the original version, even though this is often at variance with the spelling of the *Dictionnaire Jersiais–Français* (Le Maistre 1966), which is used elsewhere.) The poem is interesting as an indicator of the regional features perceived as most salient by the author – and probably by many Islanders.[16] However, as will now be demonstrated, the regional variation of Jèrriais is, in fact, far greater and more complex than this.

3.3.1. *Phonology*

I do not propose to discuss the phonology of Jèrriais in depth, as Spence (1985) and (1987) provide a comprehensive phonological description of the dialect, examining in detail the distinctive consonants and vowels of Jèrriais, permitted consonant sequences and the behaviour of the schwa. Further information on the phonological system of the dialect may also be obtained from Spence (1960: 16–28, 1957b, 1990). The purpose of this section is, rather, to outline the main instances of phonological variation that occur within the distinct sub-dialects of Jèrriais. In the first instance, however, in order to provide the reader with a point of reference, the most salient ways in which the phonological system of Jèrriais differs from that of standard French will be highlighted.

a. *Vowels*

The phonological inventory of Jèrriais contains the following vowels:

The vowel system of Jèrriais
Oral vowels

[i]	[i:]	[y]	[y:]	[u]	[u:]
[e]	[e:]			[o]	[o:]
[ɛ]	[ɛ:]	[œ]	[œ:]		
		[a]	[ɑ:]		

and the schwa, [ə].

Nasal vowels

[ẽ]	[ẽ:]		[ø̃]	[ø̃:]		[õ]	[õ:]
[ɛ̃]	[ɛ̃:]						
			[ã]	[ã:]			

(after Spence 1985: 151–2)

Since length is phonemic in Jèrriais, this means that there are seventeen oral vowel phonemes and ten nasal vowel phonemes. These are discussed by Spence (1985), who provides detailed descriptions of them and examples of minimal pairs. The most frequent context in which they contrast – indeed, the only context in the case of pairs of vowels such as [ɛ] and [ɛ:] – is word-finally, where, unlike in standard French, the short vowel is used for the singular and the long vowel for the plural hence: [rɛ]–[rɛ:] *raie–raies* ('furrow'–'furrows'). This contrast is also observed in the dialects of mainland Normandy and Picardy (Spence 1993: 46).

The vowel system of standard French
Oral vowels

	[i]		[y]		[u]
	[e]		[ø]		[o]
	[ɛ]		[œ]		[ɔ]
		[a]		[ɑ]	

and the schwa, [ə].

Nasal vowels

[ɛ̃]		[œ̃]		[ɔ̃]		[ɑ̃]

A glance at the vowel system of standard French also reveals that the Jèrriais system is the more assymmetrical of the two in that it lacks a half-open back rounded vowel, corresponding to [ɛ], and a half-close front rounded vowel corresponding to [e] and [o]. As will be seen below, however, these sounds are present in some of the localized *parlers* (3.3.1.1.a.). In terms of the low vowel [a], length is more distinctive than degree of aperture in Jèrriais.

Length is also phonemic word-finally in the nasal vowels of Jèrriais, with most contrasts again found in the context of the singular–plural distinction. In addition to this, Jèrriais has one more nasal vowel sound than standard French, namely [ẽ], which features in words such as [gardẽ] *gardîn* ('garden'), [lẽ:ʒ] *lînge* ('household linen') and [lapẽ] *lapîn* ('rabbit'). In standard French, the corresponding words would all contain [ɛ̃].

In modern French, the diphthongs of Old French and Middle French have been progressively reduced to simple vowels so that there exist only monophthongs. Jèrriais, on the other hand, contains one diphthong – [a:w], which is found only in the east of Jersey. As this never reduces to a simple vowel, Spence treats this differently from all the secondary diphthongs of Jèrriais, which he considers to be allophones of simple vowels (3.3.1.1.a.).

b. *Consonants*

The consonantal phonemes of Jèrriais

	Bilabial	Labio-dental	Dental	Affricate	Palato-alveolar	Palatal	Velar	Glottal
Stop	p b		t d				k g	
Fricative		f v	s z ð	ʧ ʤ	ʃ ʒ			h
Nasal	m		n			ɲ		
Lateral			l					
Trilled			r					

(after Spence 1987: 119)

The consonantal phonemes of standard French

	Bilabial	Labio-dental	Dental/alveolar	Palato-alveolar	Palatal	Velar	Uvular
Stop	p b		t d			k g	
Fricative		f v	s z	ʃ ʒ			ʁ
Nasal	m	n			ɲ	ŋ	
Lateral			l				

A comparison of the consonant systems of standard French and Jèrriais reveals the following points of contrast:

(i) Four consonantal phonemes are present in Jèrriais that do not occur in standard French, namely [h], [ð] and the affricates [ʧ] and [ʤ].

(ii) As with standard French, Jèrriais has never preserved any trace of Latin [h]. The Jèrriais phoneme is a borrowing from Germanic dating from the domination of Gaul by Frankish tribes in the sixth century. This 'Germanic' [h] disappeared from standard French in about the sixteenth century, although it is still heard in several varieties of regional French.

(iii) [ð] exists in Jèrriais exclusively as a result of the assibilation of intervocalic [r] (Spence 1957b). This sound change is not a feature of standard French.

(iv) In standard French, the affricates [ʧ] and [ʤ] only occur in borrowings such as *match*, *gin* and *bridge* (Spence 1987: 119). However, in Jèrriais, these sounds also occur as a result of the secondary palatalization of [k] and [g] before a front vowel, as in words such as [ʧ œ] *tchoeu* ('heart') and [dʒɛ:r] *dgèrre* ('war').

(v) In Jèrriais, [r] is a dental trill whereas in standard French it is a uvular fricative. The trilled pronunciation was common in standard French as late as the seventeenth century but had been supplanted by the uvular fricative of Parisian pronunciation by the eighteenth century. The trill is still heard in many varieties of regional French.

(vi) The velar nasal entered standard French in the twentieth century in a number of English borrowings, for example *le shopping* [ʃɔpɪŋ] ('shopping'), and is now considered to be a phoneme of the language, albeit with a restricted distribution (it only appears word-finally). The velar nasal also occurs in English borrowings in Jèrriais, some of which are well established, such as [blæŋkɛt] *blanket* ('blanket') and [diŋi] *dinghy* ('small boat'). However, it is not considered by Spence (1987: 119) to be a phoneme of Jèrriais.

c. *Glides*

Both standard French and Jèrriais have three glides, [j], [ɥ] and [w]. However, Spence notes that, in Jèrriais, there is a tendency for [ɥ] to be replaced by [w] (1960: 27).

3.3.1.1. *Geographically based variation in the vowel system of Jèrriais*
a. *Oral vowels*[17]

[i] A short close unrounded front vowel which is slightly less close than that of standard French: [pi] *pid* ('foot'). In north-east Jersey (NEJ) it is not found before a final nasal consonant, when it is replaced by [e] with some nasal resonance: [raʃen] *rachinne* ('root'); [fen] *finne* ('fine' – f. adj). In Grouville, before a nasal consonant this vowel is realized somewhat lower than [ẽ].

[i:] The same as above, but longer: [i:tr] *hître* ('oyster').[18] Long and short [i] contrast in minimal pairs such as [pi] *pid* ('foot') and [pi:] *pids* ('feet') (and *pits* ('well')).

[e] A half-close unrounded front vowel, which only contrasts with [ɛ] when word final (Spence 1985: 155). In the western (WJ) parishes of Ste Marie, St Pierre, St Brélade and St Ouen it is replaced by the half-open unrounded front vowel [ɛ]. In these parishes, therefore, there is no contrast between [e] and [ɛ]. In some parts of the east (EJ), it is often subject to slight diphthongization (to [ej]) (Spence 1993: 44): [mej] *mé* ('me').[19] In St Jean and parts of EJ, diphthongization may also occur in monosyllabic words: [lej] *les* ('the', pl.), [ʃei] *ces* ('these') and so forth. In Rozel (NEJ), some rounding may occur of the first element of the diphthong after a labial

consonant: [øj] (Le Maistre 1979b: 22; Spence 1960: 21) [me] *mé* > [møj] ('me'). As mentioned above, in St Ouen, the opposition between [e] and [ɛ] is neutralized (to [ɛ]). This variety also has fewer diphthongs and a tenser articulation than the other *parlers*.

[e:] This vowel is found in the *parler* of St Ouen, where it often replaces the [ej] diphthong. Elsewhere, it is always realized as [ej]: [bejk] *becque* ('beak') except before [r]. Spence argues that that this diphthong is not a continuation of the Northern Gallo-Romance [ej] diphthong (from Vulgar Latin tonic free ē and ĭ), since this generally reduces to [ɛ], for example [bɛð] *béthe* ('to drink') (1993: 44). It frequently occurs in words where the vowel was lengthened by the absorption of [s] or the schwa ([tejt] *tête* ('head') < Latin TESTA; [mej] *mais* ('month') < Vulgar Latin *MESE.

[ɛ] A short half-open unrounded vowel. In EJ, when stressed and before a nasal consonant, it is replaced by [æ], or, in NEJ and the south-east (SEJ), by [a], for example [kram] *crème* ('cream'). In St Brélade, this vowel is particularly open.

[ɛ:] In the WJ parishes of Ste Marie, St Pierre and St Brélade, [ɛ:] is replaced by [æ:]. In EJ it remains, except before nasal consonants where, in the west of Trinité, St Hélier and the west of St Martin, it is replaced by [æ:] (with nasal resonance) and, in extreme NEJ and SEJ, by [a:], hence [letʃɛ:r] > [letʃæ:r] in the phrase *à l'êtchèrre* ('at right angles').

[a] A short unrounded vowel, intermediate in quality between standard French [a] and [ɑ]: [ma] *ma* ('my', f.). In EJ, it is often replaced by [ɒ] before nasal consonants. In NEJ and the south-west (SWJ), when stressed it may be replaced by [ɒ] when final or followed by consonants other than nasals – for example [pɒ] *pon* ('not').

[a:] An allophone of [ɑ:]. This occurs only in the *parlers* of NEJ and SEJ, where it appears before nasal consonants. Both [a:] and [ɑ:] are rare, and are often realized as [ɒ:], particularly in EJ, hence [kɒ:] *cats* ('cats').

[ɑ:] A long open unrounded back vowel. This occurs above all in morphological alternations of the type [ka]–[kɑ:] *cat*–*cats* ('cat'–'cats'). It is replaced by [ɒ:] or [ɔ:] in EJ and in E St Jean, hence [gɒ:ʃ]/[gɔ:ʃ] *gâche* ('cake').

[o] A short half-close rounded back vowel which only occurs word-finally – except in the variety of St Ouen, where it is generally maintained in all positions. Word-medially, it is replaced by [ɔ], for example [bɔs] *bosse* ('bump'), [kɔt] *cotte* ('pig sty') (Spence 1985: 158). In St Jean and EJ it may be followed by a closer element, becoming [o:w].

[o:] is only retained in St Ouen. Elsewhere it becomes diphthongized to [o:w], hence [ʃo:wz] *chose* ('thing') (Spence 1985: 159). In EJ, this diphthong is often replaced by [a:w], hence [ʃa:wz] ('thing').

[u] A short close rounded back vowel which has a tendency to diphthongize to [wo] before palatal or prepalatal elements, for example [bwoji] *bouoilli* ('to boil'), [bwɔʃ] *bouoche* ('mouth'), [rwoʒ] *rouoge* ('red'). Diphthongization also occurs before [λ], which has become [l] in a secondary final position, [katwol] *catouoille* ('a tickle'); [mwol] *mouoille* ('to wet' 3sg.) and before [ð] from intervocalic [r], especially in non-tonic syllables, hence [swɔði] *souothis* ('mouse'); [wɔðɛl] *ouothelle* ('ear').

[u:] As above but longer. When lengthened due to the loss of another sound, this vowel has a tendency to diphthongize preconsonantally, hence [kwɔ:te] *couôter* ('to cost'). However, diphthongization does not occur in all parts of Jersey. In WJ (St Ouen, St Pierre, St Brélade, Ste Marie) the simple vowel is realized, hence [mu:k] *moûque* ('housefly'), whereas in EJ a diphthong is present, hence [mo:wk] (St Jean, St Laurent and Trinité) ([ma:wk] in Grouville and St Martin). An exception to this is the word *crôte* ('crust'), which is pronounced [kro:wt] in all *parlers*.

[y] A short close rounded front vowel which, in some words, diphthongizes to [wœ:], for example [wœ:le] *hueûler* ('to shout'); [twœ:ði] *tueûthie* ('a difficult task'). In SWJ the vowel is more open. In EJ it is replaced by [ø] or, in the extreme east, [øy] when final.

[y:] As above but longer and less common. It contrasts with [y] in singular–plural distinctions such as [kjy]–[kjy:] *cliu–clius* ('a small piece of cloth').

[œ] A short half-open rounded front vowel. In the *parlers* of SWJ [œ] is more open and less rounded. In EJ, the sound is replaced by [ø].

[œ:] In the *parlers* of SWJ (St Brélade and St Pierre), [œ:] is more open and less rounded than in standard French. The vowel does not occur in EJ, where it is replaced by [øy] when final, for example in the past participles of verbs such as *pouvier* ('to be able to'), *saver* ('to know') and *vaie* ('to see'), or [ø:] before a consonant. It is frequently replaced by [aj] in the south of St Jean, the north of St Hélier, the west of Trinité, St Martin, Grouville and St Sauveur, hence [saj] *seûr* ('sure'); [ajðaj] *heûtheux* (happy'); [dejmejlaj] *dêmêleux* ('comb'). It also becomes [æy] in a narrow transition zone between the *parlers* of the east and west. This comprises parts of north-east Trinité, St Hélier, St Laurent and St Jean. In EJ forms, the vowel is realized as [øy] after [r], hence [brøy] *breue* ('foam'); [røy] *reue* ('wheel'). Similar developments are attested in Lower Normandy: for example, Lechanteur (1948: 121) mentions the occurrence of diphthongs such as [aœ] and [œy] in words such as *deux* ('two'). In Les Landes (NWJ), the vowel unrounds and becomes even more open, hence [dɑ:] *deux* ('two'); [bɑ:r] *beurre* ('butter').

[ø] A short half-close rounded front vowel, an allophone of [œ]. It occurs before a final nasal in all *parlers*, hence [jøn] *ieune* ('one'); [løn] *leune* ('moon'). In EJ, [ø] is found before other consonants and word-finally and in the latter position may even become [øy], hence [tʃøraʒ] *tchoeurage* ('knot-weed'?).

b. *Nasal vowels*

Jèrriais has five nasal vowel sounds:

[ẽ] A half-close front unrounded nasal vowel. This is generally more open in EJ and, according to Le Maistre (1979a: 17), can also be replaced by the diphthong [aj], hence [lapaj] *lapîn* ('rabbit'). In the centre of the Island and in NEJ (Rozel) it is replaced by [ɛ̃], hence [lapɛ̃]. When final, the vowel can become more rounded in St Jean ([lapø̃]), although Le Maistre notes that this sound is only to be heard in the speech of older people (1979a: 17). In SEJ (La Rocque) it is often followed by a closer front element, giving a nasal diphthong [ẽj] or even [ø̃j], with rounding of the first element, for example [bẽg] *bîngue* ('basket') > [bø̃jg]; [lapɛ̃] *lapîn* ('rabbit') > [lapø̃j].

[ɛ̃] A half-open front unrounded nasal vowel. In extreme SEJ and NEJ this is replaced by the open unrounded nasal front vowel [ã] hence, [fɛ̃] *faîm* ('hunger') > [fã] ; [krɛ̃ʃi] *craînchi* ('to sift') > [krãʃi].

[ã] An open back nasal vowel which is somewhat more rounded than in standard French. In NEJ (Rozel) the vowel is often replaced by [ɔ̃], hence [grã] *grand* ('big') > [grɔ̃].

[õ] A half-close back rounded nasal vowel. The quality of the vowel is particularly close in NEJ and SEJ (La Rocque), where it frequently diph-thongizes to [õw], hence [fõw] *fond* ('bottom'); [mõwte] *monter* ('to go up').

[ø̃] A half-close front rounded nasal vowel which appears in words such as [rø̃] *run* ('space') and [lø̃di] *lundi* ('Monday').

As length is phonemic in Jèrriais, these phonemes also have long counter-parts, which contrast with them word-finally in noun plurals.

3.3.1.2. *Geographically based variation in the consonant system of Jèrriais*

The consonant system is more uniform throughout the *parlers* than that of the vowels.

(i) [ɲ] occurs word-finally only in NWJ, where it is still to be found in this position in the speech of the older generation, for example [viɲ] *vîngne* ('vine'). It is generally pronounced in the intervocalic position all over the Island, although in parts of EJ it may be replaced by [j]: for example [mijunɛt] *mîngnonnette* ('mignonette') but [miɲunɛt] also exists (Spence 1993: 56).

(ii) [r] When intervocalic, [r], the voiced dental trilled consonant, often develops to [ð] in St Brélade, St Ouen, Ste Marie, St Pierre, northern St Jean and parts of Trinité and St Martin,[20] or, alternatively, to [z] or [s]: *êp'thon*, *êp'son* ('spur') (Le Maistre 1966: 211).[21] In NEJ, the speech of certain people is characterized by the interchangeable use of [r] and [ð] in these contexts, but no such development traditionally occurs in St Laurent and southern parts of Trinité and St Martin. The development of intervocalic [r] to [ð] is not found in Serquiais, even though, as mentioned above, Sark was colonized from Jersey in the sixteenth century. This suggests that the development in Jèrriais post-dates this event.[22] When in contact with other consonants, [r] has often taken on the articulation of those consonants to produce combinations of double consonants, hence [brɔddi:] *brod'die*[23] ('embroidery'); [lejssa] *laîss'sa* ('he will leave') (Spence 1993: 53), although this does not occur with velars and labials. In parts of St Martin, intervocalic [r] is said to develop to [z] in all contexts.[24] However, Spence claims never to have heard this realization and my data, likewise, revealed no sign of this, despite the fact that at least one of my informants came from Lé Faldouët, which Spence suggests might represent the linguistic area in question (1987: 122).[25] In words which ended in Latin -URA or -ATURA, intervocalic [r] becomes [z] even in NEJ, and Brasseur notes that in La Moie 'nous avons relevé quelques traces d'un traitment en [l]', although he adds that 'le particularisme semble en voie d'extinction' (1978b: 286 n.6).[26] Where the etymological source was Latin *-rr/-tr /-dr*, [ð] is not substituted for [r] in any *parler* (Spence 1990: 213–14), so that [r] is retained in words such as [bɑːr] *barre* ('bar'), [mɑːri] *mârri* ('angry'), [bar] *bar* ('bass') and [par] *part* ('part'), where it was never intervocalic. However, if the clusters simplified early on in Old French, then assibilation to [ð] does take place, for example Latin PATREM > OFr. *pedra* > *père* ('father') ([pɛð] *péthe* in Jèrriais).

The assibilation of intervocalic [r] has far-reaching consequences for Jèrriais, both phonological and morphological, including the formation of the future and conditional tenses. These are explored in detail in Spence (1957b) and (1987), which also discuss other contexts which always or never provoke assibilation and speculate whether, in fact, this phenomenon is increasing or decreasing in Jèrriais (see also Spence 1990: 213).

In NWJ (St Ouen), [ð] may also be substituted for [z] in a word such as [mɛðõ] *maîson* ('house') ([me(j)zo] elsewhere), or in liaison forms such as [deð weðjo] *des ouaîsieaux* ('birds'), where there is no etymological connection between [z] and [r] (Brasseur 1978b: 283–5). However, replacement of this kind seems to be sporadic rather than regular and Spence (1993: 54) suggests it may be due to a form of hypercorrection. Le Maistre (1993: 15) notes that, by now, this feature has disappeared from the speech of most people.

(iii) *Consonant + [l] clusters*
This phenomenon was studied in the Calvados area of Normandy by Guerlin de Guer (1899) and in the Cotentin by Lechanteur (1968: 195–8).

In these areas, as in many parts of Jersey, the [l] of such clusters frequently undergoes palatalization to [j], for example, [kjo] *clios* ('field'). In St Ouen, however, the process is less advanced and the more conservative form [kʎo] is still to be heard amongst older speakers. St Ouen also retains the [ʎ] pronunciation word-finally in words such as [fiʎ] *fil'ye* ('daughter') whereas elsewhere in Jersey, [ʎ] has become depalatalized to [l].[27]

3.3.1.3. *Jersey's 'linguistic pockets'*

In addition to the broad east–west differences cited above, it is also worth listing the specific phonological differences that have been reported for the Island's so-called linguistic pockets.

a. *Lé Mont Mado*

  (i) Nasal e lowered before a nasal consonant

b. *Rozel/Lé Faldouët*

  (i) After a labial consonant, final [e] of monosyllables > [øj], hence [me] *mé* ('me') > [møj].

  (ii) In Rozel, front nasal vowels are very open: [ẽ] > [ɛ̃]; [ɛ̃] > [ɑ̃] hence [lapẽ] *lapîn* ('rabbit') > [lapɛ̃] and [fɛ̃] *faîm* ('hunger') > [fɑ̃].

  (iii) In Rozel, [ɑ̃] is often replaced by [ɔ̃], hence [grɑ̃] *grand* ('big') > [grɔ̃].

  (iv) The word for a 'bee' is *ain* (derived from the Latin APIS). Elsewhere on the Island it is normally *môque* or *moûque à mi/myi* ('honey fly') (Spence 1993: 23)

  (v) [e] with some nasal resonance is found before final nasal consonants in place of the [i] of other *parlers* , hence [fen] *finne* ('fine' – f. adj.)

  (vi) In Lé Faldouët, but not in Rozel, intervocalic [r] > [z], hence Latin PATREM > [pɛz] ('father').

c. *La Moie* (SWJ)

  (i) [u] diphthongizes to [wo(w)] when word final, hence [fwo(w)] *fouo* ('oven'). This does not occur, however, with the word for 'knees', which is [ʒnu] and not the expected [ʒnwo(w)] (Le Maistre 1993: 2).

  (ii) The 3sg. feminine disjunctive pronoun (*elle* in standard French; *lyi/yi* in Jèrriais) is pronounced [ljɛ] or [jɛ], whereas elsewhere in the Island it is pronounced as [lji] or [ji]. This seems to be a vestige of the Norman form *lié* < Vulgar Latin *-ELLEI.

  (iii) The Old French *-ier* and *-iel* endings generally reduce to [i] in EJ and much of WJ. In St Ouen (NWJ) the form heard is [ji] and in La Moie it is [jɛ]. For example, *pommyi* ('apple tree'), which is *pommier* in standard French, has the forms: EJ/WJ [pumi] or [pɔmi]; NWJ [pomji]; but La Moie [pɔmjɛ]. Similarly, *myi* ('honey'), *miel* in standard French, is EJ/WJ [mi]; NWJ [mji]; La Moie [mjɛ]. Spence suggests that

this phenomenon is due to the fall of the final consonants [l] and [r] having occurred later in the west of the Island (1993: 21).
(iv) The pronunciation of [ɛ] is extremely open, hence [krɛm] *crème* ('cream') > [kram].
(v) Intervocalic [r] may sometimes be replaced by [l].
(vi) [œ:] is more open and less rounded than in standard French.
(vii) [a:] and [ɑ:] tend to close to [ɒ:] as in EJ, hence [pɒ:] *pon* ('not') (Spence 1985: 157).

d. *Les Landes and L'Étacq* (NWJ)

(i) [œ:] unrounds, giving forms such as [dɛ:] *deux* ('two'), [bɛ:r ɛ dõɛ:] *beurre et des oeus* ('butter and eggs'). In some parts of Les Landes (but not in L'Étacq) the vowel is even more open, yielding forms such as [dɑ:] *deux* ('two'), [bɑ:r] *beurre* ('butter').
(ii) [ɛ] closes to [i] when in contact with a following [ð], hence [iðaɲi] *ithangnie* ('spider's web') and [tʃiðy] *tchéthue* ('plough').

e. *La Rocque* (SEJ)

(i) This *parler* contains nasal diphthongs, not seen anywhere else on Jersey: [ẽ] > [ẽj] or [ø̃j]; [õ] > [õw] hence [bẽg] *bîngue* ('basket') > [bø̃jg]; [brẽʒ] *brînge* ('broom') > [brø̃jʒ]; [fõ] *fond* ('bottom') > [fõw] ; [mõte] *monter* ('to go up') > [mõwte]. This is a phenomenon commonly found in Guernésiais (Sjögren 1964: xxxviii).
(ii) After a labial consonant, the first element of the secondary diphthong [ej] (< [e:]) may become rounded, hence [øj]. For example [møj] *mé* ('me').

3.3.2. *Lexis*

The previous section has shown that the *parlers* of Jèrriais show both phonological and phonetic variation, with regional differences apparent in the inventory of contrastive phonological units as well as in the local realization of some phonological units. Different kinds of variation are also to be found in the dialect's lexis, with some words varying somewhat randomly all over Jersey, for example *car'nas* [karnɑ:], *cagu'nas* [kagnɑ:] and *cad'nas* [kadnɑ:] ('padlock'); *triste* [trist], *tristre* [tristr] ('sad'); but others display variation which is clearly localized, as table 3.1, reproduced from Spence (1993: 22–3), illustrates.

To touch briefly on the domain of morphology, Le Maistre (1979a: 3) notes that certain third person plural past historic forms are restricted to St Ouen, for example *i' vidrent* ('they saw'), *il' eûdrent* ('they had'), *i' trouvîdrent* ('they found'), *i' vindrent* ('they came'), *i' fûdrent* ('they went') (for *i' vitent*, *il' eûtent*, *i' trouvitent*, *i' vintent* and *i' fûtent* elsewhere on the Island). However, he adds that only a few dozen or so speakers still use them. These forms are also commonly found in *Histouaithes et gens d'Jèrri*

Table 3.1 Lexical variation in Jèrrais

WJ	EJ
acouo [akwo]	oucouo/ aucouo (and aucouore, according to the *Dictionnaire Jersiais–Français* (Le Maistre 1966)) 'atill'
bandé	haûlinne [haulin] 'line from lobster-pot to surface'
ca(r)drinnette	cardrounnette 'goldfinch'
câgnon 'whipple-tree'	câgnon or caîllon [kɔ:jõ] 'chain locking beam of plough to plough-carriage'
câlée (and fourcée)	fourcée 'litter (mainly of piglets)'
cliav'ter [kjavte]	SEJ marânder 'to attend to lobster- and crab-pots'
corlieu [kɔrljœ]	courlieu [kurjø] 'curlew'
couarder	couinner '(of hen) to be on the point of becoming broody'
couardérêsse	couinnerêsse, couinnarde, couinne, couarde 'broody hen'
couvèrt [kuvɛr], couvèrcl'ye [kuvɛrkj]	couercl'ye [kwɛrkj] 'lid, cover'
NWJ couvèrtuthe	EJ, most WJ lief [jɛf] 'roof'
NWJ drove, WJ dovre	dovre, drogue and douvre 'dry drain' (cf. Fr. douve)
feunmi (St Ouen feunmyi)	EJ conré (and funmi) 'manure'
gaveleux (NWJ gavelot)	gavelyi [gavji] (pl. gacelièrs) 'cradle of scythe (rack fitted for gathering corn into sheaves)'
SWJ, NWJ houter [hu:te]	haûter [houte] 'to doze'
hueûlîn m. [wœ:lẽ]	pihangne [pihan] f. 'spider crab'
jutcheux	jutchas 'perch'
lîngnon [liɲõ]	lîn'non 'snood of fishing line'
migoût [migu:]	migaût [migou] 'store of eating apples'
moueu (pl. moueurs)	moué 'hub of wheel'
moûler [mu:le]	maûler [maule] 'to chew'
moûque [mu:k]	môque [mouk] 'fly'
ôsaine [ouzɛn]	ôsanne [ouzan], SEJ oûsaine/ oûsanne 'window-pane'
paînfais m.	bênarde f. 'hogweed'
papillote	papillon, SEJ paouillon [paupijõ] 'butterfly'
paqu'nôte	pâsserole, pâssecole 'ladybird'
pèrreuse f.	couerte f. 'pile of sea-weed weighed down by stones'
pêtre m.	aithangnie (NWJ ithangnie) 'spider' (in WJ, aithangnie means 'spider's web', as araignée did in O. French. The word pêtre is derived from the same root as pédestre – the spider has a lot of feet!)
NWJ pieuvre	Other WJ, EJ peuvre, peurve
pônchet, NWJ pânchet	pônchi, paûchi [pauʃi] 'thumb'
puchot	paîme f. 'scoop'
sétchi, s'tchi	sitchi 'to dry'
tchênelle	gliand [gjã] 'acorn'
vanné	pitounne 'scallop, queen scallop'

('Stories and people of Jersey') and *Jèrri jadis* ('Jersey yesteryear') (Le Feuvre 1976, 1983), which are, to date, the only substantial volumes of prose published entirely in Jèrriais and which were written by George Le Feuvre, who, like Le Maistre, was a native of St Ouen.

3.3.3. *Discussion*

Jèrriais clearly displays a large amount of internal variation although, as Spence notes, 'the general trends of linguistic development in the island and in the Cotentin continue to remain surprisingly close. There are few, if any, secondary developments in Jèrriais which are not found in identical or similar form over areas, large or small, of Lower Normandy', and he goes on to list and discuss some of these (1957a: 85–9). Moreover, as seen in section 3.2., the dialect also shares with Mainland Norman dialects a number of morphological and syntactic features which, Spence speculates, are of 'considerable antiquity' (1957a: 87–8).

As suggested in Langlois' poem, the presence of regional differences in Jèrriais does not pose problems of intelligibility. In the first place, despite vocabulary differences of the kind mentioned above, the majority of lexical items remain the same throughout Jersey. Moreover, the small size of the Island means that people from all over Jersey are accustomed to conversing with speakers from different parishes and, furthermore, since the phonetic differences in question occur in predictable contexts, speakers become used to recognizing correspondences between their *parler* and those spoken elsewhere and 'converting' one into another. For example, when we were discussing different words, people often told me 'we say this in our parish but people in Parish X say Y', and even the most unobservant speaker of Jèrriais could easily tell whether someone's *parler* was from the east or the west of Jersey. The regional variation is, therefore, well known within the speech community and seems to prove unproblematic vis-à-vis communication (cf. section 4.3.2.2.).

The decline of Jèrriais means that fewer people are speaking the different *parlers* and, on the face of it, it would seem likely that the varieties spoken in more urban areas of the Island, which have been Anglicized longest, would be the ones to disappear first. However, examination of speaker numbers and their distribution throughout Jersey reveals a more complex picture. In 1949, Le Maistre stated that there were no Jèrriais-speaking children left in St Brélade, St Clément, Grouville or St Sauveur and that in St Hélier no child had been brought up on Jèrriais for at least fifty years. In St Laurent and St Pierre, dialect-speaking children were something of a rarity, and although there were more in Ste Marie and St Jean, in Trinité the dialect was also starting to disappear amongst schoolchildren. In St Martin, children with an active knowledge of Jèrriais were to be found but their numbers were decreasing steadily (Lechanteur 1949: 213). At the time of Lechanteur's enquiry, St Ouen was the parish that contained most Jèrriais-speaking children, but it is plain that, even fifty years ago, the rural *parlers* were losing the fight against English. Today, this pattern continues. The 1989 Census, which, as mentioned in chapter 2, is the only one to date to have contained a question regarding the ability of respondents to speak Jèrriais,

Table 3.2 Jèrriais speakers by parish

Parish	Speakers	Total population	Speakers as a proportion of total (%)
Grouville	240	4,173	5.8
St Brélade	577	9,275	6.2
St Clément	425	7,205	5.9
St Hélier	1,352	27,549	4.9
St Jean	324	2,420	13.4
St Laurent	376	4,415	8.5
St Martin	300	3,271	9.2
Ste Marie	193	1,442	13.4
St Ouen	477	3,461	13.8
St Pierre	415	4,209	9.9
St Sauveur	725	12,795	5.7
Trinité	316	2,594	12.2
Total	5,720	82,809	6.9

Source: after the 1989 Census of Jersey, p. 16

revealed that speaker numbers did not exceed 14 per cent of the total population in any parish (see table 3.2).

As may be seen from table 3.2, the town–country divide was still apparent in 1989, with more rural parishes averaging around 13 per cent Jèrriais speakers while the town parishes had an average of 5–6 per cent. From this, Jersey's rural parishes would seem to be resisting twice as well as more urban ones but, when the actual figures are scrutinized, it becomes apparent that, numerically, more speakers are actually living in parishes such as St Brélade and St Sauveur (not to mention St Hélier) than in the so-called 'bastions' of Jèrriais. Le Maistre's prediction that Jèrriais 'survivra quelque temps dans "la vieille pâraisse dé Saint-Ou" quand le reste de l'île l'aura oublié' (Lechanteur 1949: 214) and that 'c'est là [à St Ouen] que . . . auront lieu les funérailles de la langue Jèrriaise' (Lechanteur 1949: 213–14) is, therefore, by no means guaranteed to come true.[28]

Another cause for concern among revitalizers must also surely be that, despite Le Maistre's description of the parish of St Ouen as 'la forteresse de la langue' ('the language's fortress') (Lechanteur 1949: 213) the Census figures show that, in 1989, this parish had just 0.4 percentage points more speakers as a proportion of the total population than St Jean and Ste Marie. Although, by sheer force of numbers, Jèrriais is likely to survive longer in St Ouen than in these two parishes,[29] it will only outlast the town parishes if, as is admittedly likely, given the greater density of speakers and therefore the enhanced possibilities of transmission, the 10 per cent of the Island's speakers who, in 1989, were aged 15–39 mostly live in St Ouen. If the distribution of this age-group is more or less uniform throughout the different parishes then, all else being equal, Jèrriais may cease to be spoken more or less simultaneously across the Island.

If Jèrriais disappears area by area then regional variation will lessen. This has already been seen with regard to the so-called 'linguistic pockets' mentioned above, which, even in the heyday of Jèrriais, were comprised of a relatively small number of speakers. In 1947, in a paper entitled 'The Jersey language in its present state', given to a meeting of the Jersey Society in London, Le Maistre stated that although:

> 'lé mouêtîn'[30] is still spoken it is about to disappear as all the children of school age speak only English. These remarks apply equally well to La Rocque where 'lé rotchais' is heard only from the lips of the older generations. As regards Faldouët, though some children speak 'lé faldouais' their number is dwindling fast . . . The Mont Mado district . . . is also rapidly becoming anglicized . . . 'lé landîn'[31] is still extensively spoken by everyone including the children. (1947: 7)

By today, there exist very few people who can speak any of these highly localized varieties. Les Landes is still probably the most thriving linguistic pocket but, admittedly, the term 'thriving' may only be applied to *lé landîn* relative to other such varieties of Jèrriais. Spence identifies the *parlers* of La Rocque and La Moie as having very few remaining speakers (1985: 157 n.13). Indeed, in 1996, I was fortunate enough to be able to speak to Miss Kathleen Marté l'Boutillier, who was recognized as being the only remaining speaker of *lé mouêtîn*. She died in the summer of 2000.

Coupled with the decline of the so-called 'linguistic pockets' is the phenomenon of what I will term 'dialect mixing' on the Island. Le Maistre commented more than twenty years ago on the fact that regional variation was becoming less distinct, stating that many people whose parents were not both natives of the same part of the Island usually had a 'mixed form' of speech and noting that such a phenomenon was much more frequent than in former times (1979a: 14). This 'mixing' is a consequence of the Islanders' increased mobility, which, in its wake, has led to more contact with people from different parishes and has put an end to the norm of marrying within one's parish (cf. Schmidt 1991: 114–15). This suggests an interesting line of enquiry and will be explored further in chapter 6.

3.4. JÈRRIAIS: LANGUAGE OR DIALECT?

The question of what constitutes a language and a dialect has provoked much discussion among linguists. The main reason for this is the apparent impossibility of distinguishing between such varieties on purely linguistic grounds. As Matisoff states,

> Even if one rejects the flippant definition of a language as 'a dialect with an army and a navy', it is still undeniable that the distinction between

language and dialect is primarily a sociological and psychological matter, rather than something that can be decided by purely linguistic criteria. (1991: 193)

The case of Czech and Slovak is a good counter-example to disprove the frequently made claim that mutual intelligibility makes two varieties dialects whereas its absence means that they are different languages – for we unfailingly refer to these as 'languages' even though they are usually mutually comprehensible and, furthermore, there is no doubt whatsoever that there exists less of a communication barrier between these 'languages' than between the so-called 'dialects' of Chinese. It is also clear that the whole concept of mutual intelligibility is a highly problematic issue – some dialect speakers will understand each other better than others and, in any case, there usually exists a dialect continuum, with speakers of adjacent varieties more likely to be able to communicate with each other than those more geographically removed from one another.

Distinguishing languages from dialects is often as much a political issue as anything else. Elcock notes how, towards the middle of the last century, Moldavian, a variety spoken over part of Bessarabia, was claimed as a 'language' of the former Soviet Union (1975: 498) whereas, from a purely philological standpoint, it was difficult to classify it as anything other than a dialect of Daco-Rumanian. Psychological and sociological factors clearly feature largely in the equation, as do attitudes towards a variety, on the part of both the speakers and those outside the speech community, for there is a tendency among non-linguists to consider dialects as subordinate or inferior varieties and, accordingly, for the term to acquire negative connotations.[32] Such considerations are completely irrelevant to linguistics, where the terms 'language' and 'dialect' are non-judgemental and carry no implications of superiority or inferiority. Both are functionally adequate linguistic systems and, in many cases, varieties that are today considered as 'languages' started life as dialects: two cases in point close to home being standard French, which began life as the Francien dialect (Lodge 1993), and standard English, which was formerly the East Midland dialect (Leith 1983: 32–57). Jèrriais is generally considered to be a dialect by its linguistic commentators (Spence 1957a; Liddicoat 1990) but a language by the revitalizers (Le Maistre 1947; Birt 1985). The political overtones for the revitalizers are obvious: sociopolitically, calling a variety a 'language' is felt to impart greater status, perhaps even rendering the variety in question more 'worthy' of saving.

Using the criterion of mutual intelligibility, it is clear that the varieties spoken in the Channel Islands, in Normandy and indeed over the whole *langue d'oïl* (Northern French) area qualify as dialects of French. However, as mentioned above, the adequacy of this criterion is questionable – as exemplified by the fact that most WJ varieties show a far greater degree of mutual intelligibility with those spoken in Lower Normandy and with standard French than those of EJ.

Petyt (1980) put forward two additional criteria to distinguish between a language and a dialect, namely the existence of a written form and the question of whether the same political allegiance is shared by their speakers. In the case of Jèrriais, these criteria raise more problems than they solve. To consider first the matter of a written form: although there existed no literary tradition for Jèrriais before the nineteenth century, since, until this time, it was not fashionable to write in local languages (Spence 1993: 42), it was seen in chapter 2 that Wace, the celebrated twelfth-century poet, is known to be a native of Jersey – although, as mentioned in that chapter, the additional supra-regional characteristics in his language make it impossible to claim that what he was writing was Jèrriais. Written texts in Jèrriais abound from the nineteenth century,[33] but show no consistency between themselves – each author has an idiosyncratic orthographic system and words are frequently spelt as they would be pronounced in the writer's native part of the Island, a practice still found today in the contemporary quarterly, the *Nouvelles Chroniques du Don Balleine* (see section 5.3.3.). Thus, although a written form of Jèrriais is commonly found in the nineteenth century, in practice this serves to divide, rather than unite, the *parlers*. For Petyt's second criterion, political allegiance, however, the converse is true, for although the Islanders identify with their parish at a local level, there is no question that their main loyalty is to the Island as a whole, and it is certainly not allied to that of France.[34]

The use of established criteria, therefore, does not prove particularly helpful in establishing which label we should assign to Jèrriais, and it may be more useful to consider the question from a different angle. In the Old French period, Norman was on a par with Champenois, Picard and the other varieties spoken in the Northern Gallo-Romance area. Of these varieties – usually termed dialects on the grounds that they were spoken across a relatively restricted area – one, Francien, the variety spoken in the Ile de France area, was, for sociopolitical reasons, elevated to the status of standard French, which we distinguish from the other varieties by giving it the label 'language', a term which denotes its changed sociopolitical status and symbolic function as linguistic unifier of the territory known as France. Part of the process of becoming standardized as a language involves codification. The aim of this is to make the standard language a more or less homogeneous entity. This is rarely the case with dialects – the briefest glance at a dialect map shows that, unlike the boundaries of a standard language, which are usually politically delineated, those of a dialect will be less clear cut, with dialects often merging gradually with another as part of a continuum. Dialects, therefore, are rarely homo-geneous and, although a high degree of mutual intelligibility may be found within the area of their extension due to the existence of a 'common core' of linguistic features, different points in their territories will often show some variation from one another.

Localized, mutually intelligible varieties with low socioeconomic status, either with or without an over-arching standard, may be more appropriately described as dialects than languages, and this, I suggest, also holds true for Jèrriais. However, although at present the former term seems to be more appropriate than the latter, developments during the past few decades have meant that the situation may be starting to change. As will be seen in chapter 5, in recent years, the publication of a comprehensive Jèrriais–French dictionary containing some 20,000 entries, the *Dictionnaire Jersiais–Français* ('Jèrriais–French Dictionary') (Le Maistre 1966; hereafter DJF), a Jèrriais grammar (Birt 1985) and two volumes of prose (Le Feuvre 1976, 1983) in the variety spoken in NWJ have led to a situation where this variety (St Ouennais) is beginning to emerge as a linguistic 'first among equals' with respect to the other *parlers*. In view of this, it is perhaps worth considering whether St Ouennais may legitimately start being considered as standard Jèrriais.[35]

Haugen's schema for the standardization of languages (Haugen 1966) identified four main stages, namely selection, codification, elaboration of functions and acceptance. These steps have been identified in, among others, the creation of standard French (Lodge 1993). If this schema is applied to modern Jèrriais, it is clear that the linguistic stages of the process, namely selection and codification, are already under way. The sociopolitical stages of standardization are somewhat less advanced: Jèrriais is undoubtedly being introduced to new domains but, as will be discussed in chapter 5, its presence in some of these is decidedly limited so that, as yet, it is difficult to claim that the variety has undergone a full elaboration of functions. As regards Haugen's fourth stage, acceptance, although there is no objection to the *parler* of NWJ becoming the 'first among equals' or to the DJF becoming the normative work of reference throughout the speech community, due to the fact that Jèrriais has, until very recently, been excluded from the classroom (Spence 1993: 3), it is extremely unlikely that native speakers of other *parlers* will adopt St Ouennais themselves, for the purposes of either speech or writing. Thus, the only people who will simultaneously both accept and make use of the St Ouennais-based standard will be the second-language learners, who have no possibility of learning, and indeed do not have much contact with, any other variety.

After centuries of being spoken on Jersey, therefore, Jèrriais is finally becoming standardized. As will be discussed in chapter 5, language planning in recent decades has ensured that the stages identified by Haugen as crucial to the emergence of a standard are, at least, under way, even if not yet complete.[36] This seems to suggest that, if Jèrriais lives long enough and if, crucially, sufficient institutional backing may be obtained to further the sociopolitical parts of the process, then it may, in time, be appropriate to refer to the variety as a language. However, as the following chapter will begin to demonstrate, at present time does not appear to be on the side of Jèrriais.

4

A SOCIOLINGUISTIC PROFILE OF THE JÈRRIAIS SPEECH COMMUNITY

4.1. INTRODUCTION

Although the 1989 Census was, for the first time, able to establish numbers of Jèrriais speakers, their age and parishes of residence, it did little more than elicit information on a yes/no basis regarding an individual's ability to speak Jèrriais, and provided no information regarding the nature of the speech community in terms of literacy skills, intergenerational transmission of Jèrriais, attitudes towards the variety and the domains in which it was most frequently used. Thus, it has not hitherto been possible to build up a reliable portrait of the nature of the dialect's speech community. In an attempt to compensate for this, a questionnaire addressing the above areas was administered to fifty adults, all of whom were native speakers of Jèrriais and who had lived on Jersey for most of their lives.

4.2. METHODOLOGY

The fieldwork-based chapters of this study rely on data obtained from one set of informants via a three-part interview comprising a sociolinguistic questionnaire (analysed in this chapter), a tape-recorded conversation (analysed in chapter 6 and in part of chapter 8) and a lexical questionnaire (analysed in chapter 7). The sampling technique described below, therefore, holds good for all the above chapters.

a. *Sampling technique*
Fieldwork-driven studies of minority varieties often encounter problems in securing a sample that is both large enough and representative enough of the speech community to make the results meaningful. Given the fact that only some 7 per cent of the population of Jersey still speak Jèrriais, it was not possible to select informants by means of a random sampling technique such as that used by Labov (1966) in the Lower East Side of New York City. Moreover, in the tape-recorded part of the study, I was aiming to try and observe how informants normally spoke when not being observed – in other words, I wanted to overcome, or at least to minimize, what Labov termed the 'observer's paradox', namely the problem of finding out through systematic observation how people speak when not being systematically

observed (1985: 209). This was potentially a serious problem, given my status as an outsider who wanted to gain access to a restricted speech community for which Jèrriais was not normally a variety used to strangers, and for whose members the dialect could potentially be a cause of stigmatization. The only technique that seemed to go any way towards tackling these problems was the so-called 'friend-of-a-friend' technique, which was devised by Lesley Milroy in the course of her work on the urban vernacular of Belfast and which is described in detail in Milroy (1980).

Milroy's solution to the observer's paradox was to become part of the system that she was observing. This was achieved by being introduced to it as a 'friend-of-a-friend' rather than in a formal capacity as a researcher. By using this technique, therefore, the researcher aims to avoid being identified as an outsider, with all the associated connotations of power and formality and, instead, seeks to become accepted by interviewees by virtue of association with a mutual friend (Milroy 1987: 66).

In order to use this sampling technique, it was necessary to gain a foothold in the community by establishing contact with someone willing to act as a 'linchpin' by introducing me to a number of friends and acquaintances, who, in turn, would introduce me to their friends and acquaintances, and so forth. In this way, I was able to gain access to several social networks within the Jèrriais speech community and, thereby, a large number of different speakers. Clearly, as the importance of the initial 'linchpin' is paramount, a great deal of care is needed in the selection process. In this case, the 'linchpin' chosen was quite a prominent figure in the Jèrriais revitalization movement. Such an individual, it seemed, would by definition know a large number of Jèrriais speakers. Moreover, it was hoped that this association with a young pro-Jèrriais campaigner who had learnt Jèrriais as a second language might make my eagerness to hold a conversation in Jèrriais seem more understandable to many informants.

Although the friend-of-a-friend technique is well established (Milroy 1980), it has not escaped criticism (Williams 1992: 191). However, working in the field of minority languages, Ball and Müller have expressed the following opinion:

> It is often found that social networks of minority language speakers are fairly dense, in that it is the social network (rather than geographical areas) that maintains the usage of the language. In this case, if researchers can gain access to such a network, therefore, they can obtain linguistic data from many members of the network, and an analysis of a set of networks will probably be representative of the speakers of the minority language in that community as a whole. (1992: 246)

As will be demonstrated, this technique is highly suitable for eliciting data when the object of study is a restricted, even stigmatized, variety. In the first place, given the fact that the number of speakers of Jèrriais is not high, it is extremely likely that a more random sampling technique would have failed to produce an adequate number of informants during the fieldwork period. Moreover, since, as stated above, Jèrriais is not considered by speakers as a variety to be used with strangers, it is likely that the use of a different sampling technique would have led to more reluctance on the part of informants to participate in my study, whereas, with this method, the fact that informants were given a familiar point of reference seemed to help keep down the number of refusals. Furthermore, it could be argued that the 'friend-of-a-friend' technique has itself an in-built degree of randomness, as the choice of people to whom the researcher gets introduced is beyond her or his control.

Using this technique, fifty adults were interviewed, all of whom were native speakers of Jèrriais who had been born on the Island and who had lived there for most of their lives. The social network method of data collection had the inevitable repercussion of yielding informants who were concentrated in one part of the Island. However, this tendency was not unadvantageous in that it was sufficient to break into a network in one parish to obtain an adequate sample of informants from that parish.

Milroy's work on the urban vernacular of Belfast showed that the closer an individual's ties were with their local community, the more closely his or her language approximated to localized vernacular norms (1987: 78, 106). However, Dorian's study of the Gaelic spoken amongst a relatively homo-geneous population in East Sutherland revealed well-established patterns of intra-village and intra-speaker variations that had no correlation with social factors (Dorian 1994b). The conflicting results of these two studies means that it is not completely safe to assume that, due to the dense network ties that are to be found in the parishes of Jersey, the speech of one member of a network is necessarily similar to that of another. However, as the research method involved breaking into networks from several parishes, the speech of the native speakers interviewed did, at least, reflect tendencies present in different parts of the Island, rather than concentrating on one area alone. It is hoped that this made the sample more representative of the Jèrriais speech community.

The make-up of the sample was as follows (according to parish of origin):

St Ouen	12 informants
Trinité	10 informants
St Martin	8 informants
St Laurent	7 informants
St Jean	6 informants
Ste Marie	4 informants
Grouville	1 informant
St Hélier	1 informant
St Brélade	1 informant

No informants were located in the parishes of St Pierre, St Clément or St Sauveur. Of those interviewed, thirty were male and twenty were female. Nineteen informants were aged 70 and over, eighteen were aged 60–9, twelve were aged 40–59 and one was aged 20–39. A profile of the speakers is given in appendix 1.

As can be seen above, social networks were broken into in six of the twelve parishes. Moreover, given that, according to the the 1989 Census, speakers of Jèrriais are most heavily concentrated in percentage terms in St Ouen, St Jean, Ste Marie and Trinité (cf. table 3.2), it is not surprising that, again in percentage terms, most of the informants also came from these parishes. Although it was not a prerequisite that informants lived in the same parish as they had been born in, due to the strong parish-based attachment prevalent on Jersey, and the relative ease with which it is possible to choose exactly one's preferred area of residence, given the fact that distances on the Island are so small, it emerged that thirty out of the fifty informants interviewed had lived all their life in their parish of origin. This statistic made it possible to undertake a study of what I have termed 'dialect mixing', which is considered in section 6.4.3.

b. *Procedure*
The use of questionnaires to gather data is a common feature of socio-linguistic studies (Dorian 1981; Mackinnon 1977; Carruthers 1999). The advantages and limitations of this technique are, however, self-evident. Questionnaires are easy to distribute and to analyse but the inevitable self-reporting on the part of informants means that there is no assurance as to the complete reliability of what they say.

As the questionnaire represented the only practical way of eliciting information about informants' use of Jèrriais, it was decided to administer the questionnaire to each informant orally rather than giving it to them to take away and fill in themselves. This ensured that I was on hand to help with any comprehension difficulties that arose and prevented informants from comparing their responses with those of other people, with the consequent temptation to 'redo' questions. Of course, it also meant that a full return was guaranteed.

Another frequently levelled accusation is that questionnaires elicit stereo-typed responses. This might have been problematic if the aim of this chapter had been to obtain an empirically accurate portrayal of the Jèrriais speech community, where it was important that every result reported should reflect precise numerical information about that community. However, given the fact that the sample represents a small percentage of the speech community, even were the numerical accuracy of all the results able to be guaranteed for this sample, it would be somewhat imprudent to claim that these were then able to be further generalized to the speech community as a whole. The results presented in this chapter, therefore, are intended to represent general trends at large in the community rather than precise numerical information, and the scores themselves should be interpreted not as exact statistics pertaining to the speech community but rather as conveyors of the tendencies revealed. Finally, as sociolinguists such as Labov have shown (1985: 117–18), it is often interesting to see what people *think* they do as well as what they actually *do* do.

In an attempt to ensure success in this part of the survey, the questionnaire used was one which had been tried and tested on two prior occasions. It was essentially that devised by Fañch Broudic and had first been used in a survey of the linguistic practices and language attitudes of 1,000 people throughout Lower Brittany (Broudic 1991). I also had some personal experience of using the questionnaire during a study undertaken of the situation of Breton in the *commune* (rural administrative district) of Plougastel-Daoulas (Jones 1996) and was therefore aware of its potential pitfalls. This meant that I was well placed to be able to make the necessary adjustments required in order to use the questionnaire in a Jèrriais context.

Whereas the original questionnaire had aimed to elicit information about both Breton speakers and non-Breton speakers, in this instance the study was limited to the Jèrriais speech community.[1] Thus, although not all the results obtained in this chapter are identical in focus to those obtained in Jones (1996) and Broudic (1991), many of them are, in fact, directly comparable. Using questionnaires of a similar format to collect data on minority languages may prove to be a profitable strategy in that it facilitates inter-language comparison, which may have a bearing on subsequent language planning.

4.3. RESULTS

4.3.1. *Ability to use Jèrriais in everyday life*

4.3.1.1. *Daily use of Jèrriais*

Although all those interviewed spoke Jèrriais fluently, and as their native language, only 34 per cent made regular use of the dialect on a day-to day basis and, as table 4.1 demonstrates,[2] a mere 18 per cent stated that they used

Table 4.1 'How often do you speak Jèrriais?'

Frequency	% (number)
More often than English	18% (9)
As often as English	66% (33)
Less often than English	16% (8)

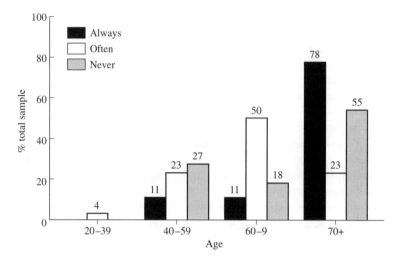

Figure 4.1 Daily use of Jèrriais correlated with age

Jèrriais more often than English. This indicates the progressive Anglicization that is taking place on the Island, since it is likely that an individual who has acquired Jèrriais but who hardly ever uses it may represent the last generation of fluent speakers within his or her family. It was also noteworthy that 78 per cent of those who spoke Jèrriais as their main everyday language were aged 70 and over.

Figure 4.1[3] indicates that the age of informants was clearly related to the frequency with which they spoke Jèrriais. Only those aged 70 and over used the dialect on a daily basis to any significant degree. Nevertheless, although it did not function as an everyday means of communication to such an extent for informants aged 40–69, Jèrriais was still quite widely used by the members of this group, for whom it is likely that the dialect had functioned as a home and community language during their childhood. This suggests that networks of relatives and friends still exist for people of this age. Most significant of all, however, was the near total absence of informants under the age of 40. Although there undoubtedly exist native speakers under this age,[4] the fact that I was only able to locate one such individual, despite asking repeatedly, indicates that they are few and far between. The absence of such speakers is particularly noticeable given that speakers aged 40–59 are not uncommon.[5] Although Jèrriais did not cease to be spoken overnight and had been in decline for centuries (see chapter 2), such a salient change in the nature of the speech community suggests the occurrence of a significant sociopolitical event which has left its mark on the Island and, given the age-group involved in this case, it seems that these results reflect the sharp decline in speaker numbers that occurred in the wake of the Second World War.

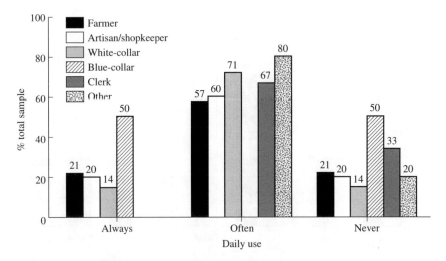

Figure 4.2 Use of Jèrriais according to socioeconomic status

The fact that Jèrriais was found to be used equally by people from all walks of life is also indicative of its widespread use in the community prior to the Second World War (see figure 4.2). This differs from the findings in Brittany, where use of Breton tended to be restricted to workers in the agricultural sector (Jones 1996: 53–4).

4.3.1.2. *Use of Jèrriais by parish*

The 1989 Census records that the speakers of Jèrriais were most heavily concentrated in percentage terms in the parishes of St Ouen, St Jean, Ste Marie and Trinité, with St Laurent, St Martin and St Pierre forming an intermediate tier between these four and the urban parishes of Grouville, St Brélade, St Clément, St Hélier and St Sauveur (cf. table 3.2).

Although it was only possible to analyse data with regard to the parishes of St Ouen, St Laurent, Trinité, St Jean and St Martin, as the samples obtained from other parishes were too small, it was interesting that the vast majority of informants from all these parishes made frequent use of Jèrriais – presumably due to the existence of more opportunity to speak their native tongue and less need to resort to English than in the urban parishes. Significantly, the informants who claimed to speak Jèrriais more than English all came from St Ouen, St Martin and Trinité (figure 4.3).

4.3.1.3. *Reading proficiency*

Of the sample, 70 per cent could read Jèrriais proficiently (figure 4.4). Given the fact that the dialect was not taught in schools before 1999 and has long ceased

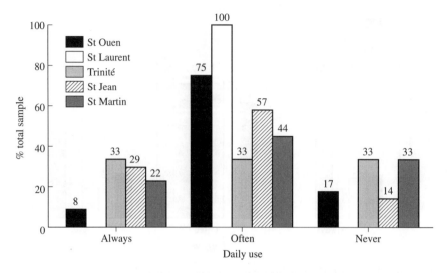

Figure 4.3 Frequency of use of Jèrriais correlated with parish of origin

to be used in church (see chapter 2), this percentage seems quite high.[6] It may be attributable to the fact that standard French is taught as a compulsory part of the primary school curriculum from the age of 7 onwards. As Jèrriais and standard French are both Northern (*langue d'oïl*) varieties, it is likely that ability to read the latter facilitates the task of reading the former. When asked whether they could read Jèrriais, it was not uncommon for informants to state that they could but with the caveat that the ease with which they did so often depended on the writer. Although Jèrriais has arguably been

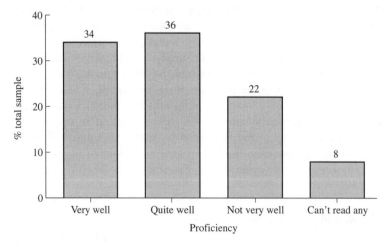

Figure 4.4 'Can you read any Jèrriais?'

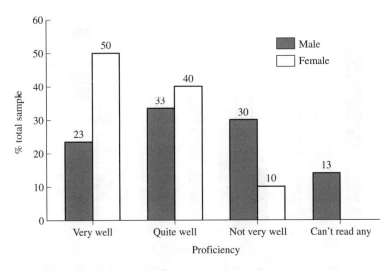

Figure 4.5 Ability to read Jèrriais correlated with sex of informants

standardized since the appearance of the *Dictionnaire Jersiais–Français* (see section 3.4.), the absence of any formal means of teaching it has meant that the standard spelling has not been enforced – or even prescribed – to any significant degree. The result of this is that writers often develop their own system, based on their particular sub-dialect (see section 3.3.), and it is therefore to be expected that uninitiated speakers will have less difficulty in reading a graphy based on their own *parler*.

When ability to read was correlated with the sex of informants (figure 4.5), it emerged that women's skills in this area were more advanced than those of their male counterparts, nearly half of whom were unable to read the dialect without difficulty. The reasons for this gender-based discrepancy are at present unclear.

When ability to read was correlated with the parish of informants (figure 4.6), it was found that those with the greatest reading proficiency came from St Ouen, a parish where, as seen in table 3.2, the concentration of Jèrriais speakers in percentage terms is among the highest on the Island (13.8 per cent). Figures obtained for St Jean, where 13.4 per cent of the population speak Jèrriais, were also high, as were those for St Laurent, even though only 8.5 per cent of its population has any knowledge of Jèrriais.[7]

It was not surprising to find that, as table 4.2 indicates, the most proficient readers of Jèrriais were also those individuals who spoke the dialect most frequently, while those illiterate in the dialect also tended to be those who spoke it least.

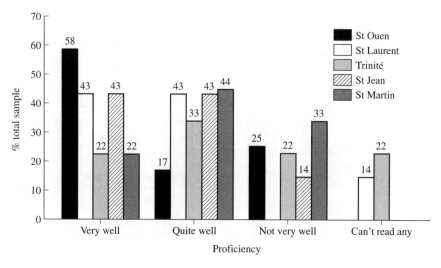

Figure 4.6 Ability to read Jèrriais correlated with parish of origin

Table 4.2 Reading proficiency in Jèrriais correlated with frequency of use

Frequency of use/ reading proficiency	Always: % (number)	Often: % (number)	Never: % (number)
Very well	23.5% (4)	64.7% (11)	11.8% (2)
Quite well	16.7% (3)	66.7% (12)	16.7% (3)
Not very well	18.2% (2)	54.5% (6)	27.3% (3)
Can't read any Jèrriais		25.0% (1)	75.0% (3)

4.3.1.4. *Writing proficiency*

One in five of the sample was able to write Jèrriais without difficulty, with just over half of those interviewed claiming not be able to write the dialect at all (figure 4.7). However, it is possible that these statistics may, in fact, overstate the Jèrriais' ability to write their dialect in that, as with the question on reading skills, several informants claimed not be able to write 'official' (i.e. standard, DJF-based) Jèrriais but rather used their idiosyncratic system.[8] These figures also revealed a sex-based discrepancy, with women again ahead of men in terms of their writing proficiency (figure 4.8). When writing skills were correlated with parish of origin, St Ouen and St Jean emerged as the parishes with the largest number of people able to write the dialect and the fewest non-writers (figure 4.9). Table 4.3 indicates that most of those who felt able to write most competently used Jèrriais as

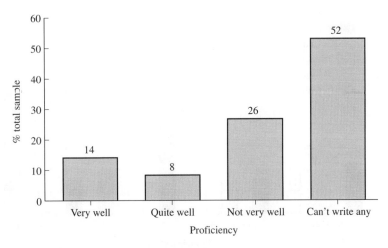

Figure 4.7 'Can you write any Jèrriais?'

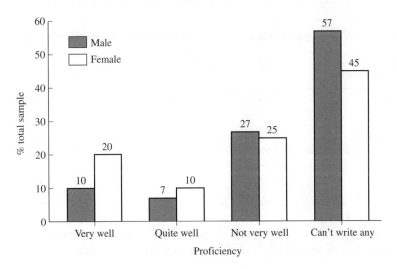

Figure 4.8 Ability to write Jèrriais correlated with sex of informants

their main language, whilst over half of those who spoke English more regularly than Jèrriais were unable to write the dialect.

4.3.2. *Contexts in which Jèrriais is spoken*

As all speakers of Jèrriais are bilingual, they potentially have a choice of language every time they speak. Since choice is inevitably influenced by the

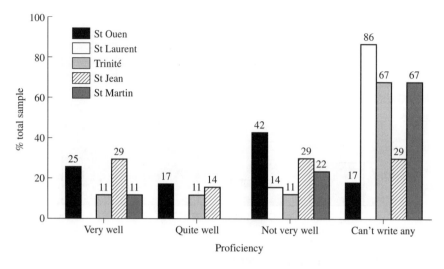

Figure 4.9 Ability to write Jèrriais correlated with parish of origin

Table 4.3 Writing proficiency in Jèrriais correlated with frequency of use

Frequency of use/ writing proficiency	Always: % (number)	Often: % (number)	Never: % (number)
Very well	42.9% (3)	57.1% (4)	
Quite well	25.0% (1)	75.0% (3)	
Not very well	15.4% (2)	53.8% (7)	30.8% (4)
Can't write any Jèrriais	11.5% (3)	61.5% (16)	26.9% (7)

context of the situation and the person whom they are addressing (Mertz 1989: 114; Dorian 1981: 76; Appel and Muysken 1993: 23), information about contexts most and least likely to provoke use of Jèrriais enabled the identification of the variety's strongest and weakest domains.

4.3.2.1. *Interlocutor*

The results indicated clearly the progressive Anglicization of the Jèrriais speech community that took place during the twentieth century. Table 4.4 indicates that all informants spoke or had spoken Jèrriais to their grand-parents and nearly all of them did or had done so to their parents, yet only 62 per cent and 54 per cent respectively of those who had brothers and sisters spoke the dialect to their siblings and even fewer used the variety with their own offspring (17 per cent and 27 per cent respectively of those who had either a son or daughter). Jèrriais is therefore considered as an appropriate

Table 4.4 'To whom do you speak Jèrriais?'

Interlocutor	% (number)[a]
Grandparents	100% (50)
Mother	98% (49)
Father	98% (49)
Friends	86% (43)
Brother	62% (16)
Sister	54% (15)
Neighbours	54% (27)
Partner	51% (24)
Daughter	27% (10)
Colleagues	22% (5)
Son	17% (5)
Grandchildren	12% (3)
Employer	0%

[a] The percentages here are of the sample eligible to respond to the question.

variety to use with one's family, but the decrease in its use in this domain is also evident: despite the fact that the purpose of the figures used here is to indicate general trends involved rather than any precise numerical value, the language shift that has taken place over three generations is plain to see, and although 12 per cent of informants who had grandchildren declared that they spoke Jèrriais to them, in practice this turned out to consist of teaching them the occasional word as something of a novelty rather than holding any form of conversation.

It goes without saying that the linguistic ability of a speaker's partner also has repercussions for the transmission of Jèrriais, for if that partner cannot speak the dialect it is unlikely that it will become the variety used in the home (Mougeon and Beniak 1989: 292; Kibrik 1991: 259). This is particularly noteworthy, since the reduction in speaker numbers throughout the nineteenth and twentieth centuries has meant that Jèrriais speakers have become statistically less and less likely to have a Jèrriais-speaking spouse.[9]

The fact that 86 per cent of the sample also used the dialect on a regular basis with friends corroborates the findings above, namely that Jèrriais is felt to be suitable for close relationships. Moreover, it reflects the close network ties that exist within the Jèrriais speech community in that many native speakers have other native speakers as friends. There may be several reasons why only 54 per cent used the dialect to neighbours, the most obvious being the latter's relative competence and/or confidence in Jèrriais; but it is also the case that the language of one's partner can be a factor in determining whether English or Jèrriais is used with one's neighbours, and once the initial linguistic choice has been made, it is rarely changed. Of course, unlike the case with one's friends, one does not usually choose one's neighbours and, in more Anglicized parts of the Island, these are statistically more likely not to be able to speak Jèrriais, especially if they are under the age of 40. However, since more than half of the Jèrriais speakers interviewed did actually use the dialect in this domain, it is clear that Jèrriais is also deemed to be appropriate for this type of relationship, which, like that of family and friends, is solidarity- rather than power-based.

Whilst Jèrriais was occasionally used to colleagues in the workplace, it was not spoken at all with an employer. This may be attributable to a reason such as the employer not being able to speak Jèrriais, but it might also reflect a feeling among Jèrriais speakers that the dialect is not an appropriate variety for power relationships (cf. Jones 1996: 55–6). It is, however, necessary to introduce a caveat here in that a discrepancy was found between people who worked or who had worked on the land and those who worked or had worked in offices or businesses. Many of the former owned or had owned smallholdings and did not therefore have an employer as such. Moreover, they seemed to use Jèrriais or English indiscriminately with their employees according to the linguistic abilities of their interlocutor. The 'employer' category is, therefore, based on the answers of thirteen informants who worked in offices or businesses, mainly in St Hélier. That these informants considered Jèrriais as a wholly inappropriate variety to be used with their employers indicates how the change in lifestyle and employment of the Jèrriais speakers is also affecting their use of the dialect.

4.3.2.2. Setting

Nearly all the speakers interviewed stated that they would readily use Jèrriais when speaking to people from other parishes (table 4.5), confirming that the phonological and lexical differences that exist between the different *parlers* (see section 3.3.) do not pose any major problem for communication. Such ease of inter-regional communication contrasts with the situation in other minority-language contexts. For example in Brittany, a study of the Breton spoken in the *commune* of Plougastel-Daoulas revealed that only 38 per cent of those questioned stated that they would use Breton with a native speaker from elsewhere in Brittany (Jones 1996: 56–7; cf. Hindley 1990: 216

Table 4.5 'Where do you speak Jèrriais?'

Setting	% (number)
With people from other parishes	94% (47)
Leisure	88% (44)
Work	54% (27)
Family	50% (25)
Local shops	12% (6)
Supermarket	8% (4)
Bank	4% (2)

on the sitation in Eire). The fact that regional differences are seen as an impediment to communication in Brittany though not in Jersey is probably due to the much greater diversity of forms in the former and also the fact that, on Jersey, both the geographical and numerical size of the Jèrriais speech community is small, which means that it is not uncommon for speakers to encounter features not found in their own *parler*. Although Breton is a language marked by dialectal differentiation, there exists an exaggerated feeling on the part of many Breton speakers that their variety of Breton is not intelligible to people from any other part of Brittany and vice versa, whereas in practice, it is likely that, given some effort, communication would be possible (J. Le Dû, p.c.).[10,11] On Jersey, however, although a diversity of forms is also to be found, given the small size of the Island, speakers are used to encountering such variation and do not perceive it as problematic and, consequently, it seems to offer no impediment to communication (cf. Boretzky 1994: 71).

As regards the other types of setting examined, although it was clear that Jèrriais was spoken most frequently during leisure time, 54 per cent of those interviewed also made – or had made – some use of it on a regular basis in the workplace. The results obtained in section 4.3.2.1. were confirmed in that the family was again revealed as a setting conducive to the production of Jèrriais, although as was observed in table 4.4, usage tended to vary in this domain according to which member of the family was being addressed. Further evidence of the Anglicization of the parishes was revealed by the fact that only 12 per cent of those interviewed regularly made use of Jèrriais in their local shops (and most people took pains to point out that this represented a big change vis-à-vis their youth). It came as no surprise that these informants all lived in St Ouen, St Jean and St Martin. At 8 per cent and 4 per cent respectively, the supermarket and bank were clearly not felt to 'belong' to the Jèrriais world.

With the exception of the domain of work, which was influenced by the particular nature of Plougastel-Daoulas, setting was found to influence the use of Breton and Jèrriais in a similar way (cf. Jones 1996: 56–9). In both communities, there appeared to be a psychological distinction in the minds of speakers governing the use of the minority variety that was based on a focus inwards towards the speech community or outwards towards the world beyond. Any suggestion on my part that the dialect might be used in a setting that was not identifiable with the established Jèrriais 'world' was greeted with mirth and sarcasm or a feeling that the dialect was inadequate for such purposes. As one informant put it, 'That'll be they day when we speak Jèrriais in a bank', or another, 'We don't have the words for that in Jersey French.'

4.3.3. *The way in which Jèrriais is transmitted*

4.3.3.1. *Parents*

Given that the entire sample was comprised of native speakers, as expected, it was found that all informants had learnt Jèrriais from their parents within the family setting. As will be discussed in section 5.4.1., 1999 was a landmark year for Jèrriais in that, for the first time, the dialect was taught in school. Before this, Jèrriais had never been taught in the Island's schools, even as an option, with the consequence that the school has never represented a possible means of language transmission. Although evening classes have provided a locus for learning Jèrriais in recent years, their success has been limited and they have not succeeded in producing fluent speakers who adopt Jèrriais as the language of the home. The recent introduction of the dialect into primary schools – albeit on an extra-curricular basis – represents a first step in the process of revitalization and will undoubtedly help kindle interest and enthusiasm among young people, but it remains to be seen whether such action will help re-establish the inter-generational chain of transmission, which is vital if Jèrriais is to remain alive.

The extent to which Jèrriais is being lost among speakers of the same family is represented in table 4.6, where it was revealed that 72.2 per cent of all speakers who spoke or had spoken Jèrriais to their parents regularly did not ever speak Jèrriais to their children. The language shift that has occurred over two generations is striking and, due to the absence of all but an embryonic movement for language maintenance (see chapter 5), no compensatory strategies are in place which could stem and make good this ebb of speakers. Such a rapid depletion from one generation to the next indicates that time may be starting to run out for Jèrriais and makes the need for a coherent and immediate programme of officially backed language planning imperative. The 'tip' (Dorian 1981: 51) towards English has already taken place and, if no action is taken, the downward spiral of speakers is likely to continue with the passing of every year.

Table 4.6 Inter-generational transmission of Jèrriais by parents who spoke Jèrriais regularly to their own parents

Frequency	% (number)[a]
Jèrriais spoken to children often	13.9% (5)
Jèrriais spoken to children sometimes	13.9% (5)
Jèrriais never spoken to children	72.2% (26)
Total	100.0% (36)

Notes: n/a 14
a The percentages here are of the sample eligible to respond to the question.

Table 4.7 Age of parents speaking Jèrriais to offspring

Age	Jèrriais spoken often/sometimes to offspring: % (number)[a]
20–39	0%
40–59	11.1% (1)
60–9	25.0% (3)
70+	40.0% (6)

[a] The percentages here are of the sample eligible to respond to the question.

Further evidence of the age-gradation within the process of shift was revealed when the ages of those who spoke Jèrriais to their offspring were examined (table 4.7). Most of them were aged 60 and above.[12]

4.3.3.2. *The role of the school*

From the above discussion, it is clear that the school has hitherto exercised no positive influence whatsoever on Jèrriais and, indeed, it was seen in chapter 2 that it has actually had quite the opposite effect. The cross-tabulation of the present age of informants (and their children) with their linguistic ability on starting school shows that between half and three-quarters of the sample interviewed were unable to speak English when they started school (figure 4.10). However they were, without exception, bilingual at the end of this period. This indicates that, although it may not have been the only factor behind the Anglicization of the speech community, the school has nevertheless played a significant role in this process.

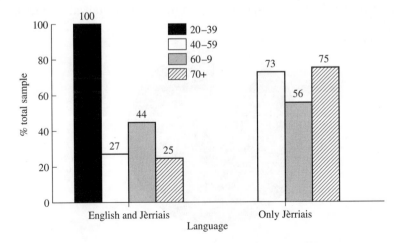

Figure 4.10 'When you started school, which language(s) could you speak?'

4.3.4. *Attitudes towards Jèrriais*

Within the field of sociolinguistics, the study of language attitudes has long been investigated via a number of methods, both direct (questionnaires, interviews, scaling techniques) and indirect (the matched guise test: Lambert, Hodgson, Gardner and Fillenbaum 1960). The importance of this area of research stems from the fact that people's attitudes towards a linguistic variety can be shown to influence their opinion of its speakers (Watson 1989: 44–5; Rouchdy 1989: 94) and their ability to acquire it (Gardner 1982). Trudgill's investigation of Arvanitika has shown that the attitude of its speakers towards their own variety could have important repercussions for its fate (Trudgill 1983), and Fishman (1991: 174) notes that positive attitudes towards a minority language on the part of the speakers of the dominant variety can help its revitalization.[13]

From my first encounter with Jèrriais, it became apparent that the dialect was seen by many of the Islanders as contrasting with the variety that they termed 'Good French' (i.e. standard French), with this very label implying that Jèrriais is perceived to be an inferior variety. In order to determine the prevalence among the current speech community of any such attitude, which might be affecting the dialect's linguistic prosperity, it was decided to include some questions on language attitudes in the questionnaire survey.

The fact that 90 per cent of those questioned were of the opinion that measures should be put in place in order to preserve Jèrriais reflects the unequivocal support that exists for the dialect among its speakers (figure 4.11). Although, on the face of it, this might appear to be predictable, it should be pointed out that, in Brittany, although native speakers were willing to pay lip service to the notion that Breton should be preserved, it was found that, in practice, the non-Breton speakers were often more supportive than the native speakers of some of the revitalization measures

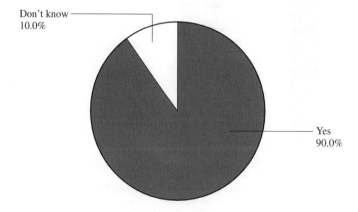

Figure 4.11 'Do you think that Jèrriais should be preserved?'

that had been established. Hence, it seems that, if the native speakers of an obsolescent variety consider it to be a hindrance to social advancement or a badge of backwardness they may be reluctant to support its revitalization (Kuter 1989: 80; Jones 1996: 66–7, 68–9). This groundswell of support at the grassroots level is, therefore, a major plus point in support of the movement for language maintenance in Jersey, for, as Grenoble and Whaley point out, 'a strong commitment to revitalization will have an impact on the viability of a language' (1998: 54) and 'the motivation of the population to maintain or revive a variety is crucial' (1998: 51).[14]

On being asked whether, in their opinion, Jèrriais would, in fact, succeed in being preserved, a more pessimistic picture appeared, with only one in five informants replying positively and half the sample expressing the belief that the dialect would probably die (figure 4.12). Some typical comments were: 'Jèrriais is simply not used any more', 'It's been shunned by a whole generation' or 'Jersey French doesn't boost your chance of employment.' There exists a clear discrepancy, therefore, between the hopes and the expectations of Jèrriais speakers regarding the future of their dialect. No significant difference of opinion was recorded on the basis of parish.

Due to the discrepancy found in the Plougastel-Daoulas survey between willingness to preserve their language in the abstract and actual support for established language-planning action (Jones 1996: 63–70), Jèrriais informants were also asked their opinion about more concrete measures pertaining to language maintenance. By doing this, it was hoped to determine whether or not the reactions manifested in figures 4.11 and 4.12 had been genuine declarations of support for Jèrriais or merely automatic responses.

The first such issue examined was the idea of teaching Jèrriais in school. As mentioned above, Jèrriais was introduced into the Island's primary schools in 1999. As surveys were undertaken to gauge the level of support

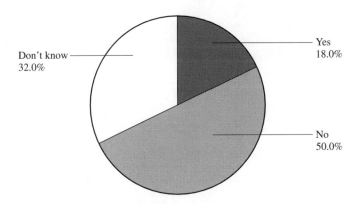

Figure 4.12 'Do you think that Jèrriais will be preserved?'

for this measure prior to the lodging of this proposal in the States, this was quite a topical issue at the time of the data collection.

Two-thirds of the sample declared themselves in favour of the inclusion of Jèrriais as a subject on the school curriculum, with 16 per cent against and a fifth of those asked remaining undecided (figure 4.13). Those in favour of teaching Jèrriais explained their choice with reasons such as 'It's part of our heritage' and 'It's the language of our Island', whilst those against declared that Jèrriais was 'a matter for the home, not for school', and expressed fear that learning the dialect might hinder progress in other subjects: 'The world is competitive and the curriculum is already loaded with essential subjects' or 'They [the children] need Good French since we're so near to France – Jersey French would mix them up.'[15] One informant merely exclaimed 'What's the point? Who will teach it? There's no one for them to speak it to anymore.' In spite of these negative views, figure 4.13 shows that, in fact, the overall result in this section corroborated the more abstract expression of support for the dialect illustrated in figure 4.11. Such findings offer encouragement to those involved in the Jèrriais education initiative, as the replies suggest widespread approval for further action to be taken in this area – and a willingness to support the inclusion of Jèrriais as a fully fledged part of the curriculum.[16] Given that literacy is generally seen by many people as an important factor in the revitalization process (Grenoble and Whaley 1998: 31), this would represent a positive step for Jèrriais.

Of those who declared themselves in favour of the presence of Jèrriais in school, one-third even went as far as saying that they thought that it should be included as an obligatory subject of study (figure 4.14). This was matched by another third who thought it should have the status of an option and a further third who remained undecided. Those who supported the compul-

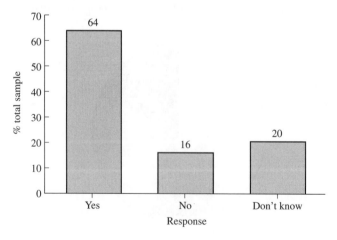

Figure 4.13 'Should Jèrriais be included on the primary school curriculum?'

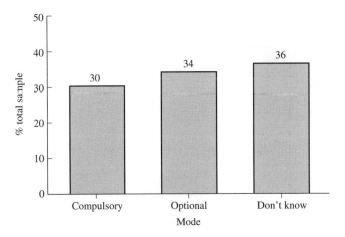

Figure 4.14 'Should the study of Jèrriais be compulsory at school?'

sory study of Jèrriais cited reasons which ranged from the aesthetic – the importance of Jèrriais to the cultural identity of the Island and its people – to the pragmatic – 'It's the only means left to prevent Jersey French from dying.' Those who remained undecided regarding which course of action to take stated that, in their opinion, children would be better off learning a European language such as German or Spanish rather than a variety that could be spoken only on a small island, or that learning Jèrriais would hinder a child's acquisition of 'Good French', which was evidently seen as the more important of the two varieties. Once again, this reflects the pervasive influence of the world 'without' for the Jèrriais speakers, and the feeling that the pragmatic implications of their proximity to France are more profitably addressed than a nostalgia for a distant cultural identity of the world within the Island.

Even more support was forthcoming for the introduction of regular television programmes in Jèrriais, with 82 per cent of the sample declaring themselves in favour of this measure and only 8 per cent against (figure 4.15). The most frequently given reason against the proposed measure was that the audience would be too limited. At present, the only provision for television programmes in Jèrriais is the one-hour slot which is given by Channel TV to Jèrriais and Guernésiais in alternate years.[17] Although one hour of Jèrriais television every two years is of little value to language maintenance, the biennial broadcast is important in that it does, at least, represent an H domain[18] which Jèrriais has penetrated and, in fact, in this case the increased status given to Jèrriais in the minds of its speakers by the fact that the dialect is deemed suitable for use in this – modern – domain far outweighs the linguistic benefits. It remains to be seen whether the claim that television and radio exposure significantly aids language learning by giving learners more

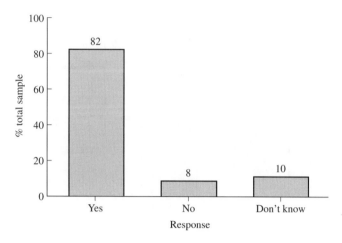

Figure 4.15 'Should there be regular television programmes in Jèrriais?'

fora for exposure to the second language (Jones 1993: 210) will be taken on board by the States of Jersey, and whether they decide to fund more Jèrriais television broadcasts as a corollary to the Jèrriais education initiative.

It was noteworthy that, when questioned about the value of Jèrriais television programmes, no informant introduced a caveat to their answer concerning the variety of Jèrriais used. This represents a marked contrast to the results obtained in Brittany, where Breton speakers who were in favour of increasing the number of hours in which Breton should be broadcast added the proviso that, for reasons of intelligibility, their support was for broadcasts made in their own variety (Jones 1996: 68). The fact that such a view was not prevalent amongst Jèrriais speakers is further confirmation of the fact that, despite the differences that exist between the *parlers* of Jèrriais (see section 3.3.), these do not pose problems for comprehension – even at a psychological level, unlike the situation in other minority language contexts (see section 4.3.2.2.).

The final area in which speakers' attitudes towards Jèrriais were examined involved bilingual road signs. Although many of the Island's road names are in Jèrriais or standard French, all road direction signs are in English. The provision of bilingual road signs has formed an important part of the revitalization campaign for many minority languages in that, despite having no tangible effect in terms of speaker numbers (Fishman 1991: 162), it endows the variety with a certain 'official' status and provides it with a high-profile context and an immediate presence in the community. Although, in some ways, bilingual road signs could be seen as a mere trapping of little consequence in the process of revitalization, their presence has, in fact, taken on quite a symbolic importance – and their introduction has even met with fervent opposition in some quarters (Jones 1996: 68–70).

In view of the fact that the Section de la Langue ('Language Section') of the Société Jersiaise ('Jersey Society') had recently campaigned successfully for the right to put up bilingual welcome signs in the airport and harbour (section 5.3.2.), it was hoped that this question would elicit strong views.

Just under half of those questioned supported the idea of bilingual signs on all roads throughout the Island, as 'It reflects the fact that there are two languages spoken here' (figure 4.16). This was closely matched by the 40% who were opposed to the idea and who cited reasons such as 'There's not enough people left who could read them' or 'French is the official language not Jersey French so it's right to have that' and 'French should be used – to be correct.' One native speaker rejected the idea of bilingual signs on the grounds that 'Jersey people wouldn't be able to read them.' Such a simple statement captures in a nutshell the problems faced by the revitalizers.

4.4. CONCLUSION

The aim of this chapter has been to construct a profile of the Jèrriais speech community at the turn of the twenty-first century. It has shown that, although many people still conduct a significant part of their lives in the dialect, the pool of native speakers is depleting in the wake of the 'tip' towards English.

Individuals' parish of origin has been shown to have a bearing on, first, their likelihood of being able to speak Jèrriais and, secondly, the contexts available for them to do so on a daily basis. However, despite Le Maistre's prediction that the last native speaker of Jèrriais will probably die in St Ouen (Lechanteur 1949: 213–14), it is important to recognize that, in terms of

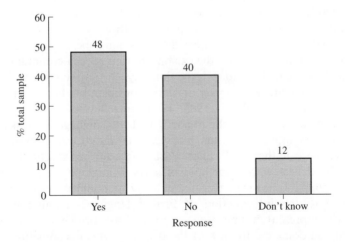

Figure 4.16 'Should Jèrriais feature on all the Island's road signs?'

native ability in the dialect, it is people's age rather than their parish which is significant. Native speakers may be easily located in St Ouen, Ste Marie, St Jean and Trinité but, below the age of 40, they are as thin on the ground in these parishes as elsewhere.

The questionnaire survey also illustrated the abrupt and near total cessation of mother-tongue transmission that took place in the second half of the twentieth century. Unlike the case in, for example, many of the Celtic countries or Canada (Jones 1998a; Mackinnon 1977; Maguire 1991; Cummins and Genesee 1985), there exist as yet no compensatory measures to put fluent speakers back into the community, although perhaps the introduction of Jèrriais in the primary school represents a first, preliminary, step towards this. A variety cannot survive if transmission has ceased and surely this must represent the primary, and pivotal, aim of any revitalization campaign. The future – and very existence – of Jèrriais therefore is contingent upon a concerted and structured movement for language main-tenance aimed at (re)introducing the variety into the community at large via a whole range of domains, of which the most crucial are, undoubtedly, those of the family and the neighbourhood, in order to try to 'kick start' the transmission mechanism, which surely represents the acid test in respect of successful maintenance. Given the current position of Jèrriais, this must represent a mammoth task.[19]

Jèrriais is, however, fortunate in that, by and large, its speech community is positive in its attitude towards its maintenance. This is often far from the case – for, in the words of Kuter, 'Those most likely to resist efforts to defend or promote a language such as Breton are often the very people who best know the language' (1989: 80). Moreover, as Grenoble and Whaley point out, 'Even with community level commitment, revitalization is never completely independent from the attitudes of the majority culture' (1998: 52). For Jèrriais to survive, therefore, it is vital that the dialect's profile in the community should be raised and positive attitudes fostered towards its future. Furthermore, such positive attitudes must permeate the Island's anglophone community, since the existing Jèrriais speech community needs to be enlarged, and this can only be done by drawing 'converts' from the anglophone population who may not have considered hitherto that Jèrriais was relevant to them. Boyd (1985: 17) claims that the attitudes of the dominant majority towards the minority and the language it speaks play a large part in the fate of the latter. It is clear that the education system has a role to play here, in that, if all children are taught Jèrriais at school, this may provide the dialect with a toe-hold of sorts in anglophone families. Any degree of support, however passive, is likely to establish an environment favourable to the introduction of further language-planning measures, which will represent a first step in raising the profile of Jèrriais and expanding its domains. In view of the disparity which is sometimes found between vocal and active support for a minority language (Dauenhauer and

Dauenhauer 1998: 67; Fishman 1991: 124), there is a need to ensure that the 'sayers' are also 'doers' or else what, at first, may seem a promising language-maintenance campaign could ultimately prove unsuccessful. This will be returned to in chapter 5.

It was noteworthy that, even among the most ardent supporters of Jèrriais, doubts were raised as to whether the dialect would survive. All the positive attitudes in the world cannot compensate for a lack of linguistic infrastructure and, at present, the depletion of speakers is so advanced – especially among those who form part of the Island's working population – that it is surely pertinent to reflect upon the extent to which revitalization methods could be implemented, even if they were to be put in place. There is no point in having a Jèrriais-medium school unless there are enough teachers to staff it, or bilingual forms unless there exist people who can process them. What would be the point of increasing Jèrriais viewing hours on the television if no one were to watch them, or publishing Jèrriais books if no one were to buy them? Admittedly, the revitalization of Cornish and Manx seems to be occurring after a fashion despite a far worse starting point than that of Jèrriais, which, at least, has a generation of native speakers left.[20] However, there is no denying that the present situation on Jersey is something of a race against time, in that it is far more difficult to resurrect a speech-variety in a contextual vacuum than to revitalize one that still has native speakers. As will be discussed in the next chapter, language-planning measures are starting to be put in place but the time to act is long overdue. Dorian draws attention to the dangers of postponing such action: 'Having waited too long before undertaking to rally support for threatened languages, we may find ourselve eulogizing extinct languages whose living uniqueness we had hoped instead to celebrate' (1998: 21). It is a timely warning. For Jèrriais to survive, the undoubted goodwill that exists towards the dialect must be converted into affirmative actions. Apathy, even on the part of the well-meaning, will ultimately prove to be the dialect's death-knell.

5

LANGUAGE PLANNING ON JERSEY

5.1. INTRODUCTION

Although the previous chapter provided a clear illustration of the speaker reduction observable for modern Jèrriais, it also indicated that there exists a groundswell of support on Jersey in favour of language maintenance. This chapter examines the emergence of the Jèrriais revitalization movement, which has been instrumental in initiating a series of language-planning measures to promote the dialect.

5.2. LANGUAGE PLANNING

The term 'language planning' was introduced to the literature by Einar Haugen (Haugen 1959). Today, the field is recognized in its own right and, as such, enjoys a large body of literature. Its definition and aims have been discussed widely (Cooper 1989; King 1999: 111; Gorman 1973: 72; Nahir 1984: 294; Rabin 1971: 277–9; Hornberger 1989: 7) as have the agencies behind it (Lewis 1983: 323; Spolsky and Boomer 1983: 244; Daoust-Blois 1983: 212; Rabin 1983: 53; Nyati-Ramahobo 1998: 56; Cooper 1989: 108). As it is beyond the scope of this chapter to engage in any terminological debate,[1] for the sake of convenience I will adopt the broad definition given by Cooper, who sees language planning as 'deliberate efforts to influence the behavior of others with respect to the acquisition, structure or functional allocation of their language codes' (1989: 45). Although, as its name suggests, the focus of language planning is always a speech variety, its aims are typically non-linguistic and involve targets such as 'consumer protection, scientific exchange, national integration, political control, economic development, the creation of new elites or the maintenance of old ones, the pacification or cooption of minority groups and mass mobilization of national or political movements' (Cooper 1989: 35). In situations of language obsolescence, however, language planning is often used as a means for securing language maintenance and revitalization (Hindley 1990; Jones 1998a; Puga 1996; Ballart 1996), and official bodies, governmental agencies and legislation may all be set up in support and for the promotion of the minority variety within the speech community.

Kloss (1969) and others have identified two main foci for language planning, namely status planning and corpus planning. The case of Jersey is of interest in that no official state-controlled body exists to contribute to either of these areas, which are both in the hands of a small, non-linguistically trained, group of enthusiasts. This chapter examines the progress they have made hitherto, suggests some possible avenues for the future and discusses the factors determining the success or otherwise of the movement.

5.2.1. *Status planning*

According to Kloss, status planning involves those 'primarily interested in the status of the language, whether it is satisfactory as it is or whether it should be lowered or raised' (1969: 81). In other words, it is concerned with the position of one variety relative to that of other varieties. This is distinct from corpus planning, which, according to Kloss, modifies 'the nature of the language itself, changing the corpus as it were', via changes in vocabulary, orthography and structure (1969: 81). It will be immediately apparent that although, in theory, these categories may be treated as distinct, in practice, the distinction between them may often be blurred – as Rubin states, 'Doesn't a change in spelling or grammar often constitute a change in status? Does a change in variety belong to status or corpus planning in fact?' (1983: 341; cf. Fishman 1983: 382).[2]

Status planning usually occurs 'when changes in the functional allocation of a community's language are seen as desirable' (Cooper 1989: 120). It is by no means exclusive to new or developing nations, although it has certainly been carried out in countries such as Israel and Ireland. Rubin reports on how the process has also been witnessed in 'many seemingly monolingual, developed and older nations and regions', which 'have begun to reconsider the status of minority or non-official languages and in many cases made efforts to change the status and allocation of use of these languages' (1983: 330). In fact, case studies have shown status planning to be an on-going process that often provides the impetus for corpus planning as part of an almost circular process. For example, section 46 of the Government of Wales Act 1998 requires the Welsh devolved Assembly to give equal treatment to English and Welsh. This has led to the creation of standard terminology in Welsh in specific subject areas relating to the Assembly's jurisdiction and, in turn, these new lexical creations will enable the language to be used in a number of new domains.

Cooper argues in favour of yet another focus for language planning, namely acquisition planning, which may be seen as a sub-division of status planning specifically aimed at increasing the number of speakers of the variety in question (1989: 33). This is frequently seen in situations of language obsolescence, where the process may be an integral part of reversing language shift (cf. Fishman's eight-stage planning model (1991: 395), discussed in section 5.8. below).[3] Promotion via the education system often forms a central focus of any revitalization campaign (Jones 1998a; Lewis 1983: 323; Spolsky 1989), but the latter also involves the use of the threatened language in high-profile domains such as street signs, advertisements, large chain stores, forms, cheque books and official documents. Ellis and Mac A 'Ghobhainn question the usefulness of such measures in combating language shift – 'a language cannot be saved by singing a few songs or having a word printed on a postage stamp' (1971: 144) – in that, by themselves, these are unlikely to increase speaker numbers. However, by giving prominence to a variety in domains from which it has hitherto been absent, the value of such measures as image-builders is considerable (Bentahila and Davies 1993: 367). Moreover, continually confronting people with the minority variety makes them accustomed to it as a 'normal' and expected part of the community. Increased familiarity may encourage people to learn the variety or, at the very least, lessen their indifference towards it. By this token, therefore, even the most trivial status planning is far from meaningless for an obsolescent language.

5.2.2. *Corpus planning*

As mentioned above, corpus planning involves changes in the language itself. Although its effects are seen most saliently and immediately in the lexis, Fishman illustrates how the term has been extended to refer to change ranging from the development of entire linguistic varieties to the modification of number and pronoun systems and the simplification of verbal and phonological patterns (1983: 109). Nyati-Ramahobo (1998: 55) sees the goals of this type of planning as 'to modernize, purify or reform a language'; however, in the words of Fishman, the process is in practice 'a delicate balancing act' (1983: 117). Care must be taken to harmonize the old with the new, or else this can create problems within the speech community which, at its worst, can lead to a breakdown in communication (Jones 1998a: 314–24).

As has been seen in section 5.2.1. above, in situations of language obsolescence, status planning can give rise to corpus planning – the introduction of a variety into a domain from which it has hitherto been absent will necessarily lead to the need to elaborate terminology that will render its use possible, but there is no use having such terminology if it is impenetrable to the majority of the speech community. It is therefore vital for corpus planners to remain in touch with their public, for a lack of care in this area can serve to undermine the work of the status planners. This has been seen, for example, in the case of Breton television programmes, which are often not watched by the intended target audience of native speakers on the grounds that the Breton broadcast is too academic (Jones 1996: 67–8). A similar accusation has also led to action being taken to simplify the 'highbrow' language of Welsh-medium television programmes (Jones 1998a: 274).

In situations of language obsolescence, corpus and status planning are often found together, acting as complements to each other to maintain the threatened variety. Their operation will now be considered in relation to Jèrriais.

5.3. AGENCIES OF LANGUAGE PLANNING ON JERSEY

The agencies behind language planning can take many shapes. Sometimes, the necessary decisions are taken by a single individual, such as Ataturk in Turkey, and at other times, they lie in the hands of a group of people, as with the Académie Française, which is seen as the main regulator and controller of standard French in France. As in the case of the latter, this agency may be an official one,[4] but occasionally language planning may occur without the existence of an overseeing official body (Spolsky and Boomer 1983: 244). Language planning may also be supported by legislation (Schlyter 1998).

On Jersey, language planning receives, at best, a tentative backing from the state. The only real support given in this area to date has been to an initiative to introduce Jèrriais into the last two years of the primary school on an optional, extra-curricular basis – a project originally destined to run for two years (see section 5.4.1.). Apart from this, as mentioned above, language planning has hitherto been left to enthusiastic individuals and groups with no official status or experience in this area and has proceeded in rather an *ad hoc* fashion. Most efforts to promote Jèrriais are realized via the following three organizations.

5.3.1. *L'Assembliée d'Jèrriais*

This society was founded in 1951 by twenty-seven Jèrriais speakers, including Dr Frank Le Maistre (author of the DJF; see sections 3.4. and 5.3.3.), with the aim of 'la consèrvâtion dé l'usage dé la langue Jèrriaise par touos les mouoyens pôssibl'yes'. It was further stated that 'Toute personne intérêssie dans l's objets d'l'Assembliée peut êt' membre' (quoted in Hublart 1979: 62).[5] The Assembliée d'Jèrriais (lit. 'the meeting of Jersey people') prides itself on its emphasis on Jèrriais – the minutes of all its meetings are taken, and recorded, in the dialect and, since 1952, quarterly bulletins, the *Bulletîn d'Quart d'An dé l'Assembliée d'Jèrriais*, have been published, which contain poems and short stories in Jèrriais as well as official reports by members of the committee. Although financial problems led to the suspension of this publication between 1977 and 1989, membership of the Assembliée has grown considerably over the years (to more than 160 in 1997 – although, admittedly, this figure represents only a small fraction of the present Jèrriais speech community). The Assembliée's contribution is to status planning rather than corpus planning. It organizes social events on a

monthly basis, has forged close links with its counterpart on Guernsey
(L'Assembllaïe d'Guernésiais), and has brought Jèrriais into the religious
domain by organizing an annual carol service in Jèrriais, 'Neu Leçons et
Cantiques dé Noué' ('Nine Lessons and Christmas Carols'). Although not a
dynamic force in revitalization in that there is little attempt to be proactive
on the part of Jèrriais, the Assembliée d'Jèrriais provides a regular
opportunity for its members to speak the dialect and a context in which
Jèrriais is, for once, seen as primary.

5.3.2. *La Société Jersiaise – La Section de la Langue Jèrriaise*

The Island's biggest society, La Société Jersiaise ('The Jersey Society'), has
existed since 22 January 1873, its date of foundation surely representing in
itself a sign that nineteenth-century Islanders were feeling that their culture
was under threat. Today, the Société boasts many branches such as
vernacular buildings, botany, entomology, environment, garden history,
marine biology, ornithology and archaeology. However although in the
Société's first bulletin (1873) a language committee is shown to have existed
and it was, by all accounts, active until the early 1900s, no specific provision
was made for Jèrriais during most of the twentieth century. This changed in
1994 when four members of the Société, none of whom was a native speaker
of Jèrriais but all of whom were concerned about the disappearance of the
dialect and many local traditions, started meeting on a monthly basis to
discuss a possible plan of action. The decision was taken to found a branch
of the Société which would 'encourage the use and study of the native
language and culture' (Société Jersiaise: Section de la Langue 1995) and the
first meeting was held on 24 May 1995. The Section de la Langue Jèrriaise
was intended to complement, rather than to compete with, other organizations established in support of Jèrriais, and the meetings focus on reading
from Jèrriais literature, studying vocabulary – especially less commonly
known terms in domains such as the names of flora and fauna – devising
ways to raise the public awareness of Jèrriais and learning about local
customs.

   As well as providing a forum for learning about Jèrriais, the Section de la
Langue Jèrriaise has been consciously proactive on its behalf and, since its
foundation, has lobbied successfully for the presence of Jèrriais on signs in
the airport and harbour (achieved 1998). At the time of writing, it is asking
for the dialect to be incorporated on the Island's phone cards and stamps.
The Section also helped to lobby for increased Jèrriais air time on BBC
Radio Jersey (1997; see 5.4.2.2. below) and for bilingually printed milk
cartons to be delivered to the Island's schools (1999). Although such
measures will not, in themselves, have an immediate effect on speaker
numbers, by giving the dialect a presence in such high-profile locations,
they help to render it familiar to non-Jèrriais speakers and to reinforce the

image of Jersey as a bilingual island. Although initially, the presence of Jèrriais in these 'new' domains may be seen as something of a novelty, the more it occurs, the more the novelty value will diminish and it is hoped that, ultimately, there will be a reversal of norms – with the exclusion of Jèrriais becoming the exception.

The Section de la Langue Jèrriaise has also sought to present the dialect on a wider stage. It was prominent in the campaign for Jèrriais to feature in the opening ceremony of the 1997 European Inter-Island Games and has forged links with the Association Jersey–Coutançais ('Jersey–Coutances Association'). The Section was also instrumental in the foundation of the Congrès des Parlers Normands et Jèrriais ('Congress of Norman and Jersey Dialects') on 12 October 1996, and it has ensured that Jèrriais has been represented in minority language conferences (such as Visionet, 1996, and the fourth European conference on immersion programmes, September 1998). A recent project has been to launch Jèrriais on the World Wide Web, at http://www.societe-jersiaise.org/geraint/jerriais.html, and, to date, there are some 1,700 *pages Jèrriaises* ('Jèrriais pages') to be found at this site.

As far as corpus planning is concerned, the Section de la Langue has recently produced a Jèrriais volume in the 'First Thousand Words' series, a vocabulary for children providing essential terminology (Huëlin and Nichols 2000). The aim of this book is two-fold: to supply many of the basic terms in a user-friendly way and also to show that, contrary to the belief of many of its traditional native speakers, Jèrriais is well suited for use in all domains of modern life. To this end, it has been necessary for many of the terms found in 'modern' domains, such as computer terminology, to be coined (see section 5.5.). The Section de la Langue has, therefore, set itself the task of modernizing the dialect's vocabulary. In the absence of professional assistance and support from the States, this is no mean task. Words are created during special meetings by individuals who are united by their concern to preserve Jèrriais but who have no actual linguistic training. Moreover, the invented terms are given no real scrutiny before they become 'officialized' by the Société and disseminated within the speech community (most directly via the education initiative). Inconsistencies, therefore, can and do happen. This may seem an unsatisfactory way to proceed but, given the absence of any support (or interest) on the part of the States in this area, there is no other option available. For the revitalizers, it is truly a case of do or the dialect dies.

5.3.3. *The Don Balleine Trust*

The Don Balleine Trust was created from a substantial legacy left by Arthur E. Balleine (1864–1943) for the study of Jèrriais. By publishing books in the dialect, the Trust has contributed to status planning but, as will be seen, by supporting the publication of volumes of prose in Jèrriais and metalinguistic works on the dialect, it has also been one of the main agencies behind the standardization of Jèrriais.

As with the Section de la Langue Jèrriaise, no trained linguist oversees the work of the Trust. Its executive committee consists of four parish officers (*connétables*) who are nominated by the twelve parish *connétables*, a secretary and a number of co-opted members, Jèrriais authors and others interested in the promotion of the dialect. Over the past thirty-five years, as well as its quarterly *Chroniques du Don Balleine* and, more recently, its *Nouvelles Chroniques du Don Balleine*, the Trust has published a number of works with the aim of promoting Jèrriais and, at the same time, providing a record of the dialect for posterity. Its first major publication was the *Dictionnaire Jersiais–Français* (DJF) (1966). As mentioned in section 3.4., this is a Jèrriais–French dictionary containing some 20,000 words and was written by Frank Le Maistre, a farmer from St Ouen who spent twenty-five years collecting the words for what was a labour of love. Le Maistre is one of the foremost figures in the movement to preserve and promote Jèrriais and he was awarded an honorary doctorate for his work by the University of Caen.

The DJF was a milestone in the history of Jèrriais in that, for the first time, it enabled the spelling to be fixed and the forms of words to be determined definitively. But perhaps more valuable than this was the fact that, by setting down the dialect in this way, the DJF gave Jèrriais the status it had hitherto lacked, enabling its speakers to consider it as a variety in its own right rather than a mere variant of standard French. The codification of Jèrriais was carried further in 1985, with the appearance of *Lé Jèrriais pour tous* ('Jersey French for all') by Paul Birt, a translator in the University of Wales, Bangor. This doubled as a grammar of Jèrriais for the existing speech community and a textbook for beginners and, following the lead of the DJF, confirmed the St Ouennais variety as the basis of standard Jèrriais, a variety whose existence, despite not having much relevance for the existing speech community, was essential if any hope was to be entertained of teaching the dialect at school.

In addition to its contribution to standardizing Jèrriais, the Don Balleine Trust has also tried to record the regional variation that exists within the Island by publishing five cassettes with accompanying booklets that focus on the distinctive pronunciation of the different sub-varieties. It has also published *A brief history of Jèrriais* (Spence 1993), a work examining the dialect's historical linguistic development, and the only two substantial volumes of prose to have appeared entirely in Jèrriais: *Jèrri jadis* and *Histouaithe et gens d'Jèrri* (Le Feuvre 1976, 1983). A recent project, *Jersey Norman French is fun* (Tapley 1998), based on a Welsh model, is a light-hearted, user-friendly book which seeks to appeal to beginners and to provoke interest in the dialect among the English-speaking community. The Trust's most recent publication to date, *Mille ditons en Jèrriais* (Huëlin,

Vibert and Lucas 2000), is a book on the sayings and proverbs of Jèrriais. Since 28 September 1978, the Trust has also published a series of occasional contributions in Jersey's daily newspaper, the *Jersey Evening Post* (see section 5.4.2.1. below).[6]

The publication of work in and about Jèrriais enhances the prestige of the dialect and thus forms part of status planning. Another major contribution in this area on the part of the Trust has been the appointment of a Jèrriais language teaching co-ordinator, who began work in January 1999 with the remit of introducing Jèrriais into the primary school as an extra-curricular subject over a period of two years (see section 5.4.1. below). By expanding its role in this way, the Trust has now placed itself firmly at the heart of the revitalization movement.

5.4. Jèrriais status planning: recent developments

It will be seen from section 5.3. that Jèrriais status-planning initiatives, such as the Assembliée d'Jèrriais, have been around for many decades. It is also clear that, for many years, such initiatives aimed to record the dialect for posterity and to offer fora for the use of Jèrriais by its native speakers without having much concern for its revitalization. However, recent years have witnessed a change in strategy, with a focus on increasing the existing pool of speakers and taking Jèrriais into new domains. This section concentrates on new developments in the fields of education and the media.

5.4.1. *Education*

Evening classes have been held in Jèrriais at both beginner and advanced levels since 1967. The classes are subsidized by the States' Education Department and the Assembliée d'Jèrriais. Although numbers are not high – the average is around fifteen pupils per class – it could be argued that the culture spread by the evening classes is, in many ways, more important than the actual classes themselves in that their influence extends far beyond those who actually attend them. For example, the students play an active part in promoting Jèrriais in events such as Lé Vier Marchi ('The Old Market'),[7] and the Sethée Jèrriaise ('Jèrriais Evening') of the Eisteddfod in November.[8] December 1991 also saw the first edition of *Lé Crapaud Avanche* ('The Toad Marches Forward'),[9] a 'newspaper' produced by some evening-class students, which was intended as a light-hearted look at Island life and times in order to promote awareness of Jèrriais to a wider public, and on 23 March 1995 the students started an occasional column in Jèrriais in the *Jersey Evening Post* entitled 'Plein l'Pagas' ('A Basketful'). Responsibility for this column has since been taken over by another group concerned with promoting Jèrriais, the Congrès des Parlers Normands et Jèrriais.

Despite the structured approach to the acquisition of Jèrriais offered by the evening classes, in practice these were insufficient to produce a significant increase in speaker numbers. Moreover, the students attracted tended to be predominantly adults. In order to target large numbers of younger students, there was a need to teach Jèrriais in school.

Although Spencer (1986) mentions the existence of a Jèrriais club for children at the primary school of St Jean parish, the idea of teaching Jèrriais as a fully fledged school subject never received any official backing. Even so, indicators cropped up from time to time that there would be support for such a move within the community, such as when, in November 1994, Channel TV asked the question 'Should Jèrriais be taught in schools?' as part of its weekly vote-line and obtained 690 votes in favour to 69 against.

In 1996, a report on the situation of Manx was brought to the attention of the States' Education Committee. This report described how 1,000 school-children on the Isle of Man were studying the language, and stated that a GCSE examination in Manx was about to be introduced despite the fact that Ned Maddrell, the last surviving native speaker of Manx, had died in 1974. Feeling that if Manx could be taught in this way in the absence of native speakers then it was high time to introduce Jèrriais into the schools of Jersey, Senator Jean Le Maistre, son of the author of the DJF, lobbied for a proposal calling for the teaching of Jèrriais in the primary school to be put before the States. It was agreed to test the water and, in 1997, questionnaires were distributed to the parents of all the Island's primary school pupils. When an overwhelming 790 positive replies were obtained, the proposal was put to the States and was passed with only one dissenter, who expressed fears regarding possible adverse effects on the progress made by pupils in standard French. The successful proposal contained provision for the establishment of a two-year pilot programme to teach Jèrriais, under the direction of a Jèrriais language teaching co-ordinator. Jèrriais would be taught on a voluntary, extra-curricular basis for thirty minutes per week, to pupils in their last two years of primary education. The teaching programme was to be run jointly by the Don Balleine Trust and the States' Education Department. Anthony Scott Warren, a staunch supporter and promoter of the dialect, who had himself learnt Jèrriais as a second language, was appointed as the first Jèrriais language teaching co-ordinator and began work in January 1999. Classes started the following September at twenty schools throughout Jersey and were attended by some 170 children. The coursebook used, Lé neu c'mîn ('The new road') (Scott Warren 1999), was adapted from the Manx 'Bun Noa' series and was successfully piloted during a seven week trial at Grouville primary school.

At the end of its first full year, the general feeling amongst schoolchildren and their parents was that the Jèrriais education programme had proved both desirable and a success. At the time of writing, the programme has just been awarded a further five years of funding, which will enable Jèrriais to be introduced on the same basis into the secondary school, a domain from which the dialect has been virtually excluded. Indeed, the only presence it has had hitherto in this area has been when, in September 1998, a series of ten Jèrriais lessons was taught as an option in one comprehensive school's enrichment programme for sixth formers. This was run by members of the Congrès des Parlers Normands et Jèrriais and although the take-up was low (eleven students), the fact that it was included in the programme at all indicates the change in climate. The additional funding has also enabled the employment of a second Jèrriais teacher for four days per week as from November 2000.

As a corollary to the introduction of Jèrriais in the primary school, in 1999 Pierre Le Moine, a former president of the Federal Union of European Nationalities, applied for Jersey to join the European Bureau for Lesser Used Languages (EBLUL). A representative from the Congrès des Parlers Normands et Jèrriais attended a meeting of the Bureau as an observer on 9 September 1999, and presented information on the background and developments of Jèrriais, particularly in education, broadcasting, literature and bilingual signage. Although the fact that Jersey is not an official member of the European Union precludes it from acceding to full member status of EBLUL, its observer status at the meetings means that the Island is able to share in the organization's programme of fostering the preservation and development of minority languages, albeit to a limited degree.

5.4.2. Media

5.4.2.1. The Jersey Evening Post

Jersey's only daily newspaper, with a circulation of some 23,000, has published regular columns and other articles in Jèrriais for many years. Although resident in North America, George Francis Le Feuvre (known by the *nom de plume* George d'la Forge), the author of *Jèrri jadis* and *Histouaithes et gens d'Jèrri* (see section 5.3.3.), was a regular contributor, and more than 900 of his articles were published before his death in 1984. Another famous exile, Sir Arthur de la Mare, a former diplomat who lived most of his life outside the Island, wrote a regular column in Jèrriais, 'Contes d'eun Ervenu' ('Tales from a Returner'), when he finally settled in Trinité parish after retiring from the Foreign Office.[10] Since his death in the mid-1990s there has been no one regular contributor but, as mentioned in sections 5.3.3. and 5.4.1., two or three articles in Jèrriais are supplied per month by advanced students of Jèrriais, the Don Balleine Trust or the Congrès des Parlers Normands et Jèrriais.

5.4.2.2. Radio

Until recently, the provision for Jèrriais in the *Jersey Evening Post* exceeded by far that given to it in other forms of the media. For many years, the only

Jèrriais presence on the radio was in the form of the *Lettre Jèrriaise*, broadcast for five minutes per week, often early on Sunday morning. However, in recent years, BBC Radio Jersey has taken heed of the lobbying for an increase in its provision of Jèrriais broadcasts. For example, in 1997, the Section de la Langue of the Société Jersiaise joined forces with the Congrès des Parlers Normands et Jèrriais to conduct a survey in which people were asked whether they would like more air time to be given to Jèrriais, and about their preferences regarding subject matter and time slots for such programmes. The support given to increasing the existing air time allocated to Jèrriais was such that on Friday 29 November 1997 a new series, *Les Crapauds Avanchent* ('The Toads March Forward'), was launched on BBC Radio Jersey. This twenty-minute programme is broadcast once a fortnight, thereby trebling at a stroke the existing Jèrriais air time. In addition to this, Anthony Scott Warren, the Jèrriais language teaching co-ordinator, has been given a weekly, half-hour slot in which he teaches Jèrriais lessons. These are backed up on the World Wide Web (at http://www.jerriais.ifrance.com).

5.4.2.3. *Television*

Jèrriais television broadcasting has, nevertheless, been slow to develop. As seen in section 4.3.4., existing provision by Channel TV allows for sixty minutes of air time per year to be allocated to the dialects of the Channel Islands, which means that, in practice, Jèrriais and Guernésiais are both given one hour every two years. This must surely represent an immediate area for action for the revitalizers, especially in view of the potential value of television in reinforcing the ground covered in the classroom.

5.5. JÈRRIAIS CORPUS PLANNING

Corpus planning in modern Jèrriais has focused mainly on expanding the lexis. In order to illustrate the processes of word creation used, the comparatively new domain of Jèrriais computer terminology will be analysed.[11]

5.5.1. *Borrowings*

If a new concept or object is introduced into one speech community through contact with another, then the word for that concept or object may be borrowed alongside it, as borrowing often represents a more convenient alternative to neologism.[12]

In the case of French, the phenomenon of borrowing is almost as old as the language itself – with even the earliest texts, such as the ninth-century

Sequence of St Eulalia and the twelfth-century *Chanson de Roland*, revealing examples of borrowed words used for new concepts:

(1) *Melz sostendreiet les empedementz*
     *Qu'elle perdesse sa **virginitét***
     'She would rather endure torture than lose her purity.'
     (*The Sequence of Saint Eulalia* ll.16–17. The borrowing is from Latin.)

(2) *E **gunfanuns** blancs e vermeilz e **blois***
     *Es destres muntent tuit li **barun** de l'ost*
     '[They are carrying] white, red and blue pennons;
     On the right all the barons of the army mount on horseback.'
     (*The Chanson de Roland* ll. 1800–1. The borrowings are from Germanic.)

Borrowing is often criticized by purists as 'corrupting' a language. This has been highly prevalent in the case of standard French, with the Loi Toubon (1994), which imposed penalties for the use of English borrowings in French, providing an extreme example of this. However, such puristic attitudes have been prevalent for centuries: for instance, in his *Traicté de la Con-formité du langage François avec le Grec* of 1565, the French scholar Henri Estienne bemoaned the number of Italianisms which had penetrated French. Although lexical borrowing is a frequent outcome of contact between two peoples, and hence two linguistic varieties, negative attitudes towards borrowings are commonly seen in situations of language obsolescence, where the act of using a term from the dominant language is seen as 'selling out' (Jones 1981: 49).

Revitalization campaigns often take great pains both to replace borrowings from the dominant language with creations indigenous to the obsolescent variety (Jones 1995: 429) and to ensure that indigenous coinages, rather than borrowings, are used to fill any lexical gaps that may exist, typically in 'modern' domains – and this whatever the repercussions vis-à-vis the comprehension of its native speakers. For example, in an attempt to rid Breton of words felt to be too obviously reminiscent of French, new words have been created based on intricate procedures of derivation (cf. Hovdhaugen 1992: 58 on Samoan borrowings in Tokelauan). Unfortunately, many of the new coinings are inaccessible to a large proportion of native speakers (see Jones 1995: 428–9 for Breton, Dorian 1994a: 486 for Scots Gaelic, and Dorleijn 1996: 48 for Kurmanci). In short, for a speech community, lexical borrowings are often the most salient markers of interference and people are quick to take action on these while often failing to notice other changes, in areas such as syntax (Huffines 1991: 127).[13] It was therefore surprising to find several borrowings from English among the newly created Jèrriais terminology in the domain of computer technology. Although some words had clearly undergone orthographic assimilation (for example *lé compiuteu* ('computer'), *la frême* ('frame') and *lé printeu*[14] ('printer')), others were borrowed from English in an orthographically unmodified form, albeit with the addition of an article (*lé software, l'e-mail*).

Despite the presence of these English borrowings, borrowed terms in this domain came, for the most part, from standard French. These had all been made to 'look' Jèrriais by subsequently undergoing phonetic adaptation in order to conform with the phonotactics of the dialect (*brantchi* (Fr. *brancher*, 'to plug in'), *cliavé* (Fr. *clavier*, 'keyboard'), *distchette* (Fr. *disquette*, 'floppy disk')), although in some cases, only orthographic modification had occurred (*un êcran* (Fr. *écran*, 'screen')). Despite the fact that *all* borrowings, from English or from standard French, have the same net result in that they introduce non-indigenous elements into Jèrriais, in the eyes of the planners, the latter is seen as a more legitimate donor-language, given the common roots of Jèrriais and standard French as *langue d'oïl* varieties.

Giving preference to borrowings from varieties other than the dominant, 'threatening' language is, of course, not exclusive to Jèrriais. In his study of modern Breton, Hewitt mentions that borrowings from Welsh, another Celtic language, are used freely by revitalizers but that even long-standing, commonly found borrowings from standard French are consciously avoided (1977: 38–9). Moreover, since it is relatively simple to work out regular phonological correspondences between cognates in standard French and Jèrriais, it is possible for the revitalizers to claim that the standard French borrowing, modified according to the phonotactics and morphological patterns of Jèrriais, is how the indigenous Jèrriais form would probably be, had it existed.

With certain words, it is not possible to tell whether borrowings have been taken from English or from standard French. This may be because the words used by standard French are themselves English borrowings (*Internet* ('Internet'; Fr. *Internet*), *scanneu* ('scanner'; Fr. *scanneur*), *modem* ('modem'; Fr. *modem*)) or calques on English (*boîte de dialogue*, ('dialogue box'; Fr. *boîte de dialogue*), *disque dur* ('hard disk'; Fr. *disque dur*)).[15] They may also belong to the class of so-called 'international' words (*serveux* ('server'); *curseu* ('cursor'); *programme* ('program'); *moniteu* ('monitor')). In view of the ambiguity surrounding the donor-language in these cases, such words are incorporated unproblematically into teaching material given to children (for example, *lé journaliste* ('journalist'); *lé microphone* ('micro-phone'); *la télévision* ('television')), whereas in this context, unequivocal English borrowings usually tend to be avoided.

5.5.2. *Calques*

Calques are loan-translations. They involve a word or an expression being translated literally from one language into another so that, despite being less obvious initially, due to the fact that its constituents are all indigenous to the borrower-language, the word may be considered just as much a borrowing as those described in section 5.5.1. above. A famous example of this phenomenon may be found in the case of the word 'skyscraper', which has yielded the following calques: *gratte-ciel* (French), *rascacielos* (Spanish), *grattacielo* (Italian), *wolkenkratzer* (German) and *nebo skrjób* (Russian). Calques may involve syntax as well as the lexis (Jones 1998a: 82–6) and are very common in contact situations. They may be found in both 'healthy' and 'obsolescent' languages, and the only prerequisite for their occurrence seems to be the presence of enough bilingualism in a community to make translation of the foreign term possible (Winter 1992: 213).

Although calques, therefore, represent borrowings every bit as much as taking a word 'wholesale', as it were, from a donor-language, the fact that they 'look' indigenous makes them more acceptable to Jèrriais language planners than the use of a borrowing. Calques on English abound in 'modern' domains and, in the case of computer terminology, may sometimes be preferred despite the availability of a standard French term that could have been borrowed. Calques on English found in this domain included: *l'ithangnie* ('spider's web') for '(World Wide)Web',[16] *sauver* ('to save'; standard French has *sauvegarder*), *la page d'siez-mé* ('homepage'; standard French has *la page d'accueil*). In one case, where standard French had also used an English calque, namely *le tapis de souris* ('mouse-mat'), the calque found in Jèrriais (*la natte à souothis*) differed in terms of one of its constituents, despite the fact that the word *tapis* also exists in the dialect with the same meaning as in standard French (= 'rug'/'mat'). The use of *natte* and not *tapis* to convey the meaning of 'mat' in this case therefore suggests that English, and not standard French, has formed the basis for this calque. 'Drop-down menu' is rendered in Jèrriais as *lé m'nu tchiyant* (lit. 'falling menu'; cf. standard French *le menu déroulant*). As there is no Jèrriais term for 'drop-down', an approximate alternative has been used, making this Jèrriais term, in practice, more of a descriptive sentence than a calque.

5.5.3. *Extension of the meaning of an existing word*

Another common method used to express new meanings is extending that of an indigenous term (McMahon 1994: 192). Thus in Jèrriais, *la souothis* now comes to denote a 'computer mouse' as well as the animal, in exactly the same way as in (and along the lines of) English and standard French. Similarly, *tabl'ye* is used for 'a computer-generated table', *mèrcheux* for 'a computer bookmark', *dotchument* for 'a computer document', *f'nêtre* for 'a computer window', *memouaithe* for 'computer memory' and *èrchergi* for 'reloading a computer program'. In certain cases, the Jèrriais word used may differ from that used in standard French, thus 'scrollbar' (*flèche à défiler* in standard French) is *èrchelle* ('arrow') in Jèrriais, 'link' (*liaison* in French) is *lian* ('the link of a chain') in Jèrriais, and 'to download' (*télécharger* in standard French) is *déchergi* ('to unload') in Jèrriais.

5.5.4. *Jèrriais coinage*

Only one word pertaining to computer terminology may be seen as a Jèrriais coinage, making this the least common by far of all the processes of word creation in this domain. Moreover, even this instance was not a true example of creation *ex nihilo*, as the word involved – *maître-pêtre* (lit. 'spider-master') – clearly has links with its English equivalent 'Webmaster'. It is possible that the creation of this term may have progressed along the following lines: after rejection of the French term, *administrateur de site Internet*, on perhaps the grounds of length, a calque may have been considered, such as *maître-ithangnie*. Since, in EJ, the term *ithangnie* denotes the spider as well as the web (see section 3.3.2.), it is possible that the WJ term *pêtre* (which only denotes the spider) may have been suggested as an alternative to *ithangnie*. *Maître-pêtre* may have been accepted as the final version due to its 'catchy' internal rhyme, despite the fact that, in practice, the meaning of the seemingly transparent compound is somewhat confusing.

5.5.5. *Summary*

The field of computer terminology has served as an example of a 'modern' domain which has involved Jèrriais corpus planning during the past few years. As has been seen, calquing and borrowing represent the most commonly used strategies of word creation, although, when they are taken from standard French, borrowings tend to be assimilated to conform to the sound and morphological patterns of Jèrriais, probably in order to make them 'look' authentic. Borrowings from standard French had been used more than any other means of word creation in the coursebook *Lé neu c'mîn*,[17] which, as in the case of much minority language teaching material, tends to avoid 'wholesale' borrowing from the dominant language (in this case English). However, while borrowing from the dominant language is clearly not the preferred strategy of the Section de la Langue of the Société Jersiaise either, it seems to be better tolerated by Jèrriais language planners than is the case with many other varieties, both endangered (Breton, Welsh) and 'healthy' (standard French). Indigenous Jèrriais coinages are rarer; however, the slightly peculiar *maître-pêtre* is not typical. *Lé neu c'mîn* contains several more transparent coinages – for example *lé téléfanatique*, a compound comprising elements borrowed from standard French but agglutinated, presumably on the basis of the English word 'tellyaddict'.[18]

5.6. WILL LANGUAGE PLANNING BE SUCCESSFUL?

The corpus planning being undertaken for modern Jèrriais has provided a means for the dialect to be used in all the domains required of a speech-variety in the twenty-first century. Moreover, thanks to the status-planning initiatives that are at last under way, Jèrriais is now beginning to penetrate some hitherto uncharted domains, although it is clear that, for the dialect to have any real chance of surviving, these must represent no more than the tip of the iceberg. Even if we grant that this is indeed the case, the success of Jèrriais language planning will still be contingent upon several factors, the most salient of which will now be discussed.

5.6.1. The role of the school

The school is often given a central place in campaigns to revitalize obsolescent varieties (Jones 1998a; McDonald 1989), due to its ability to impart knowledge of these varieties to large numbers of children, who are seen as representing the variety's future. The role of the school in language planning has been debated widely with respect to the process of reversing language shift and it is clear that it can produce undoubted benefits, such as altering the functional allocation of a variety, increasing its domains of use and thereby its status (Hornberger and King 1996: 438), or stemming the decline in speaker numbers among the young, thereby preventing a generation gap (Edwards 1984: 256-7). Indeed, it has been shown that introducing a dying variety into the school can be worthwhile even if the revitalization campaign is not likely to succeed, in that it can lessen the negative attitudes towards the variety and its speakers and lead to greater self-awareness on the part of the minority speech community (Dorian 1987: 64-5).

However, it is also true that the school cannot operate alone to provide a 'quick fix' for obsolescent varieties. In the first place, although it is possible to increase numbers of Jèrriais speakers in the short term, there is no guarantee that teaching the dialect in schools will ultimately alter its fate by re-establishing the intergenerational chain of transmission. Studies in Eire have demonstrated that, where there was no opportunity to speak the language, children who had learnt Irish in school were quick to forget it (Ó Riagáin 1988: 38). As Bentahila and Davies point out, although secondary bilinguals do have some symbolic value for the language, increasing the number of speakers is meaningless if these are largely made up of non-native speakers who have neither the occasion nor the inclination to use the minority language (1993: 365; cf. Ballart 1996: 15).[19] Hornberger and King (1996: 433) also see successful revitalization as dependent on joint and mutually reinforcing initiatives in and outside the classroom (cf. Dorian 1987: 61; Spolsky 1989: 102; Fishman 1991: 371). For Jèrriais to become revitalized, therefore, there is, at the very least, need for the activities within the classroom to be complemented by opportunities to use the dialect outside the learning context, and for any hope of transmission to become re-established, it is desirable that the current provision is transformed into some form of immersion education. As Cooper states, 'Not only exposure to the language but also incentive to learn it is greater when it serves as medium than when it serves merely as subject of instruction' (1989: 161).

A second point to consider is the nature of the variety to be taught in the schools. As illustrated in section 3.3., despite the fact that Jersey measures some 45 square miles, Jèrriais is far from homogeneous. It is immediately divisible into two main varieties (EJ and WJ) and even these may be broken down further (see map 3) into more localized forms. There is, therefore, the question of whether children from different parts of the Island should be taught their own local variety of Jèrriais – and the desirability, and practicality, of learning a localized variety of what is already a minority speech-form – or whether it is better to teach a standardized variety, even though this might represent a different form of the dialect from that which is historically spoken in a particular area. Of course, if standardization is the preferred option, there is also the question of how this process should be achieved.

5.6.2. *Standardization*

On the question of introducing minority varieties in school, Dorian mentions that if, by means of a lucky accident, a localized dialect does get on to the curriculum, it is usually a variety which little resembles the standard language, leading to a dilemma for the teachers as to which variety they should teach. Teaching the dialect may cause problems in that the teacher may not control the variety adequately or, if it is uncodified, may not know how to write it down, and the school authorities are sure to be even less pleased at the prospect of a localized form of the minority language being taught than they would be at the idea of teaching the minority variety itself (1978a: 651). This scenario is equally applicable to Jèrriais: lack of resources makes it impractical to engage teachers (even if they were to be found) and to produce teaching material for every different sub-dialect. Furthermore, despite the general perception that differences between the sub-dialects did not pose a significant obstacle to communication (see section 4.3.2.2.), this late on in the day, it seems of limited use to create a cohort of younger speakers with any ready-made in-built barriers that might hinder free intra-group communication. This makes teaching a standard form of Jèrriais seemingly unavoidable. However, if not handled properly, standardization can be detrimental to the variety in question (Jones 1995), creating controversy and resentment among those who should be its supporters.

The creation of a standard can take place via one of two ways. Either it is produced on the basis of one dialect, which then becomes a linguistic 'first among equals' (Lodge 1993), or else it can emerge from a non-geographically locatable composite of several dialects (Jones 1998a: 260–9).

The standardization of Jèrriais has followed the first of these paths. It is a relatively recent development, whose origins lie in the fact that the DJF was written by a native speaker of St Ouennais and that, by coincidence, the only two substantial volumes of prose to be published entirely in the dialect were also written in this sub-variety. When the first major grammatical work on Jèrriais (Birt 1985) was published, it was therefore not surprising that, as mentioned in section 5.3.3., St Ouennais was chosen as its basis as, in the words of the author, the variety which 'In many ways . . . has asserted itself as the standard form of Jèrriais' (Birt 1985: 2).

The elevation and codification of St Ouennais therefore happened quite fortuitously and, when a standard variety was called for by the introduction of Jèrriais in school, it was readily at hand. As there exist no official bodies to monitor and make linguistic pronouncements on the dialect, the existence of the DJF has been sufficient to secure St Ouennais status as 'first among equals' and, as no work of this kind has ever been undertaken in any other *parler*, its place is uncontested.

Chance, then, has meant that Jèrriais has avoided many of the problems often inherent in the selection of a variety to be standardized, and both the creation and imposition of standard Jèrriais have been relatively unproblematic, a situation which would seem very much to be the exception rather than the rule (cf. Richards 1989: 109; Hornberger and King 1996: 433). Moreover, given the sociopolitical circumstances of the dialect, it is unlikely that a rival candidate will ever emerge. Since many native speakers are illiterate in Jèrriais, the proposed standard spelling, too, often an area of controversy and deeply entrenched opinions (Jacobs 1997; Rabin 1971; Spolsky and Boomer 1983: 248), has been accepted without question, with the DJF once again considered to be the main arbiter of usage – despite the fact that it is not always consistent, probably due to its author never having received any linguistic training. Given the fact that speaker reduction is so advanced, it is unlikely that the promotion of St Ouennais in school over other sub-varieties will have any detrimental effect on the latter, and the fact that all the *parlers* are generally mutually intelligible means that there are unlikely to be any difficulties with cross-generational communication, unlike those witnessed in Brittany (Jones 1998a: 296–333).

5.6.3. *The approval of the speech community*

A third factor governing the success or otherwise of language planning on Jersey is the approval of the speech community for the measures taken. This is probably the most important factor of all, for just as a variety cannot live without the will of its speakers, so no reform or other change is likely to be successful without their consent. One need only look at the case of Irish in Eire to see that, in spite of the huge amounts of money allocated to revitalization and the numerous government agencies that were established to this end, the fact that, ultimately, the person in the street saw no real need for the language to survive was to prove its downfall.

As has been seen in the case of Welsh, it is extremely important that support for the revitalization process is mustered both within and without the community of native speakers (Jones 1998a: 328). In chapter 4, the desirability of involving the non-native speech community in the revitalization venture was discussed. Clearly, it is also important to engage the support of the remaining native speakers, for failure to secure this will result in a situation akin to that found in modern-day Brittany, where the language is being revitalized in the name of the 'traditional' speakers by a group of predominantly non-native speakers but with neither group having much to do with the other (Jones 1998b: 135). As Fennell states:

> A shrinking language minority cannot be saved by the actions of well-wishers who do not belong to the minority in question. . . . It can be saved only by itself; and then only if its members acquire the will to stop it shrinking, acquire the institutions and financial means to take appropriate measures, and take them. (1981: 39)

Fennell's comments indicate one of the main problems behind revitalizing an obsolescent language – not only do the native speakers need to approve of the campaign but they must also engage actively in language-planning measures. As seen in chapter 4, support from outside the speech community is beneficial in that it creates an atmosphere of goodwill towards the variety and the planning measures – and may even attract new 'converts' – all of which is undoubtedly conducive to revitalization, but, for all the regret that this group of speakers may feel regarding the demise of the minority variety, they can often not be counted on in terms of active support. This was witnessed in the Breton *commune* of Plougastel-Daoulas, where many non-Breton-speaking parents declared themselves to be in favour, in principle, of optional Breton classes in school but stated that their sons or daughters were unlikely to take advantage of their availability (Jones 1996: 67; cf. Hornberger and King 1996: 432). Striking a balance between approval from within and without the speech community therefore seems to be the most desirable strategy.

The approval of the indigenous speech community is extremely important in the domain of corpus planning, for any new words created will be used only if they are actually understood. Indeed, corpus planners often fail to recognize that merely inventing a word is not enough to ensure that it will be used and that, if sufficient care is not taken with corpus planning to ensure acceptance on the part of the native speakers, this can actually undermine efforts at the status-planning stage (see section 5.2.2.). There is no purpose in inventing new words if no one uses them, and Jèrriais corpus planners would do well to test 'new' Jèrriais vocabulary on native speakers in order to determine its acceptability, a strategy that is currently being advocated for language planning in several countries (Richards 1989: 113).[20]

The coercive power of any language planning body rests, as Cooper puts it, 'on the consent of the governed' (1989: 78). However, consent alone is not always enough. The advantages of engaging the support of the anglophone speech community are self-evident. Nevertheless, even though their numbers are small, it is essential that the existing Jèrriais native speakers also be mobilized in active support of both corpus- and status-planning measures. The rapid depletion of the pool of such speakers would make it, in theory, possible for revitalization to go ahead without any consultation with the indigenous speech community being strictly necessary – for in twenty years or so, very few native speakers will still be alive and, if revitalization measures are successful, the learners will predominate. However, given that Jèrriais is unlikely ever to represent anything other than a second language to the learners, if the variety they learn has little to do with that which is currently spoken on the Island, this makes the revitalization somewhat academic rather than practical in its aims. As has been seen in Brittany, alienating the present cohort of native speakers by using a variety which they have difficulty in understanding, and therefore limiting learners to in-group communication with themselves, is, in certain respects, to start undertaking language revival while revitalization is still possible (cf. Jones 1995). This is why the adoption of 'authentic' St Ouennais as a linguistic 'first among equals'-type standard, rather than promoting a synthetic amalgam based on the various sub-varieties, is, in this particular context, probably the best strategy by far.

5.7. IS REVITALIZATION POSSIBLE?

It is by no means guaranteed that, once in place, language-planning measures will succeed in revitalizing a variety by somehow putting back the clock and restoring the obsolescent variety to its old self.

In fact, this is probably an unattainable goal. Planning measures, almost by definition, will do anything but restore Jèrriais to its old self. Although corpus planning may seek to 'undo the linguistic results of extensive interaction with the contact language' (King 1999: 126) and thus return the variety to its perceived healthier former state, status planning is more likely to transform Jèrriais than to restore it (Bentahila and Davies 1993).[21] Thus, Jèrriais may be penetrating domains from which it has hitherto been excluded, such as education, the media and religion, but, as Bentahila and Davies state, 'Despite all the energetic campaigning and the impassioned rhetoric of revivalist leaders, it would seem that the chances of returning a declining language to its old domains in a restored speech community are slim' (1993: 368). They go on to make the point that this is especially the case when, for pragmatic reasons, such campaigns tend to focus outside rather than inside the home, when, of course, this very domain has represented one of the constant strongholds of the obsolescent variety (1993: 371–2).

In the same vein, the speech community itself may be transformed rather than restored as a result of language planning. As has been discussed many times, in Western societies it is typically the middle classes who champion the cause of revitalization (Macnamara 1971: 85; Jones 1998a: 314; Dorian 1987: 63; McDonald 1989: 214), whereas the bulk of the traditional speakers of most obsolescent languages come from the working classes. Moreover, the movement is often found at its strongest outside the heartlands in those areas which are undergoing most language loss (Fennell 1981: 38), and the variety the 'new' speakers learn may have no historical tradition within the particular territory in question. They may, therefore, often be at odds with the 'traditional' speech community in terms of their geographical location, social backgrounds, the nature of the variety they speak and even their reasons for speaking it. As McDonald has commented on the situation in Brittany:

> the militant world and the popular world have different 'Bretons'. They are not talking the 'same' Breton; they are not talking about the same thing in commentary upon Breton; they do not have the same social value of Breton; they do not share the same level of education or the same linguistic and social sensibilities and competences. They are not, we might say, speaking the same 'language'. (1989: 279)

The potential for resentment and polarization is plain to see. Jèrriais may have fortuitously avoided the problems often encountered with the creation of a standard but, if the revitalization campaign ever gathers sufficient momentum to produce new adult speakers, care must be taken to ensure that the speech community is held together.

Although the revitalization campaign is likely to transform the nature of both Jèrriais and its speech community, it is nevertheless undeniable that language planning can create a variety of the dialect suitable for use in the twenty-first century and provide contexts in which it can be used. However, the ability to secure actual usage of a variety such as Jèrriais is clearly contingent upon the extent of its decline. As Dorian found in relation to East Sutherland Gaelic (1987: 61), even if sufficient resources were available to instigate all the necessary planning measures, and although it might prove possible to revitalize some form of standard, the fact that the last native speakers who could assist with these ventures would be likely to have died before such measures were fully established would lead to a difficulty in reinstating the use of a localized *parler*. As demonstrated by table 3.2, therefore, the fact that it is no longer possible to find large numbers of native speakers all over the Island makes restoring the use of the localized forms of Jèrriais less likely.

Moreover, for any form of Jèrriais to become even moderately used by second-language learners, there must be both a need and an incentive. The dialect has lost its primary *raison d'être*, namely as a tool of communication, and the restoration of its use will depend upon whether it succeeds in acquiring a secondary function that is important enough – and exclusive enough to it. One of the most likely candidates to fill this role is ethnic identity (Garzon 1992: 64). If Jèrriais can be identified as a quintessential part of Island identity – an emblem of 'groupness' and a focus of national loyalty on a par with, say, a flag or a national anthem – then this symbolic role may well serve as a springboard for its use. The problem, of course, is to ensure that its practice extends beyond the ceremonial, for this would not be sufficent to change any interpersonal or familial patterns of language use (King 1999: 122–3). Of course, emphasizing the link between language and identity will result in increased use of the former only if speakers actually view their ethnicity in a positive light. If they consider a variety as a leash tethering them to a stigmatized self-image, such a course of action will only succeed in hastening the variety's decline (Dorian 1978a: 653), and it is for this reason that language planning should also encompass an element of what Pool terms 'identity planning' (1979: 5).

Stronger than identity in terms of kick starting revitalization are concrete and well-publicized economic incentives (Dorian 1987: 60–1). These typically act more effectively than cultural and political motivation, for individuals content to learn a language for the 'feelgood' factor alone are few and far between. However, even economic incentives are by no means a sure bet – as witnessed once again in the case of Eire, where, for all the efforts of the Dublin government to initiate policies of positive discrimination, making financial reward available to families and communities who attain a certain level of proficiency in Irish, the language is still dying (Hindley 1990: 168). Nevertheless, in the right climate, when the community in question identifies positively with the minority variety and perceives a real need for its maintenance, incentives of this kind can be powerful arms for revitalization – as long as they are used wisely in encouraging people to speak the aforementioned variety rather than alienating them for not doing so.

Use of Jèrriais will only increase if there are sufficient opportunities outside the classroom for it to be spoken. It is always surprising to see how often sole responsibility for reinstating a variety within a community is given to the schools and evening classes, when these tend to involve using a language only passively, in a restricted context and for a relatively small proportion of each day. Realization that such provision is not sufficient for revitalization has led the Welsh Language Board, established as part of the 1993 Welsh Language Act, to state as one of its goals the creation of an atmosphere conducive to the use of Welsh in communities throughout Wales. The past decade or so has seen the establishment of fifteen community-based initiatives such as Menter Iaith Myrddin and Menter Aman

Tawe, which aim to provide the societal promotion of Welsh – Fishman's 'family–neighborhood–community arena' (1991: 374) – needed to reinforce the work done in the classroom (Campbell 1992).

In summary, therefore, revitalizing Jèrriais may be possible but any assessment of its success will depend on how its goals are perceived. The revitalizers should not aim to recapture a prior 'golden state' of the dialect or to reinstate it in all its domains. Languages are constantly changing – and revitalizing ones are no exception. After all, of what use would nineteenth-century Jèrriais be in the twenty-first? Revitalizing Jèrriais in any shape or form is a gargantuan task and talking at this stage of reintroduction in the home is probably no more than a pipe dream. However, setting the sights to a more realistic level and creating a positive environment in which the dialect may be nurtured, together with establishing it as an important part of Island identity and providing sufficient motivation for its use, might be as good a start as any.

5.8. CONCLUSION

After a period of very little action in support of Jèrriais, the past few years have, therefore, witnessed an intense burst of language planning with two statable, and connected, aims, namely putting Jèrriais on an official footing for the first time and, more fundamentally, keeping it alive. The first of these aims is, admittedly, easier to attain than the second but, as Dorian (1987) illustrates, the efforts invested in language planning on Jersey will not be in vain even if, ultimately, the maintenance campaign does not succeed, for they will have helped impart knowledge of the Island's culture and history to a wide audience and immeasurably enhanced the prestige of Jèrriais both inside and outside the indigenous speech community.

It is difficult to make an accurate prediction of the fate of any variety. There exists no grand plan for language maintenance or revitalization, and different fates can befall languages with ostensibly similar sociopolitical circumstances. This does not, though, preclude us from identifying certain steps which can improve the chances of survival of a minority variety. Nevertheless, such measures may be numerous and varied, often dependent upon contexts particular to an individual variety and unable to be generalized 'wholesale' to other varieties. A useful benchmark of the progress made by Jèrriais, which will, at the same time, allow the dialect to be compared in a reasonably objective manner to other minority varieties, is provided by mapping its current situation onto Fishman's Graded Intergenerational Disruption Scale (GIDS) (1991: 87), which is intended to give an indication of a variety's prospects for maintenance. It clearly represents no more than one view of the situation, but offers an indication both of the work that has already been done for Jèrriais and of the road ahead:

Toward a Theory of Reversing Language Shift
STAGES OF REVERSING LANGUAGE SHIFT:
SEVERITY OF INTERGENERATIONAL DISLOCATION
(read from the bottom up)

1. Education, work sphere, mass media and governmental operations at higher and nationwide levels.
2. Local/regional mass media and governmental services.
3. The local/regional (i.e. non-neighborhood) work sphere, both among Xmen [speakers of the obsolescent language] and among Ymen [speakers of the dominant language].
4b. Public [i.e. state-run] schools for Xish [the obsolescent language] children, offering some instruction via Xish [the obsolescent language], but substantially under Yish [the dominant language] curricular and staffing control.
4a. Schools in lieu of compulsory education and substantially under Xish [the obsolescent language] curricular and staffing control.

II. *RLS* [Reversing Language Shift]
to transcend diglossia, subsequent to its attainment

5. Schools for literacy acquisition, for the old and for the young, and not in lieu of compulsory education.
6. The intergenerational and demographically concentrated home–family–neighborhood: the basis of mother tongue transmission.
7. Cultural interaction in Xish [the obsolescent language] primarily involving the community-based older generation.
8. Reconstructing Xish [the obsolescent language] and adult acquisition of X S[tandard] L[anguage].

I. *RLS to attain diglossia (assuming prior ideological clarification)*
(Fishman 1991: 395)

Fishman's scale is intended to be read from the bottom up. Stage 8 represents the most advanced degree of language attrition possible in a community and stage 1 is described as 'the end of a long and difficult haul' (1991: 107), where language shift has, to all intents and purposes, been reversed.[22] It is not intended that every revitalization movement should start at stage 8 and work through to stage 1 (1991: 109). The scale serves, rather, as a means by which a variety's position can be gauged, enabling the identification of potential areas for future action. However, this is not the only function of the GIDS scale. Throughout his work, Fishman stresses what he calls 'the proper sequencing of efforts' in the process of reversal of language shift and advises revitalizers to ensure that all the stages 'below' them on the scale are achieved before attempting to progress to the next (1991: 111). The GIDS scale, therefore, presents a context in which successful reversal of language shift can take place, depicting the way forward for the language but stressing the importance of reinforcing each stage adequately.

In terms of status planning, Jèrriais has already cleared many of the hurdles on the GIDS scale. Stage 8 has not proved necessary, as the Jèrriais language model has never been inaccessible to the community. Stage 7, similarly, has never been lost altogether and indeed, as mentioned in section 5.3., any slippage that may have taken place was made good, to a certain extent, many decades ago with the establishment of L'Assembliée d' Jèrriais, the Eisteddfod, and more recently the Section de la Langue Jèrriaise of the Société Jersiaise. Evening classes go some of the way to attaining stage 5, and the diglossia that has existed on the Island for may centuries is gradually starting to be transcended with the recent initiative for the presence of Jèrriais in state-run schools (stage 4b) and in local mass media (stage 2).[23] Despite the relatively recent start of its revitalization campaign, therefore, Jèrriais is attaining the upper echelons of the GIDS scale. However, it is also evident that this has been done without any systematic clearance of the 'lower' hurdles. Stages 3 and 4a have not been broached and neither, crucially, has stage 6. The high profile of stages 4a to 1 and the immediate rise in status they give to an obsolescent variety make them attractive targets for revitalizers and, as has been mentioned, the school, in particular, is a common target for such movements in the West. However, Fishman warns against concentrating immediately and exclusively on the upper stages of the GIDS scale since, for all their high status, they do not lead directly to inter-generational mother-tongue transmission and, in fact, may cause confrontation and rivalry with the dominant language community at a time when the obsolescent variety is in no position for this (1991: 112–13). For Fishman, then, the re-establishment of the inter-generational chain of transmission is primary and supersedes all other RLS measures:

> The favourable outcomes of Hebrew, Catalan and Quebec French *did not begin with* work, media or government . . . they began with the acquisition of a firm family–neighborhood–community base . . . what media, work sphere and government agencies and institutions can do for science, mathematics and geography . . . they *cannot* do with respect to converting a non-mother tongue into a mother tongue. (1991: 374–5)

Even though the mammoth task of getting Jèrriais a foothold in the education system and a presence in the media has now been achieved, there is therefore no time for complacency. While such steps are important parts of the revitalization process they do not, in themselves, represent a magic wand by means of which the dialect will be saved. In fact, this foothold is barely the beginning and, as Fishman advocates, it is now high time for Jèrriais to attain some of the lower stages on the GIDS scale, for, ultimately, it is these which will determine the dialect's future as they will help re-establish transmission. For all the fact that children may learn Jèrriais at school, unless they pass the dialect on to their children there is no long-term net gain.

As the vast majority of native speakers are beyond child-bearing age, and even those who do still fall into this category are not necessarily married to a Jèrriais-speaking spouse and, as mentioned above, are therefore unlikely to use Jèrriais as the language of the home, the school, *faute de mieux*, has to have a central role in the revitalization campaign. Nevertheless, it cannot and should not be relied upon to combat obsolescence. As McDonald has illustrated (1989: 208), asking parents to learn the variety their children are acquiring at school and subsequently convert their home language may be something of a tall order. However, since it is undeniable that acquisition of Jèrriais would be greatly enhanced – both practically and from the point of view of motivation – if there were frequent possibilities for it to be used in the community, the revitalizers would do well to reproduce some of the community-based initiatives that have recently been established in Wales (Campbell 1992) and Hawaii (Zepeda and Hill 1991: 145), so that the classroom becomes one of many mutually reinforcing agencies working for the revitalization of the dialect rather than a solitary basket for all the Jèrriais eggs. If the movements that already exist to promote socialization in Jèrriais were able to provide similar opportunities for child-learners, this would provide an impetus for the Jèrriais classes at school by making the dialect appear to the children as something other than a school-based variety with little practical use. Underlying all this, of course, is the question of resources, but, arguably, if a choice has to be made, it is surely better to do without some of the higher-profile status symbols of stages 4a to 1 than attempt to base these on shaky foundations. Fishman cites as a case in point the situation in Eire, where he criticizes the policy of seeking to make Irish compete with English-medium services such as local government and media rather than concentrating on 'more urgent and more intergenerationally-transmissible Stage 6, 5 and 4b enterprises' (1991: 141).

Ironically, despite the revitalization campaign, Jèrriais is currently taught on the Island far less widely – and on a less official basis – than standard French. As has been seen, the movement to promote the dialect relies for its support almost entirely on enthusiastic volunteers, whose persistent lobbying in recent years has led to enhanced prestige for Jèrriais in a number of domains. In terms of the goals of language planning, the agencies of status planning, the methodology of corpus planning and the factors determining success or failure of the revitalization campaign, it has been demonstrated that certain parallels exist between the situation on Jersey and that of countries such as Eire and Wales, where more support is forthcoming from the state. It has also been demonstrated that, in some respects, lack of official interest has worked in favour of Jèrriais. However, it is plain that without increased support from the state, the revitalization of Jèrriais can only proceed so far. Although the efforts of the revitalizers have put the movement on its feet, the state alone has sufficient resources to put in place and to sustain the necessary measures in different areas of Island life (not least in adult and child education, community initiatives, broadcasting, the work sphere and corpus planning) needed to take the existing campaign into its next stage.

The main problem is one of time. As seen in chapter 3, in 1989, 90 per cent of Jèrriais speakers were aged 40 and above. This pool is being depleted at a rapid rate and, by today, the average age of the dialect speakers is certain to be even higher. Although no revitalization measure is ever wasted, in the case of Jersey, unless such measures prove sufficient to ensure that transmission is reinstated by the time the last native speaker disappears, it will become necessary to plan for revival rather than revitalization, which is an altogether more difficult venture.[24]

6

LINGUISTIC DEVELOPMENTS IN MODERN JÈRRIAIS

6.1. INTRODUCTION

The previous chapters have concentrated on the sociolinguistic situation of Jèrriais and have demonstrated that, due to the encroachment of English, the dialect has undergone significant speaker reduction, even in its former heartlands. As previous studies have shown that, in the context of language obsolescence, the sociopolitical background may often be instrumental in precipitating large amounts of linguistic change (Dorian 1989; Jones 1998a: section 4.1.), the next two chapters seek to complement the sociolinguistic part of this study by focusing on linguistic developments that may be attested in contemporary Jèrriais.

6.2. METHODOLOGY

Its current sociolinguistic situation makes modern Jèrriais potentially open to two types of linguistic development. At one level, there is the possibility of influence from English and, at another, the existence of several sub-varieties, all in close geographical proximity to one another, provides a setting that is ripe for the occurrence of koinéization.[1] As described in section 4.2., in order to gather data for the analysis of both of these potential developments, the interviews conducted with the sample of fifty informants incorporated a period of tape-recorded free conversation between myself and the informant, which had the aim of eliciting casual speech. The informants participating in this part of the survey were therefore identical to those of chapter 4. As virtually no native speakers are to be found under the age of 40, it has not been possible to compare the speech of younger and older speakers of Jèrriais. It is also worth reiterating that, in order to qualify for the sample, informants had to have been born on the Island and to have lived there for most of their lives. As no monoglot Jèrriais speakers are still alive, all informants were bilingual in Jèrriais and English.

Since the aim of the tape-recorded conversation was to elicit casual speech, several means were used to try and reduce the effect of the observer's paradox. Hoping that the 'friend-of-a-friend' sampling technique (see section 4.2.) might already have helped reduce my 'official' status, it was further attempted to increase the atmosphere of informality by conducting the interviews in a location chosen by the informants themselves: usually their own homes. Whenever possible, I tried to interview in groups of more than one. This meant that, although usually only one partner of a married couple had been the initial 'contact', the other partner was also encouraged to participate in the conversation. In this way, I was often able to recede into the background and let informants converse together. All informants were given the opportunity to refuse being tape-recorded.

Once permission to record had been granted, the tape-recorder was switched on and left running until my departure. It was not switched off if another person entered the room or if refreshments were served. Labov indicates how these are both prime contexts for the elicitation of casual speech (1985: 87–90). In general, the subject matter of the interview was not specifically directed and informants were allowed to stray as much as they liked from the questions asked. None of the questions focused on linguistic topics but, rather, they dealt with the broad theme of life on the Island. One subject that was deliberately introduced, however, was the Occupation of Jersey during the Second World War. The aim of introducing such an emotive topic was to produce a situation not unlike Labov's 'danger-of-death' question (1985: 93), where the emotional content of what informants were saying had been found to produce less guarded speech. Trudgill (1974) found that it was not possible to use the 'danger-of-death' question as it stood in his study of the English spoken in Norwich, as the majority of his informants had never experienced such a situation. However, he adapted the question to the British context by asking informants instead to describe a situation where they had a good laugh. It was hoped that asking informants about the highly emotional subject of the German Occupation would provide a way of adapting the question to a Jersey context.

Since most of the interview was conducted in Jèrriais, it is conceivable that the fact that I am not a native speaker of the variety may have influenced the language used by informants. While this cannot be proved conclusively one way or another, I believe that it is unlikely to have happened to any significant degree, given that my proficient knowledge of standard French, coupled with intensive study of Jèrriais during the months preceding the fieldwork, meant that I had no difficulty in understanding what was said: indeed, I was even teased by some informants on account of my St Ouen-biased Jèrriais.[2] Furthermore, random 'spot-check'-type comparisons of the speech of informants when addressing each other and addressing me revealed no significant difference in terms of the features under study.

This study focuses on the speech of the native speakers of Jèrriais only. Whilst it would have been interesting to study the proficiency continuum frequently found in situations of language obsolescence, it was, perhaps, an inevitable consequence of the 'friend-of-a-friend' sampling technique that I would not be introduced to someone who was not of native-speaker ability. However, given the undoubted advantages of this technique (see section

4.2.), together with the fact that semi-speakers are often reluctant to become informants in studies of this kind (Jones 1998a: 52–3), I remain confident that the 'friend-of-a-friend' sampling method was the most appropriate technique available for the purposes of this survey.

6.3. THE VARIABLES

In accordance with the study's aim of investigating two types of linguistic development, the data were analysed for both of the following kinds of variables:

(i) linguistic features common to all *parlers* of Jèrriais, where retention or loss would indicate the presence or otherwise of language obsolescence (eight variables).
(ii) linguistic features which traditionally differed between *parlers* (five variables).

The results are also discussed in conjunction with examples of the written language, which are taken from the two volumes *Histouaithes et gens d'Jèrri* (HGJ) and *Jèrri jadis* (JJ) (Le Feuvre 1976, 1983).

6.3.1. *'Language obsolescence' variables*

As typologically related languages, English and French and, one may add, varieties thereof show a high degree of structural overlap (Mougeon and Beniak 1991: 196–7). The eight variables in this section were thus selected due to the fact that they represented points with regard to which English and Jèrriais traditionally diverge and therefore seemed to be prime candidates for change.

All the variables were binary in nature (except for variable 6.3.1.1.). In other words, they offered a clear-cut alternation between the presence and absence of language obsolescence. However, as will be discussed, it would be mistaken to consider these changes as phenomena exclusive to language obsolescence. Many of the changes observed in modern Jèrriais have also been noted in so-called 'healthy' languages. What makes them indicative of language obsolescence in this context is not their nature but rather the combination of their number, the rate at which they are occurring and the current sociopolitical environment of Jèrriais, namely territorial contraction and speaker reduction.

6.3.1.1. *Prepositions – with*

Whereas English and French both have just one form to convey all functions of the preposition 'with' (*avec* in standard French), traditional Jèrriais has three different prepositions, each of which has a distinct function. *Auve* is the unmarked form, which also tends to be used when the referent is animate, hence:

(1)   *P'têt qué d'main, j'éthons eune chance de pâler **auve** not' vaîsîn*
      'Perhaps tomorrow we will have an opportunity to speak to our neighbour'

However, when the instrumental function is being conveyed and the object is inanimate, then *atout* is used:

(2)   *Frappez l'cliou **atout** chu marté*
      'Strike the nail with this hammer'

The third preposition, *acanté*, is used to convey a comitative meaning:

(3)   *Je m'en vais **acanté** lyi*
      'I am going along with her' (Birt 1985: 166)

This separation of functions is not unique to Jèrriais and may be observed in other varieties of Norman. Although the DJF (p. 3) cites the form *quànt-et* for Guernsey (cf. *à quànté* (De Garis 1983: 214)), in practice, a two-fold opposition is found in modern spoken Guernésiais, where *dauve* is the unmarked form and, like its Jèrriais cognate form, *atou* conveys an instrumental function when the referent is inanimate. Mainland Norman has *aveu/d'avec, d'o* and *(d')aquant(et)*, although the distribution is somewhat different, with *d'aveu/d'o* expressing accompaniment, *d'o* used with material and *d'aveu* expressing the means by which something is achieved:

(4)   *No féchoune eune ormouère **d'o** du quêne*
      'One makes a wardrobe with oak wood'

(5)   *Il fait du varet **d'avec** sa vuule querrue*
      'He is doing some light work with his old plough' (UPN 1995: 117, 128)

The data were therefore examined in order to determine whether the ternary opposition of traditional Jèrriais was being maintained.

6.3.1.2. *Affirmation*

As in standard French, Jèrriais has two forms of the word 'yes': *oui*, the unmarked form, and *si*, the form used in traditional Jèrriais to give an affirmative answer to a negative question, hence:

(6)   *Tu ne sors pon ch't arlevée? – **Si-fait***
      'You're not going out this afternoon, are you? – Yes, I am' (Birt 1985: 52)

Since this distinction does not occur in English and since both of these forms can only be taken to mean 'yes' in this context, it was possible that one form might be generalized to the exclusion of the other.

6.3.1.3. *Gender*

All Jèrriais nouns are either masculine or feminine. The gender of nouns is marked by a variety of different means, such as the definite article, the indefinite article, possessive pronouns, demonstrative pronouns and adjectives, anaphoric and cataphoric pronouns, and the agreement of any adjectives used to qualify the noun. Some of these devices may be used together, such as an article and an adjective, for example. In instances such as these, therefore, the gender-marking is, in all but one case, redundant and, accordingly, the data were analysed in order to determine whether such redundancy was being eliminated, a feature often found in obsolescent languages (Dorian 1981: 136; Mougeon and Beniak 1991: 91; Jones 1998a: 65, 68, 71–2, 171–2, 179).

6.3.1.4. *Choice of auxiliary*

The perfect and pluperfect tenses in Jèrriais are formed by the use of the past participle and an auxiliary verb, normally *aver* ('to have'), although *être* ('to be') is used with reflexive verbs and with what Birt describes as 'certain other verbs which generally express motion' (1985: 54), citing *aller* ('to go'), *v'nîn* ('to come') and *arriver* ('to arrive') as cases in point (1985: 200).[3] In order to see whether both patterns were being maintained or whether one was being generalized at the expense of the other, the use of the auxiliary was examined in all verbs in the perfect and pluperfect tenses.

6.3.1.5. *The negative pronoun*

As in Mainland Norman (UPN 1995: 112) the negative pronoun, 'no one' (*pèrsonne*), historically commands a plural verb in Jèrriais. However, both Birt (1985: 193) and the DJF (p. 400) maintain that the pronoun may also be used with a singular verb. Since Guernésiais also has a similar pronoun (*autchun*), which is used with a plural verb, it seems likely that the use of the pronoun with a singular verb is a recent innovation, perhaps on the basis of English, where the negative pronoun always commands a singular verb. The data were therefore analysed to see whether, in modern Jèrriais, simplification was occurring, with one of the patterns being generalized at the expense of the other.

6.3.1.6. *Prepositions – souotre*

Birt (1985: 233) describes the use of this preposition thus: *souotre* is used 'particularly after the verb *couôrre* ('to run')':

(7) *Les deux tchians couothaient **souotre** not' pétit cat chaque fais*
     qu'i'l'viyaient dans l'gardin
     'The two dogs used to run after our little cat every time they saw him in the garden'

'However', he continues, the preposition 'is also used like "after" in English following certain verbs':

(8) *Lé Chent'nyi s'en fut **souotre** li*
     'The Centenier chased after him'

(9) *Quand i'nos vîtent, i's'mîntent à crier à tue-tête **souotre** nous*
     'When they saw us, they began shouting at the top of their voices after us'

The form comes from Old French *soentre* and its reflexes are also found in Guernésiais and Serquiais (*souventre*).

The form *auprès* ('after') (pronounced [oprɛ]/[uprɛ]) is also found in Jèrriais in contexts such as:

(10) ***Auprès** aver prîns toute chutte peine-là*
     'After having taken all that trouble'

(11) ***Auprès** tout*
     'After all' (DJF, p. 31)

However, it is not traditionally used after the verb *couôrre*, in which context *souotre* is preferred.

In English, of course, the functions of *souotre* and *auprès* are subsumed by the single preposition 'after'. The data were therefore analysed in order to determine whether the two traditional patterns were being maintained in modern Jèrriais, or whether one of these was encroaching upon the other.

6.3.1.7. *Position of adjectives*

In traditional Jèrriais, many adjectives precede the noun they qualify (Birt 1985: 43–5). Although English adjectives are also preposed, the Jèrriais construction is not generally considered to be an anglicism due to the fact that monosyllabic adjectives and also adjectives of colour are commonly preposed in Mainland Norman (UPN 1995: 36–7).[4] Although some Jèrriais adjectives may be preposed, therefore, adjective position also represents an area of divergence from English in that many common adjectives invariably follow the noun they qualify in traditional Jèrriais (Birt 1985: 44). The adjectives in the data were therefore examined in order to determine whether any shift in their position was apparent.

6.3.1.8. *The subjunctive*

In modern English, there are few distinctive subjunctive forms and even these are no longer frequently used in everyday speech. Jèrriais, on the other hand, has both a present and imperfect form of the subjunctive for every verb, although as in standard French, in the present tense the three persons singular and third person plural are homophonous with the indicative in the case of *-er* verbs.

The decline of the subjunctive mood in Jèrriais was mentioned by Le Maistre as long ago as 1947 (1947: 5). More recently, Liddicoat mentioned that the mood was being replaced by the indicative in the speech of non-fluent speakers, although he gives no details of the precise constructions involved (1990: 204).

The data were examined for use of the subjunctive in all of the contexts cited as triggers by Birt (1985: 210–14), namely (i) after verbs expressing a wish, (ii) in clauses dependent upon expression of evaluation, such as *Ch'est* + adjective + *qué* ('It's X that'); (iii) after *faller* ('to be necessary that'); (iv) after adjectival clauses containing a superlative; (v) after certain conjunctions of time, concession, purpose, condition; and (vi) in main clauses, with pseudo-subordinating *qué*.

6.3.2. *Lexical change*

A discussion of lexical change involving borrowing and calquing, phenomena associated with linguistic interference, has also been included after the analysis of the morphosyntactic variables.

6.3.3. *'Dialect mixing' variables*

The data discussed in this section involved variables whose realization traditionally differed according to geographical location. They are all phonetic in nature and are discussed in section 3.3.1. These variables involve the assibilation of intervocalic [r] and secondary diphthongization – in other words, oppositions which would be salient to most speakers.

6.4. RESULTS

6.4.1. *'Language obsolescence' variables*

6.4.1.1. *Prepositions – with*

In modern Jèrriais, the ternary opposition between *auve*, *atout* and *acanté* was found to be in a state of flux. Examination of the 485 tokens in the corpus yielded no instances at all of *atout* or *acanté*, with these prepositions having been replaced entirely by *auve* or, more commonly, by the loan-word *avec*, pronounced [əuvɛk] in EJ. *Atout* was, however, found in HGJ and JJ:

(12) *Il' 'taient faits **atout** d'la pâte dé pâté et des pommes douoches*
      'They were made with paté mixture and sweet apples' (HGJ, p. 41)

(13) *Dans nouos tentes j'avions eune pailloche bouôrrée **atout** d'l'êtrain*
      'In our tents we had a mattress stuffed with straw' (JJ, p. 102)

This might suggest that the written language is slightly more conservative than speech. However, although both *auve* and *atout* are attested – in a variety of spellings – in the *Almanach de la Chronique de Jersey* from the turn of the twentieth century, this opposition is not generally maintained in modern Jèrriais writing in, for example, the articles written in the quarterly

Nouvelles Chroniques du Don Balleine. Of course, since both HGJ and JJ are written by the same author, and no other substantial volumes of prose exist in Jèrriais with which Le Feuvre's use of *auve/atout/acanté* could be compared, it is possible that the distribution of these prepositions may reflect the author's idiosyncratic usage, rather than that of the speech community as a whole.

Although mentioned in the DJF (p. 3), no trace of the preposition *acanté* was found in either HGJ, JJ, the *Almanach de la Chronique de Jersey* or the *Nouvelles Chroniques du Don Balleine*. Moreover, it was clear that, in the work of Le Feuvre, at least, *auve* had replaced *acanté* with respect to the comitative function:

(14)   *Tchiquefais, m'n oncl'ye Dâlpheusse y' allait **auve** mé*
       'Sometimes, my uncle Dâlpheusse would go there with me' (HGJ, p. 65)

A simplification of the system has therefore occurred both in writing and, to an even more advanced degree, in speech. This may either be seen as an internal change, involving the loss of a previous opposition, which is characteristic of language obsolescence or, alternatively, it could be attributable to borrowing from standard French, calquing from English, or even a combination of these factors.[5] The minority of informants who retained *auve* to the exclusion of *avec* did not form a homogeneous group, in terms of either age or parish of origin, four coming from St Ouen, one from St Jean, one from St Laurent and one from St Martin.

6.4.1.2. *Affirmation*

The data revealed that the distinction between unmarked *oui* and its marked counterpart *si*, the latter normally used exclusively to give an affirmative answer to a negative question, was being maintained in only twenty-seven out of the forty-five tokens (60 per cent) obtained of contexts where *si* would be required historically. *Oui* was used the other 40 per cent of the time. Again, this suggests that the system is being simplified, as the meaning is equally transparent whether *oui* or *si* is used. As in section 6.4.1.1., however, this change could equally be attributed to influence from English, where only one form is used for affirmative answers, whatever the nature of the question.

As regards written usage, a certain amount of fluctuation was recorded for this variable, in that both *si* and *oui* were found in the written language as affirmative answers to negative questions:

(15)   *Mais y'a-t-i pon d'l'asseûthance? – **Oui***
       'But isn't there any insurance?' – 'Yes' (HGJ, p. 13)

(16)   *J'sis seux qu'tu n'pourôrrais pas m'aimer autant comme jé t'aime – **Si-fait**, man chièr*
       'I'm sure that you could never love me as much as I love you' – 'Yes I do, my dear' (HGJ, p. 142)

At present, it is difficult to predict with any great accuracy whether this fluctuation will continue at its present level or whether, in a few decades' time, *oui* will have gained further ground. Evidence from East Sutherland Gaelic (Dorian 1997) suggests that the more proficient speakers are unlikely to show much change in their patterns of usage but, as Dorian (p.c.) points out, change may well occur in the Jèrriais of speakers of lesser proficiency, especially those who are reasonably fluent in Jèrriais but who, nevertheless, make more use of English than Jèrriais in their everyday lives.[6] It will, however, be difficult to determine whether or not any deviations the latter group make from the historical norm in their later lives truly do represent change unless the current speech habits of this group can be documented and compared systematically with that of the most grammatically conservative group.

6.4.1.3. *Gender*

The examination of gender-marking in modern Jèrriais focused on two specific constructions, namely gender agreement in adjectives and gender-marking with referential pronouns.

a. *Gender in adjectives*

Table 6.1(a) Gender in adjectives: traditional usage

Variable	Number of tokens	Percentage of total number of tokens (tables 6.1(a) and 6.1(b))
Masculine adjective used with masculine noun	300	36%
Feminine adjective used with feminine noun	448	54%
Total	748	

Table 6.1(b) Gender in adjectives: non-traditional usage

Variable	Number of tokens	Percentage of total number of tokens (tables 6.1(a) and 6.1(b))
Masculine adjective used with feminine noun	81	10%
Feminine adjective used with masculine noun	4	0.5%
Total	85	

Total number of tokens = 833

Examination of this variable revealed that an adjective of a historically inappropriate gender was being selected in approximately one in ten of the 833 contexts examined (tables 6.1(a) and 6.1(b)), yielding examples such as the following:

(17)   *Quasiment toutes les **grands** maîsons 'taient des fermes*
       'Nearly all the big [m.] houses [n.f.] were farms'

(18)   *J'avêmes eune télé **français***
       'We had a French [m.] telly [n.f.]'

(19)   *La vie est **difféthent***
       'Life [n.f.] is different [m.]'

(20)   *Un appartément **plieine** de monde*
       'A room [n.m.] full [f.] of people'

(21)   *Fallait lé mettre sus l'hèrbe qui 'tait **sec***
       'We had to put it on the grass [n.f.] that was dry [m.]'

Also common was the use of a masculine adjective when the speaker was a woman talking about herself:

(22)   *J'suis **seux***
       'I am sure'

As can be seen from table 6.1(b), most of the grammatically incorrect usage stemmed from masculine adjectives being used with feminine nouns. The meaning of each sentence, however, was clear and, in most cases, it was merely a question of elimination of redundancy rather than the elimination of gender-marking as a whole, as gender was usually marked elsewhere in the sentence.[7] Furthermore, it is not possible to deduce from these results that gender is being eliminated from even the adjectival system of Jèrriais, as the appropriate form was selected in approximately 90 per cent of cases (table 6.1(a)). Since English adjectives do not inflect for gender, it is tempting to identify this development as a straightforward case of English influence. Nevertheless, although such an explanation may be partly true, it by no means tells the whole story. As Gadet points out, the use of the masculine form of an attributive adjective for the feminine form is commonly found in low-register French (*français populaire*) (1992: 59; cf. Sauvageot 1972: 78–81). It is also possible to argue that the generalization of the masculine form in this way is an internal simplificatory change commonly seen in obsolescent varieties (Dimmendaal 1992: 126; Jones 1998a: 64–71, 166–7, 170–6).

Admittedly, the additional presence of the use of a feminine form in place of a masculine form (as in example (20)), rare in *français populaire*, does make it likely that the change is largely motivated by English influence, with the fact that English does not change its adjective according to gender possibly leading speakers to be occasionally less than rigorous in their observation of the agreement rules of Jèrriais. However, it would probably be prudent to acknowledge here at least the likelihood of multiple causation (Thomason and Kaufman 1988: 57), as the role of language-internal factors cannot be discounted for certain. Such change is termed 'ambiguous change' by Mougeon and Beniak (1991: 218). As mentioned in section 6.4.1.2., further research will be needed in order to determine whether this historically inappropriate usage increases or not in such contexts.

The correct gender agreement was always made on adjectives in HGJ and JJ:

(23) *Il est contre toutes nouos **vielles** couôteunmes*
      'He's against all our old [f.] customs [n.f.]' (HJG, p. 9)

(24) *Y' a eune **bouanne** caûchie*
      'There's a good [f.] slipway [n.f.] there' (JJ, p. 137)

b. *Gender in referential pronouns*

Anaphoric and cataphoric pronouns have a different form to refer to masculine and feminine nouns. For instance, whereas in:

(25) *Tch'est qu'est la londgeu d'vot **gardîn**? Jé sis seux qu'**lé vôtre** a pus d'flieurs qué **l'mein***
      'How long is your garden [n.m.]? I'm sure that yours [m.] has got more flowers than mine [m.]' (Birt 1985: 280)

'yours' and 'mine' are both rendered by masculine pronouns, as the noun *gardîn* ('garden') is masculine in Jèrriais, the phrase:

(26) ***Latchelle** des deux **galettes** qu'i veurt?*
      'Which [f.] of the two biscuits [n.f.] does he want?' (Birt 1985: 128)

requires a feminine pronoun, reflecting the gender of *galette* ('biscuit'). Instances were compared of when the historically appropriate form of the pronoun was selected and when it was not (tables 6.2(a) and 6.2(b)).

Table 6.2(a) Gender in referential pronouns: traditional usage

Variable	Number of tokens	Percentage of total number of tokens (tables 6.2(a) and 6.2(b))
Masculine pronoun used for masculine noun	22	8%
Feminine pronoun used for feminine noun	217	82%
Total	239	

Table 6.2(b) Gender in referential pronouns: non-traditional usage

Variable	Number of tokens	Percentage of total number of tokens (tables 6.2(a) and 6.2(b))
Masculine pronoun used for feminine noun	26	10%
Feminine pronoun used for masculine noun	0	0%
Total	26	

Total number of tokens = 265

When the use of gender in referential pronouns was examined, it was again clear that, although in the majority of cases historically appropriate usage was being maintained, making it impossible to speak meaningfully of gender elimination here (as with the adjectives, discussed above), change was clearly afoot in that the masculine pronoun was being used to refer to a feminine noun in approximately 10 per cent of all contexts. Unlike with the adjectives, this time no instances were found of the marked feminine pronoun being generalized at the expense of the unmarked masculine:

(27) *La vie* en Dgèrnésy est comme i 'tait d'vant la dgèrre
      'Life [n.f.] on Guernsey is as it [lit. 'he'] used to be before the war'

(28) *La langue* Jèrriaise . . . j' crais qu'i dait être fait sèrvi à l'école
      'The Jersey language [n.f.] . . . I think that it [lit. 'he'] should be used in school'

This was not apparent in written usage, where the correct referential pronoun was invariably selected:

(29) *'J'criyais bein qué ch'tait **eune lettre** d'împortance!' i nouos dit, 'car **oulle** est êcrite à la machinne!'*
      'I really though that it was an important letter [n.f.]!' he said to us 'because it [lit. 'she'] is typewritten!' (HGJ, p. 10)

(30) *La mé! La même comme **oulle** 'tait dans l'temps d'mes anchêtres!*
      'The sea [n.f.]! It [lit. 'she'] is the same as it [lit. 'she'] was in the time of my ancestors!' (JJ, p. 27)

It seems, therefore, that although no there is no firm evidence that gender-marking in Jèrriais is being eliminated and replaced by a system more akin to that of English,[8] some confusion exists in this area, mainly via the masculine form being generalized at the expense of the feminine (cf. Dorleijn 1996: 58). The feminine form is, presumably, being allowed to give way in view of the low functional load it has in this context, for use of the masculine form creates little ambiguity of meaning in most cases.[9] As stated above, the change in progress is not an unequivocal case of contact-based influence in that, although influence from English, where there is no such gender distinction, has some bearing, the development under way is not inconsistent with internal simplification. It will be interesting to see whether this situation represents a 'steady state', as it seems to do in *français populaire*, or whether the loss of gender marking increases further.

6.4.1.4. *Choice of auxiliary*

When the choice of auxiliary in modern Jèrriais was considered, it was found that, as in standard French, only a minority of verbs in Jèrriais were conjugated with the verb *être* ('to be'). A more comprehensive breakdown yielded the results shown in tables 6.3(a) and 6.3(b).[10]

Table 6.3(a) Choice of auxiliary: traditional usage

Verb	*Aver*	*Être*
Rentrer ('to come back')	1	0
Sorti ('to go out')	2	0
Reflexive verbs	0	43
V'nîn ('to come')	0	30
Aller ('to go')	0	22
Èrv'nîn ('to come back')	0	6
Dév'nîn ('to become')	0	3
Naître ('to be born')	0	1

Table 6.3(b) Choice of auxiliary: non-traditional usage

Verb	*Aver*	*Être*
Entrer ('to enter')	7 (70%)	3 (30%)
Arriver ('to arrive')	8 (40%)	12 (60%)
Rester ('to stay')	3 (60%)	2 (40%)
Mouothi ('to die')	1	0

It was clear, therefore, that all reflexive verbs, together with *v'nîn* and its compounds, adhered unequivocally to the auxiliary *être* in the formation of these tenses.[11] This conforms to the usage described by Birt (1985: 200), as does that of *sorti* (which makes exclusive use of the auxiliary *aver*) and *aller* (which makes exclusive use of *être*) (1985: 200). Although the number of tokens obtained for this variable was not high, there was, nevertheless, a degree of confusion regarding auxiliary selection with *entrer*, *arriver* and *rester*, which were not used consistently with either *être*, as they would be in standard French, or *aver*.

It is noteworthy that, in the case of *arriver*, Jèrriais usage is at odds with that described for Mainland Norman. Birt describes the verb as taking *être* (1985: 200), whereas in Mainland Norman, it is said to take *avaer* (UPN 1995: 161). Furthermore, whereas Birt claims that *aver* is the auxiliary used with *entrer* (1985: 200), my data indicated that, although *aver* was statistically more likely to be chosen in this context, and was also the auxiliary used in the one instance obtained from the data of *entrer*'s compound *rentrer*, there was also evidence of some selection of *être*, probably due to the influence of standard French, with which all the Islanders are familiar (see section 8.2.) The familiarity of Islanders with standard French may also account for the use of *être* with *rester*.

Analysis of this variable therefore indicated that, although traditional Jèrriais seems to have conformed to the trend prevalent in Romance for the use of the two auxiliaries of Latin (HABERE ('to have') and ESSE ('to be')) to become levelled to HABERE alone (Vincent 1982: 91–4),[12] it is possible that influence from standard French, where the opposition between auxiliaries has been maintained via grammaticalization, may be leading to the reintroduction of *être* as an auxiliary.[13] Of course, it is also possible that the direction of the change is influenced by English – which makes exclusive use of 'to have' as its perfect and pluperfect auxiliary.

6.4.1.5. *The negative pronoun*

Analysis of constructions involving the negative pronoun (forty-three tokens) revealed that the plural verb was still being used in this construction in the majority of contexts (thirty-four tokens, or 79 per cent). Use of the singular verb, which occurred in nine contexts (21 per cent), was not found to be restricted in its geographical distribution and it is possible that it may have been introduced due to influence from French or English, both of which have a singular verb in this context (Price 1993: §551). Variation in this context was also found in writing:

(31) *Pèrsonne n'**ont** jamais seu*
      'No one has ever known' (HGJ, p. 74) [plural verb]

(32) *Pèrsonne né **sont** forchis dé l'faithe*
      'No one is forced to do it' (HGJ, p. 47) [plural verb]

(33) *Pèrsonne né **pathaît** craithe . . .*
      'No one seems to believe . . .' (HGJ, p. 59) [singular verb]

(34) *. . . et j'en doute si pèrsonne **ait** seu qué ch'tait ieux jusqu'à ch't heu*
      '. . . and I doubt whether, to this day, anyone knew that it was them'
      (JJ, p. 94) [singular verb]

6.4.1.6. *Prepositions – souotre*

In order to determine whether *souotre* and *auprès* were retaining their traditional functions in modern Jèrriais, the choice of preposition used with *couôrre* was analysed in the speech of thirty-four informants, each of whom used the construction once as part of a sentence-translation exercise conducted at the end of the tape-recorded conversation. The results revealed that *souotre* was used in only 56 per cent of possible contexts (nineteen tokens), with *auprès* used in 6 per cent of cases (two tokens). In the remaining 38 per cent of contexts (thirteen tokens), the borrowed form *après* ([apre]) was used, which is distinct from *auprès* ([oprɛ]/[uprɛ]) in terms of its pronunciation.

It was clear, therefore, that as well as a lexical item being borrowed from French in this context, reduction was taking place, with the loss of the *souotre/auprès* distinction, and the generalization of the form most like the French term. Since English, like standard French, has one preposition to cover both these functions, it may be that their combined influence is leading to the loss of this distinction in Jèrriais. Of course, it is also possible that the loss of the rule distinguishing the use of *souotre* and *auprès* may represent internal simplification.

6.4.1.7. *Position of adjectives*

a. *Adjectives of colour*

Adjectives of colour are preposed in traditional Jèrriais (Birt 1985: 43). When their position was examined in the data (fifty-six tokens), it was clear that this had not altered in modern Jèrriais, as there was not a single example of such an adjective being postposed:

(35) *Un **nièr** cat*
      'A black cat'

(36) *Un **blianc** j'va*
      'A white horse'

This, of course, is not surprising, since any contact-based influence from English would reinforce the Norman tendency towards preposition.

Adjectives of colour were also preposed in written usage:

(37) *Lus **rouoges** câsaques*
      'Their red coats' (HGJ, p. 64)

(38) *La distillâtion des **bliancs** vîns*
      'The distillation of the white wines' (JJ, p. 23)

b. *Other adjectives*

Even when adjectives of colour are excluded from consideration, the data revealed that, in modern Jèrriais, around four out of every five adjectives are preposed (table 6.4).

Table 6.4 Adjective position in modern Jèrriais
(all adjectives minus adjectives of colour)

Position of adjective	Number of tokens
Preposed	556 (79%)
Postposed	150 (21%)
Total	706

In order to determine whether this result might have been skewed in some way by a high proportion of monosyllabic adjectives and those such as *vièr* ('old'), *chièr* ('dear'), *bieau* ('beautiful') and *nouvieau* ('new'), which, according to Birt, always precede the noun they qualify (1985: 45), the data were reanalysed, this time taking into account only adjectives of two or more syllables (and discounting the *vièr* group, listed above). This left a total of 182 tokens to be considered (table 6.5).

Table 6.5 Adjective position in modern Jèrriais
(adjectives of two or more syllables minus the *vièr* group)

Position of adjective	Number of tokens
Preposed	63 (35%)
Postposed	119 (65%)
Total	182

The fact that over one-third of so-called 'long' adjectives are being preposed in modern Jèrriais points to an emerging tendency towards anteposition. This tendency became even more apparent when adjectives of nationality and the word *pâssè* ('last', 'past') were omitted (table 6.6). These are described by Birt (1985: 44) as always following the noun they qualify, and

Table 6.6 Adjective position in modern Jèrriais
(adjectives of two or more syllables minus adjectives of nationality, *pâssè* and the *vièr* group)

Postposed adjectives	Number of tokens
Nationality	48 (40%)
Pâssè	59 (50%)
Other	12 (10%)
Total	119

their occurrence was probably out of proportion with their normal frequency, given the subject matter of the interviews.

Anteposition of adjectives was also far more prevalent than postposition in written Jèrriais:

(39) *Charles Deux, . . . comme preuve dé sa **rouoyale** affection*
'Charles the Second, . . . as proof of his royal affection' (HGJ, p. 78)
(cf. expressions such as *La Cour Rouoyale* ('The Royal Court'), where the adjective is postposed)

(40) *Il 'tait un charmant corps*
'He was a charming person' (JJ, p. 95)

The data revealed that even superlatives were being preposed in certain cases:

(41) *Ieune des **plus aîsies** manniéthes est . . .*
'One of the easiest ways is . . .'

(42) *Y' a deux ou trais **vraîment vièrs** avocats qui prépathent lé contrat ieux-mêmes*
'There are two or three really old solicitors who prepare the title deeds themselves'

In the written language both postposition and anteposition of superlatives were found:

(43) *Ou crait qu'ch'est la chose **la pus împortante** dans la vie*
'She thinks that it's the most important thing in life' (HGJ, p. 11)

(44) *. . . **les pus près** pathents 'taient les preunmièrs en driéthe*
'. . . the closest relatives were first in line behind' (JJ, p. 17)

Since traditional Jèrriais had two possible locations for non-colour adjective placement, it is possible that the modern dialect is displaying evidence of internal simplification, with the generalization of one of these patterns at the expense of the other. It is clear that some adjectives are now exclusively preposed (for example *difficile* ('difficult'), *aîsi* ('easy'), *favorite* ('favourite') and *spécial* ('special')), but that others (such as *naturel* ('natural')) are in a state of flux. The fact that 'short' adjectives, adjectives of colour and the *vièr* group already formed one numerically large group that was traditionally preposed might have tipped the balance in favour of more generalized anteposition. However, it is equally impossible to ignore the fact that the pattern that seems to be winning out is that which is isomorphic with English.

Neither *pâssè* nor adjectives of nationality were ever preposed in the data (cf. Birt 1985: 44). The reason why these categories of adjectives seem to be resisting any change is unclear, although it is possible to venture tentative explanations such as the fact that well-known set expressions, such as *la langue Jèrriaise* ('the Jersey language') or *temps pâssè* ('in days gone by'), may have encouraged the maintenance of postposition in these restricted contexts.

6.4.1.8. *The subjunctive*

Table 6.7 Use of the subjunctive in modern Jèrriais

Construction	Indicative	Subjunctive
Vouler qué ('to want that')	31 (35%)	58 (65%)
Ch'est + adjective + *qué* ('it is + adjective + that')	54 (98%)	1 (2%)
Faller ('it is necessary that')	50 (41%)	72 (59%)
D'vant qué ('before')	48 (68%)	23 (32%)
Bieau qué ('although')	34 (100%)	0
Sans qué ('without')	18 (100%)	0
Pour qué ('in order that')	12 (86%)	2 (14%)
3sg. commands	0	10 (100%)

There is no doubt that the use of the subjunctive is in decline in modern Jèrriais. As demonstrated in table 6.7, the data revealed that the mood is no longer triggered in three of the contexts mentioned by Birt (1985: 210–14) and only in the case of third person singular command forms was it always present – although, unlike the case in Medieval Norman, these now always require a pseudo-subordinating *qué*. Examples of similar third person commands in Medieval Norman would be:

(45) *Venget li reis, si nus purrat venger* (*La Chanson de Roland* (twelfth century), l. 1744)
'Let the king come, he will be able to avenge us'

(46) *Aït vos Deus, ki unkes ne mentit* (*La Chanson de Roland* (twelfth century), l. 1865)
'May God help you, he who never lied'[14]

Although the subjunctive was still present in the other contexts examined, these were by no means systematic triggers. Furthermore, it was possible to establish the following hierarchy of subjunctive-triggering constructions: *vouler qué* (65 per cent), *faller* (59 per cent), *d'vant qué* (32 per cent), *pour qué* (14 per cent), *ch'est* + adjective + *qué* (2 per cent).[15] Some examples of the (i) historically appropriate and (ii) inappropriate usage found in the data are given below:

(i)

(47) *D'vant qué l's autres **aient** entré*
      'Before the others came in'

(48) *I' faut qu'i **ait** eune différente licence pouor chenna*
      'He has to have a different licence for that'

(49) *J'veurs qu'i y' **âge** pouor mé*
      'I want him to go for me'

(ii)

(50) *J'voulais qué vous **avez** arrêté pouor mé*
      'I wanted you to wait for me'

(51) *I'faudra qué j'**faisons** eune autre chose*
      'We will have to do something else'

(52) *Bieau qué ses pathents **sont** hors tchique bord*
      'Although his parents are out of the Island somewhere'

It is worth noting that the three most productive contexts for the subjunctive in Jèrriais, namely command forms, after *vouler* and after *faller*, were also among the most frequent triggers of the subjunctive in Guernésiais (Jones 2000), although there the last two constructions triggered the mood more frequently (in over 70 per cent of possible contexts). *Pour qué* also triggered the subjunctive more often in Guernésiais than in Jèrriais and *d'vant qué* and *ch'est* + adjective + *qué* proved infrequent triggers in both varieties. Unlike the case in standard French, in Jèrriais the subjunctive was not used to deny the reality of an event – both *ch'n'est pon qué* ('it's not that') and *j' n' dis pon qué* ('I'm not saying that') always triggered the indicative.

The Jèrriais subjunctive does not seem to be almost automatically triggered by a conjunction ending in *qué*. Another difference from standard French was that the use of the imperfect subjunctive was widespread in Jèrriais (table 6.8), giving rise to constructions such as:

(53) *S'il faudrait qué j'**d'meurisse** . . .*
      'If I had to live . . .'

(54) *J'voulais qu'i l'**sûsse***
      'I wanted him to know'

This tense of the subjunctive is also widespread in Guernésiais and in Mainland Norman.

No significant difference in usage was recorded for either tense of the subjunctive according to the precise verb used or indeed the person of the verb, although *nou* (3sg. impersonal pronoun) + subjunctive appeared more frequently than *jé* (1pl. pronoun) + subjunctive as the exponent of the first person plural.

Table 6.8 Use of the imperfect subjunctive in modern Jèrriais

Construction	Indicative	Imperfect subjunctive
Vouler qué	26 (35%)	49 (65%)
Ch'est + adjective + *qué*	0	1
Faller	3 (18%)	14 (82%)
D'vant qué	2 (29%)	5 (71%)

The present and imperfect subjunctive were also found in writing, where they were both triggered more regularly than in speech. It was interesting to note that, despite being completely ousted by the preposition *bieau qué* in speech, *ouaithe qué* ('although') was regularly found in writing:

(55) *Ouaithe qué j'sûsse la réponse*
    'Although I knew the answer' (HGJ, p. 12)

(56) *Ouaithe qué l'Méthodisme fûsse bein êtablyi dans l'Île*
    'Although Methodism was well established on the Island' (JJ, p. 29)

Again, this could be due to idiosyncratic usage on the part of the author.
    Although the subjunctive mood still survives, therefore, in modern Jèrriais, its decline in usage across the board is also apparent, with some contexts being affected more than others. Again, the most tempting solution is to cite contact with English, where there are few distinctive subjunctive forms, as the cause of this change in Jèrriais.[16] However, it is interesting to note that Gadet's description of the position of the subjunctive in *français populaire*, a variety which has, at best, extremely limited contact with English, reveals tendencies similar to those found in Jèrriais. For example, the context in which the Jèrriais subjunctive is most frequently found (namely after verbs of volition) is also described by Gadet (1992: 89) as widely used in *français populaire*, suggesting, perhaps, that in this context the subjunctive may still be felt to be semantically motivated. This is not to say, however, that the Jèrriais subjunctive is any more expressive as an exponent of modality than its standard French equivalent. As in standard French, it exists as a morphological category but, in the vast majority of cases, it is triggered by syntax rather than by semantics. For example, although the subjunctive is traditionally required in a sentence such as:

(57) *Jé veurs qué tu prenges chutte pomme*
    'I want you to take this apple'

substitution of the indicative for the subjunctive here will not occasion any change of meaning, as the volition is always conveyed by the matrix verb. Similarly, Gadet's assertion that in contexts other than after verbs of volition 'on tendrait à le [le subjonctif] remplacer par un indicatif'[17] (1992: 89) also held good for many of the constructions of Jèrriais (see table 6.8).

It would seem, therefore, that, once again, contact with English does not account unequivocally for the whole picture here. Although contact may well serve to reinforce a simplificatory tendency that may already be present to replace the subjunctive with an indicative in constructions of this kind, it is unlikely to be the sole motivating factor. Again, it would be prudent to consider the strong likelihood of multiple causation in this context.

Another reason why we should be wary of contenting ourselves with the contact explanation pure and simple in the case described above is the fact that further analysis revealed Jèrriais to be exhibiting a tendency found in *français populaire* and some regional varieties of French to substitute the conditional for the imperfect subjunctive (cf. Gadet 1992: 89; Brunot and Bruneau 1969: 320; Cohen 1965: 63; Grevisse 1988: §869; Jones 2000). If Jèrriais usage parallels that in other varieties as regards conditional substitution in a particular context, it is not inconceivable that the same may apply in the case of indicative substitution.

Conditional substitution in Jèrriais appeared to be more restricted than in Guernésiais, occurring primarily after verbs of volition, although a few examples of substitution were also found after *faller* and *pour qué*:

(58) *I'voulaient qué j'arêt'thais sus l'comité*
     'They wanted me to stay on the committee'

(59) *Ou voulait qu'i s'rait chouaîsi*
     'She wanted him to be chosen'

(60) *I' faudrait qué j'm'en îthais*
     'I have to go'

(61) *Pour qu'i n'éthait pon la bliaûme*
     'So that he wouldn't get the blame'

However, substitution was found to occur in roughly the same proportion of contexts in both dialects (six tokens out of seventy-five (8 per cent) in Jèrriais compared to five tokens out of sixty-one (8 per cent) in Guernésiais). Further research of the kind outlined in section 6.4.1.2. will be needed in order to determine whether conditional substitution increases or not in such contexts.

Conditional substitution was also found in the written language:

(62) *Ouaithe qué j'dévthais* . . .
     'Although I should' (HGJ, p. 98)

(63) *J'voudrais tch'i' m'éthaient donné l'nom d'Pièrre*
     'I wish that they had called me Pierre' (JJ, p. 22)

As regards the morphology of the subjunctive, Jèrriais has preserved more of the reflexes of the Medieval Norman present subjunctive, with its

-ge- extension, than Guernésiais (cf. Spence 1957a: 83). These reflexes are still common in the verbs *aller* ('to go') (*qué j'âge*); *attendre* ('to wait for') (*qué j'attenge*); *prendre* ('to take') (*qué j'prenge*); *tcheindre* ('to hold') (*qué j'tcheinge*) and *v'nîn* ('to come') (*qué j'veinge*) (Birt 1985: 208–10) (and were all attested in the data). Guernésiais, on the other hand, preserves such forms only in the case of the verb *allaïr* ('to go') (*qué j'aouche*) and possibly also in *v'nir* ('to come') (in the shape of the form [i vɛŋȝ], which was attested in data collected for a complementary survey (Jones 2000)).

Some reflexes of the Medieval Norman forms are also preserved in Mainland Norman in verbs such as *allaer* ('to go') (*que je veiche*), *veî* ('to see') (*que je veige*) and *creire* ('to believe') (*que je creige*) (UPN 1995: 171–215). The data revealed, however, that in the case of the commonly used verbs *aller* and *v'nîn*, the *-ge-* reflexes of modern Jèrriais were being replaced, either by borrowings from standard French (such as *aille* for *âge*) or by alternative forms: [ɒl] in the case of *aller* and [vɛ̃], [vɛn] or [vɛns] for *v'nîn* (1sg.).

Although the Jèrriais subjunctive is conservative in its retention of the imperfect subjunctive and of the *-ge-* reflexes of Medieval Norman forms, there is also evidence that speakers are uncertain about some of its forms. This might be symptomatic of its diminishing usage, which might itself be precipitated by the lack of distinctive subjunctive forms in spoken English.

6.4.1.9. *Summary*

The findings in this section have demonstrated that all eight features examined are undergoing linguistic change. Moreover, although contact with English, the Island's dominant language and one in which all informants were fluent, seems to be an obvious motivating factor behind all the changes outlined above, as has been demonstrated, the fact that several of these developments have also been attested in regional and low-register varieties of French means that the situation is probably more complicated than this, and it is impossible to discount the presence of internal simplification as a contributory factor to the change in progress. It is, however, equally impossible to ignore the fact that features which are absent from modern spoken English are in decline in the dialect, although, at the time of writing, none of these had been eliminated altogether.

The following section considers developments in the lexis of Jèrriais. Unlike the morphosyntactic variables discussed above, these reveal unequivocal evidence of change attributable to contact with English.

6.4.2. *Lexical change*

6.4.2.1. *Borrowings and word substitution*

Given its long history of contact with other peoples, it is no surprise that borrowings abound in modern Jèrriais.[18] However, the language from which

Jèrriais has taken most of its borrowings in the modern period is English, by simple virtue of the latter's increasing presence on the Island during recent centuries. Spence (1993: 23–9) gives an informative account of English borrowings in Jèrriais and cites examples of borrowings that are to be found today in the domains of technology (*sprayer, eune bike* (p. 24)), fishing (*bouête-hook, trâler, ridgage* (p. 27)), everyday life (*boutchet, ticl'ye, scrobbinne-broche* (p. 27)) and nature (*dgêle, du privet, spruche* (p. 28)). In view of the comprehensive nature of his account, I will limit my discussion of borrowing to a few examples of the phenomenon as they appeared in my data.[19] For more detailed information, see Spence (1993).

Before embarking on such a discussion, however, it should be stressed, by way of introduction, that borrowing between Jèrriais and English is not entirely unidirectional. However, as far as sheer numbers are concerned, hundreds of English words enter Jèrriais for every few that move in the opposite direction, so that the phenomenon is far from being freely bidirectional, as it is, for instance, in Puerto Rico (Ma and Herasimchuk 1975). Moreover, the Jèrriais loans entering English tend to be words that do not exist outside the Island's culture. Dressler (1991: 102–3) describes a comparable situation in the case of Breton and French, and Mithun (1992: 104) also mentions the presence of such words in the English of the Central Pomo communities in California. These 'folklore' words (Dressler's term) should not be taken as evidence of bidirectional borrowing.

The following examples were typical of English loan-words found in Jèrriais:

(64) *I' fallait qu'i ait eune difféthente **licence** pouor chenna*
      'He needs a different licence for that'

(65) *Ou veint d'aver lé **sack***
      'She has just had the sack'

(66) *I' faut garder les routes en bouon **èrpathe***
      'We need to keep the roads in good repair'

(67) *J'avais un **fixed bayonet** dans lé dos*
      'I had a fixed bayonet in my back'

(68) *As-tu veu man **moto**?*
      'Have you seen my motor car?'

(69) *Soulais faithe lé **grêvîn** dans lé **sâsse-paine***
      'I used to make the gravy in the saucepan'

(70) *Chenna s'en va méthiter un grand **do***
      'That will be worthy of a big do'

It will be immediately apparent that, whereas some of these borrowings have been taken 'wholesale' directly from English, others have undergone some phonetic modification during the passage into Jèrriais. For example, the word 'gravy' (69) has lost its diphthong, its final vowel has become nasalized and the English alveolar continuant has been replaced by a dental trill: [grevĩ]. Similarly, the 'r' and 'e' of the word 'repair' (66) have undergone metathesis, a process which, in Jèrriais, is extremely common in the case of these two sounds (Birt 1985: 90–4; Spence 1990: 212), and assibilation of the second [r] has taken place.

Although probably the commonest (Appel and Muysken 1993: 170–1), nouns are not the only parts of speech to be borrowed. Verbs and adjectives have also passed from English to Jèrriais and, in the process, may acquire Jèrriais morphology:

(71)   *Ou 'tait **disappointée***
       'She was disappointed'

(72)   *I'faut **applyitchi** et lé spécial group chouaîsait les cheins qui peuvent v'nîn*
       'You have to apply and the special group decides who can come'

Dorleijn (1996: 49) states that Turkish verbs are generally borrowed into Kurmanci as non-finite, tenseless forms. This was not found to be the case in Jèrriais:

(73)   *Ou **manégit***
       'She managed'

(74)   *I' **réalisaient** pon qué j'tais Jèrriais*
       'They didn't realize that I was from Jersey'

English consecutive conjunctions may also be borrowed:

(75)   *La fèrme 'tait pon bein grande **so** y avait pon la pôssibilité dé garder des vaques*
       'The farm wasn't very big so it wasn't possible to keep cows'

(76)   *I'faut qu'il éprouve à mangi **because** ses pathents sont hors dé l'île*
       'He must try and eat because his parents are out of the Island'

Borrowing of the conjunction *so* was also noted by Mougeon and Beniak in the case of Ontarian French (1991: 198–212). They describe it as an example of core lexical borrowing occurring in a setting of intensive language contact, and suggest that it may 'serve to symbolize the advanced state of acculturation of bilingual speakers who experience high levels of contact with a superordinate language' (1991: 212). Hovdhaugen also discusses borrowing of grammatical terms in Tokelauan, although this is said to be uncommon (1992: 63).

Occasionally, an English word may be borrowed to modify a Jèrriais noun or verb:

(77) *Y' avait un **very spécial** câsaque*
'There was a very special coat'

(78) *Tchi maîson est à vendre **again?***
'Which house is for sale again?'

(79) *Ch'tait pon lé **proper** cîdre*
'It wasn't proper cider'

(80) *Ch'tait un **sit down** r'pas*
'It was a sit down meal'

(81) *Eune **extra** léçon*
'An extra lesson'

Unlike the situation in Scots Gaelic (Dorian 1994a: 486), the use of English borrowings in Jèrriais does not appear to be stigmatized. This corroborates Dorian's remarks that 'in cases where a small or otherwise precariously placed language has survived longer than might have been expected, an absence of puristic attitudes may have characterized some speakers' (cf. Hamp 1989: 198–9 on Arvanitika phonology and Huffines 1989: 225 on English loan-words in Pennsylvanian German).

Le Maistre (1947: 11) mentions that an English borrowing may sometimes be used despite the existence of an indigenous Jèrriais equivalent, citing *eune swallow* as a case in point, a term which is commonly used today notwithstanding the existence of *héthonde*. In the lexical survey, described in chapter 7, this practice was found to be widespread in all domains, and especially so regarding the names of plants and flowers (see section 7.2.8.). Listed below are some examples of this phenomenon, with the indigenous Jèrriais word given in parentheses. Note that some of these borrowings (marked with an asterisk) are, by now, so well integrated into Jèrriais that they are included in the DJF, where they function as synonyms of the indigenous word:

(82) *Dévant **stèrter*** (c'menchi)*
'Before beginning'

(83) *Ou **manégit** (mênagit)*
'She managed'

(84) *J'transféthis un **coupl'ye** dé cents à St Brélade (deux cents)*
'I transferred a couple of hundred to St Brélade'

(85) *I 'taitent à maîntchi **stèrvés** (affanmés)*
'They were half-starved'

(86) *Nou n'tait pon **alloué*** dé les aver (pèrmîns)*
'We weren't allowed to have them'

(87) *Quand sa nénantième **birthday** appraichit (annivèrsaithe)*
'When his ninetieth birthday drew near'

As stated above, these borrowings occur despite the existence of native Jèrriais equivalents. In fact, sometimes speakers would use a borrowing and then 'correct' themselves, showing that they were familiar with the indigenous term despite having initially used the borrowing:

(88) *Dans lé **parish hall** . . . la salle parouaissiale*
'In the parish hall'

(89) *I' fallait **chârer** tout . . . partagi tout*
'We had to share everything'

Use of another term in place of an indigenous one is a clear indicator of lexical loss. It was found by Gal amongst the restricted-network speakers of Oberwart Hungarian (1989: 328) and by Olshtain and Barzilay among adult speakers of English living in a Hebrew-dominant environment (1991: 149). This phenomenon will be explored further in chapter 7.

Le Maistre mentions the fact that the existence of a borrowing synonymous with an indigenous term can often lead to the doublets becoming semantically differentiated. He cites, as a case in point, the example of the borrowing *cleaner*, which appeared alongside indigenous *netti*. In modern Jèrriais, the latter has retained the basic meaning of 'to clean', whilst the former has specialized its meaning to refer to the annual ritual of spring cleaning (1947: 11).

6.4.2.2. Calques

A definition and explanation of calques are given in section 5.5.2., where they are discussed in conjunction with the creation of new words in Jèrriais. In this section, the calques, like the other lexical data examined, were observed in the casual speech of informants during the tape-recorded part of the interviews described in chapters 4 and 6.

(i) As with the borrowings mentioned in section 6.4.2.1. above, on Jersey, calquing is not a unidirectional phenomenon (see section 8.3. for instances of Jèrriais syntactic calques in the English of the Island). However, the dominant position of English on the Island has led to a situation where English calques abound in the speech of all native speakers. English idioms were often translated:

(90) *I tchit bas*
'He fell down'

(91) *Dans chu respé-là*
'In that respect'

(92) *I manque les Sunday roast*
      'He misses the Sunday roast'
and other examples of calques included phrases such as:

(93) ***J'fallais** aller en cours*
      'I had to go to the lesson'

(94) *J' né crais pon qué chenna est **fait servi** un tas en Français*
      'I don't think that that is made use of much in French'

(95) *I' voulaient **tchique chose politique***
      'They wanted something political'

(96) *Pouor **garder** la langue **en allant***
      'To keep the language going'

(97) *Tu ne dévthais pon **laîssi chenna s'n aller***
      'You shouldn't let that go'

Calquing was also found in the written language:

(98) *. . . **tchiquechose doux***
      '. . . something soft' (HGJ, p. 76)

(99) *. . . **sans rînme ni raiethon***
      '. . . without rhyme or reason' (HGJ, p. 135)

(100) *Auprès la fîn d'la dgèrre, La Milice Rouoyale fut dêmobilisée **pour bouan***
      'After the end of the war, the Royal Militia was demobilized for good' (JJ, p. 97)

(ii) At times, a Jèrriais word was used as a direct translation of an English word, despite the fact that it had not undergone the same semantic extension as the English term:

(101) *J'aime **attraper** avec correspondance*
      'I like to catch up with my correspondence'

(102) *J' n' sais pon exactément comment chenna **travaille***
      'I don't know exactly how that works'

(103) *J' n' savais pon qué chenna **travaillait***
      'I didn't know that that worked'

(104) *Y'a eune route qui **couôrre** dé l'églyise à la mé*
      'There's a road that runs from the church to the sea'

(105) *Mes pathents **bouogîtent***
      'My parents moved (house)'

(iii) Like standard French, Jèrriais makes a distinction between the verbs *saver* ('to know' (facts)) and *connaître* ('to know' (people/places)). The fact that such a distinction is not found in English seems to be precipitating its disappearance in Jèrriais (cf. Jones 1998a: 187 for the loss of the same distinction by some speakers of modern Welsh):

(106) *I' n' **savent** pon les routes*
       'They don't know the roads'

(107) *J' n' **sais** pon les mots d'aut'*
       'I don't know the words any more'

Such confusion was not, however, apparent in written Jèrriais, where both verbs were always used appropriately:

(108) *J'**savons** bein qué Missis Touzé est née Lîsabé Hamptonne!*
       'We know full well that Mrs Touzé was born Elizabeth Hamptonne!' (HGJ, p. 138)

(109) *J'**connais** eune femme tchi n'pouvait pon faithe lé beurre*
       'I know a woman who couldn't make butter' (HGJ, p. 68)

(iv) There were also instances where modern Jèrriais had adopted English word order. This appears to suggest that Jèrriais lexical items are, at times, being 'slotted' into an underlying English syntax:

(110) *Ous savez tchiqu' les Boches fîtent?*
       'Do you know what the Germans did?'

(v) Preposition stranding is also common in modern Jèrriais, for example:

(111) *. . . qué j'soulais être dans l'Assembliée d'Jèrriais **avec***
       '. . . who I used to be in the Assembliée d'Jèrriais with'

(112) *I'sont allés en Angliéterre pouor quatre ou chînq ans **châque***
       'They went to England for four or five years each'

(113) *J'avais un couôsîn qué j'tais bouons amîns **avec***
       'I used to have a cousin who I was good friends with'

(114) *Y' a tant dé mots à ch't heu qu'i n'y 'a pon dé Jèrriais **pouor***
       'There are so many words that now there aren't any Jèrriais words for'

(115) *J' chèrchis **pouor***
       'I looked for (it)'

(116) *Ch'taient les femmes qu'i' v'naient **pouor***
       'It was the women that they came for'

Although the examples given above also seem to be syntactic calques on English, they are not unequivocal evidence of English interference, as preposition stranding is often found in *français populaire* (Gadet 1992: 73). Bouchard (1982) also argues against interpreting preposition stranding in French as evidence of interference from English.

(vi) However, English influence was unquestionable in sentences such as:

(117)   *Il' ont donné un tas d'sou à lé janne fréthe à Mess. Lé Bro'*
        'They gave a lot of money to Mr. Le Brocq's young brother', where
        analytic *à le* ('to the') replaces the more opaque form *au.*

(vii) The data also revealed many instances of prepositions being used in contexts with which they were not traditionally associated. Again, English influence is the most likely explanation here. In each case, the historically appropriate Jèrriais preposition is given in parentheses:

(a) *Dans*

(118)   ***Dans** les rush hours* (*duthant*)
        'In the rush hours'

(119)   *J'allons **dans** lé mais dé juilet* (*en*)
        'We're going in July'

(120)   *Être întérêssi **dans** l's affaithes dé la pâraisse* (*à*)
        'To be interested in parish matters'

(121)   *J' comprends des mots **dans** l'Espangno* (*en*)
        'I understand some Spanish words'

(b) *Pouor*

(122)   *I 'tait fèrmyi **pouor** vîngt-chînq ans* (*duthant*)
        'He was a farmer for twenty-five years'

(123)   *Payi **pouor** lé r'pas* (no preposition needed)
        'To pay for the meal'

(124)   *D'mande **pouor** J.S.* (*à pâler auve*; 'to speak with')
        'Ask for J.S.'

(125)   *I' vont **pouor** eune visite à Dgèrnésy* (historically, the verb *visiter*, with
        no preposition, would be used)
        'They are going for a visit to Guernsey'

(126)   *Sommes allés **pouor** vaie lé Formula 1* (no preposition needed)
        'We went to see the Formula 1'

(127)   *J'tais membre **pouor** d's années* (*duthant*)
        'I was a member for years'

(128)   *Sis responsabl'ye **pouor** lyi* (*dé*)
        'I'm responsible for her'

(129)   *J'avais 'té en Sèr **pouor** rester* (no preposition needed)
        'I went to stay on Sark'

(c) *Sus*

(130)   ***Sus** la télévision* (*à*)
        'On television'

(131)   ***Sus** vacances* (*en*)
        'On holiday'

(132)   *Tu peux vaie la côte dé France **sus** un bieau jour* (historically, a phrase
        such as *quand i'fait bé* ('when it's fine') would be used)
        'You can see the coast of France on a fine day'

(133)   *Aver une convèrsâtion **sus** l'téléphone* (*par*)
        'To have a conversation on the telephone'

Birt (1985: 96) also cites:

(134)   *J'ai env'yé mes vièrs souliers **hors***
        (lit. 'I've sent my old shoes out', meaning 'I've thrown out my old
        shoes') (historically, a verb such as *j'ter* would be used instead of the
        composite *env'yer hors* (lit. 'to send out')).

The calquing of prepositions was found in the speech of all informants.
Moreover, contrary to that which occurs in some situations of language
obsolescence (Dorian 1981: 101), despite the obvious influence from English,
such usage was not at all stigmatized. This was because, rather than
representing the equivalent of more idiomatic renderings, in contemporary
Jèrriais, the calques often represented the only way certain meanings could
be expressed, even by bilinguals who made more use of Jèrriais than English
in their everyday lives. It goes without saying that the above examples would
be meaningless to a speaker of Mainland Norman. Instances of English
prepositions which have been calqued into Welsh, and which parallel some
of the examples discussed above, are given in Jones (1998a: 43–4, 184–5).

(viii) The use of a second negative particle in conjunction with *pon* ('not') in
modern Jèrriais may be attributable to English influence too, as the resulting
constructions may also be considered as syntactic calques:

(135)   *Faut **pon janmais** changi chenna*
        'You must not ever change that'

(136)   *J'n'ai **pon autcheune** idée dé chein qui s'est passé*
        'I don't have any idea what happened'

(137)   *Di li dé n'**pon** **dithe** rein*
        'Tell him not to say anything'

(138)   *Ma méthe n'peut **pon** comprendre **autcheune** chose du tout*
        'My mother can't understand anything at all'

(ix) A salient example of calquing in modern Jèrriais was obtained from examining the verbs used to express age. The verb used in traditional Jèrriais, namely *aver* ('to have'), differs from that used in the English construction, namely 'to be', hence:

(139)   *J'**ai** dgiex ans*
        'I am ten years old'

Forty-four tokens were examined of 'age constructions' in Jèrriais. Although *aver* was still most likely to occur statistically, being used 89 per cent of the time, the verb *être* ('to be') was found in one in ten of all contexts. In the written language, however, *aver* was still used exclusively in constructions of this kind:

(140)   *I'dait y'**aver** septante ou huiptante ans*
        'He must be seventy or eighty years old' (HGJ, p. 68)

(141)   *Comme j'n'**avais** qu'huit ou neuv'ans, i'n'est pon difficile d'înmaginner sa rêponse*
        'As I was only eight or nine years old, it isn't difficult to imagine what his answer was' (JJ, pp. 97–8)

6.4.2.3. *Semantic borrowing*

This is another form of borrowing commonly found in the modern dialect, whereby the formal similarity between a word of English and Jèrriais has led to the latter extending its meaning to encompass that of the English term. Thus, although no lexical borrowing has occurred, semantic borrowing has clearly taken place. In the examples below, the historically appropriate word has, again, been given in parentheses. This phenomenon is termed a 'loan shift' by Appel and Muysken (1993: 165):

(142)   *Oulle **a pâssé** avec honours* (*rêussi*)
        'She passed with honours' (*pâsser* = 'to pass' (movement or time); DJF, p. 390, *pâsser par siez li* ('to pass by his house'); *pâsser san temps* ('to pass one's time')

(143)   *I' sont bein **supportés*** (*souôt'nus*)
        'They are well *supported*' (*supporter* = 'to bear'; DFJ, p. 493, *supporter un paids* ('to bear a weight'); *supporter du ma* ('to bear bad times')

Unlike the ones in section 6.4.2.2(ii) above, these examples do not represent calquing, as the English word has not been translated into Jèrriais. Rather, in these cases, it is the formal similarity between English and French that has precipitated an extension of meaning. Such generalization of a meaning in the first language (L1) to include that of another word in the L1 by analogy with the scope of meaning of the equivalent word in the second language (L2) is considered, by Seliger and Vago, as a feature of L1 attrition (1991: 8).

6.4.2.4. *Tags*

Instances were also obtained of the calquing of English tags in Jèrriais:

(144)   *Ch'est not' soeu,* **oulle est**
        lit. 'That's our sister, she is'

Tags are easily borrowed due to the fact that they are free forms, whose presence has no far-reaching repercussions on the syntax of the phrase. This phenomenon has also been noted in modern Welsh, where both English tags translated into Welsh and English tags embedded in Welsh sentences were attested (Jones 1998a: 87–9).

6.4.3. *'Dialect mixing' variables*

I will now discuss the data in relation to the second type of linguistic development outlined in section 6.2. above, namely levelling due to koinéization. This part of the investigation was all the more pertinent given the claim made by Le Maistre that regional variation in Jèrriais was declining as a consequence of the Islanders' greater mobility (1979a: 14). In this part of the study, only the speech of informants who had lived most of their lives in their parish of origin and whose parents were also native to that parish was examined. The speech of informants who had lived for some time outside their parish of origin was not analysed systematically. The reason for this was that, since different people may have lived outside the parish for different periods of time, and since some might have had closer family and social links than others with their parish of origin, it would not have been possible, within the framework of this study, to obtain a meaningful picture of the extent to which any degree of mixing found in their speech was directly attributable to their change of parish or to other factors. In St Brélade, only one informant was found who fitted this criterion. This parish has, therefore, not been included in the numerical analysis.

The data analysed in this section consist of five salient phonological features of Jèrriais which traditionally differ between the regional sub-varieties (*parlers*) and which are outlined in section 3.3.1. Clearly, the assumption underlying this part of the study is that, first, at one time in the past, each geographic region of Jersey[20] had its own distinctive variety of Jèrriais and, secondly, that any significant variability of forms that appears among speakers with stable and shared geographic histories must represent 'dialect mixing'. The assumption that there is a link between social homogeneity and linguistic homogeneity is by no means a recent one. Indeed, most analyses whereby speech is correlated to a sociolinguistic variable is based on the premise that members of a predefined social group will use language in the same general way (cf. Labov 1966).

However, before embarking on this analysis, it is perhaps prudent to insert a caveat, namely that, as Dorian (1994b) found, in rural areas with an egalitarian social structure, and where there is an absence of a well-established standard, there is often leeway for individual variation, which is frequently ignored by linguists (cf. Oftedal 1956). Dorian found that what she termed 'personal-pattern variant use' showed little correlation with kin-based social networks, which, within the villages she studied, proved to be the most powerful social groupings and therefore, one might have presumed, the social structures most likely to foster linguistic homogeneity.

The Jèrriais sociolinguistic situation clearly shows strong similarities to that described by Dorian (1994b) and, for this reason, the possibility that some of the variation encountered in this context may be attributable to personal-pattern variant use cannot be discounted: for instance, as will be seen, in the case of the assibilation of intervocalic [r], the usage of some informants was found to be entirely unpredictable. While the evidence from Dorian's study makes it impossible to rule out personal-pattern variant use completely in the case of the other four variables either, the fact that all of these involve secondary diphthongization may have some bearing here. Although each individual variable centres on a particular phonetic opposition, when viewed together, the four centre on the general *tendency* towards secondary diphthongization. This is a feature which is widespread in EJ – and which is extremely salient to native speakers from all over Jersey – but which is generally absent from the *parlers* of WJ. Secondary diphthongization is therefore tied to geographic location in the minds of speakers far more than the variables discussed in Dorian (1994b), in that, historically, the feature is not variable within all parishes (most notably, those of WJ). It is possible, therefore, that any mixing found may represent something more than personal-pattern variant use arising from a choice between two apparently 'equal' options.

6.4.3.1. *Realization of intervocalic* [r]

Intervocalic [r] often develops to [ð] in St Ouen, Ste Marie, St Pierre, northern St Jean and parts of Trinité and St Martin, whereas it is preserved in St Laurent, southern Trinité and southern St Martin (see section 3.3.1.2(ii)). Although Spence notes that, where it occurs, the replacement of intervocalic [r] by [ð] has not been carried through uniformly, he adds that the change is regular enough to be regarded as typical (1993: 54). In order to gauge the distribution of [r] and [ð] in modern Jèrriais, the data were

Table 6.9 Realization of intervocalic [r]

Parish	Number of informants	[ð]	[r]
St Ouen	7	338 (90%)	37 (10%)
St Jean	3	38 (26%)	106 (74%)
St Martin	6	156 (80%)	39 (20%)
Trinité	5	58 (36%)	105 (64%)
Ste Marie	2	97 (90%)	11 (10%)
St Laurent	6	13 (17%)	63 (83%)

analysed for all contexts in which intervocalic [r] could potentially occur, and the results are displayed in table 6.9.

From table 6.9, it becomes clear that, in the data examined for this survey, the parishes in which [r] develops to [ð] most regularly are St Ouen and Ste Marie. This fits the pattern of historical usage traditionally described for Jèrriais (Spence 1957b). Informants from these parishes substituted [ð] for [r] in approximately nine out of every ten possible contexts.[21] Of the other parishes examined, substitution was next most frequent in St Martin, where [ð] occurred in four out of every five contexts. However, since usage in different parts of this parish differs (Spence, 1993: 53, 1957b: 272–3), it is not possible to conclude anything meaningful from this. Trinité, St Jean and St Laurent showed more of a tendency to retain intervocalic [r], and no evidence was found of the Faldouais tendency for intervocalic [r] to become [z].

At first sight, table 6.9 seems to reveal the occurrence of a large amount of interdialectal interference. However, the mixing recorded for St Ouen and Ste Marie, parishes which are traditionally rather homogeneous in their use of [ð], may not be as significant as the figures suggest if we recall Spence's assertion, mentioned above, that the substitution of [ð] for [r] is not systematic in any area. However, the fact that substitution was found to be occurring in St Laurent in 17 per cent of contexts – despite the fact that, historically, this is a [ð]-less area – does seem to constitute a stronger case for dialect mixing. Even though the parish is traditionally considered to be [ð]-less, substitution was found to occur in just under one in every five contexts. Indeed, some informants from this parish were found to have a highly idiosyncratic usage, often varying between [r] and [ð] in the same word: for example the word for 'yes indeed' was rendered by these informants as both véthe ([veð]) and vér ([ver]), with [ð] and [r] occurring in free variation. As St Laurent is by no means unique in terms of the make-up of its inhabitants, this large amount of 'mixing' may well indicate that, in other areas too, the development may be more advanced than first suggested and that the 'mixing' found may be attributable to more than a simple failure on the part of the sound change to work itself through regularly in every context. It is clear that more research is needed in this area to determine the extent and the causes of any 'mixing'. At present, personal-pattern variant use seems as likely an explanation as any.

If successful, the introduction of Jèrriais in school is certain to influence the development of intervocalic [r] on Jersey. As mentioned in sections 3.4. and 5.3.3., the fact that the DJF and other teaching and reading material use St Ouennais means that the dialect is likely to become standardized on the basis of this *parler*. Should this prove to be the case, it will result in the widespread replacement of intervocalic [r] by [ð] all over the Island.

Le Maistre also mentions a sporadic development in St Ouennais whereby [ð] is substituted for [z] in words where [z] is etymologically unconnected with [r] (in, for example, *les ouaithieaux* ('birds') ([leð weðjo])) (1993: 14–15). Spence (1993: 54) sees this as a form of hypercorrection related to the fact that [ð] and [z] are both sounds that emerged as replacements for weakened intervocalic [r] (see also Spence 1957b: 283, 1987: 122). Despite Le Maistre's remarks that this phenomenon was no longer to be heard much (1993: 15), the change was recorded in the speech of eight out of the twelve informants who had been born in St Ouen, and occurred in 83 per cent of possible contexts (118 tokens).[22] No significant difference in the frequency of this [z] > [ð] substitution was observed as regards the age of informants or indeed the part of St Ouen in which they lived. Three of the four St Ouennais who had moved to other parishes had retained this feature and, in fact, were found to be using it even more frequently than those living inside St Ouen (91 per cent of all possible contexts compared to 82 per cent: ninety-eight and twenty-three tokens respectively). It is possible that, as a clearly identifiable characteristic of St Ouennais, substitution of [ð] for [z] may be consciously retained as a marker of identity in the speech of such informants, in a situation akin to that of the Chilmark fishermen of Martha's Vineyard (Labov 1985: 36–9).[23]

6.4.3.2. *Diphthongization of [u:]*

As described in section 3.3.1.1.a., preconsonantal [u:] shows three different developments within Jersey. In WJ (St Ouen, St Pierre, Ste Marie, St Brélade) it is retained, hence the form *moûque* [mu:k] ('housefly') < AMARUSCA. In EJ it diphthongizes, to either [o:w], hence [mo:wk] (St Jean, St Laurent, Trinité), or [a:w] ([ma:wk]) (Grouville, St Martin). This variable was therefore analysed in order to determine whether the developments outlined above were still occurring within their respective historical territories. As the word for 'housefly' was one of the items investigated in the part of the survey dealing with lexical erosion (see chapter 7), this provided a convenient example for analysis.

Table 6.10 illustrates that, although most informants who had remained in their parish of origin used the form historically associated with that area, there were also a few instances of dialect mixing, when a form traditionally associated with another part of the Island was used. This occurred most

Table 6.10 Pronunciation of *moûque* ('housefly')

Parish	Number of informants	[mu:k]	[mo:wk]	[ma:wk]
St Ouen	7	5 (71%)	2 (29%)	0
St Jean	3	0	3 (100%)	0
St Martin	6	0	4 (67%)	2 (33%)
Trinité	5	0	5 (100%)	0
Ste Marie	2	2 (100%)	0	0
St Laurent	6	0	6 (100%)	0

frequently with the [a:w] diphthong, historically associated with St Martin and Grouville. Although six informants had been born and had lived all their lives in St Martin, the form [ma:wk] was used by only two of these, with the remaining four all using [mo:wk]. While it is, of course, possible that the small number of informants involved in this part of the study might be having a bearing on these findings, it would not, however, be unusual for a local minority form to lose ground to a non-local one if the latter were used by greater numbers of people. Given the fact that St Martin is a parish in which numbers of speakers of Jèrriais have declined dramatically,[24] speakers in the parish would therefore not only have fewer opportunities to hear the local form but also, via contact with people from nearby parishes such as St Jean and Trinité, they would be more likely to encounter the most widespread form ([mo:wk]). (Grouville, the other parish in which [a:w] traditionally occurs, has also undergone a sharp decline in speaker numbers: see table 3.2.) Of course, it is also possible that informants may have adopted the form [mo:wk] rather than the more local [ma:wk] by virtue of a grandparent or even a close friend coming from a different parish.[25]

As far as the other parishes were concerned, such 'mixing' was far less prevalent. Indeed, the only other instance of the phenomenon was found in the case of St Ouen, where [mo:wk] was found to replace [mu:k], another minority form, occasionally. It is possible that the relatively high concentration of Jèrriais speakers in St Ouen has not been without influence in the preservation of the [mu:k] form in that part of the Island, even though the latter has the most restricted distribution of the three forms in table 6.10.

6.4.3.3. *Diphthongization of [o:]*

Spence (1985: 152–3) states that in EJ (Trinité, St Hélier, St Sauveur, St Martin, Grouville and St Clément), there exists a diphthong [a:w] which is the reflex of the combination of [a] and the [w] that arose from the vocalization of preconsonantal [l] (cf. Latin TALPA > Jèrriais [ta:wp] ('mole')).[26] In WJ (St Jean, St Laurent, Ste Marie, St Pierre, St Ouen and St Brélade), this is replaced by [o:w] (or frequently by [o:] in St Ouen), hence the forms [to:wp] and [to:p].

Table 6.11 Diphthongization of [o:]

Parish	Number of informants	[o:]	[o:w]	[a:w]
St Ouen	7	57 (66%)	30 (34%)	0
St Jean	3	8 (15%)	45 (83%)	1 (2%)
St Martın	6	9 (12%)	23 (29%)	46 (59%)
Trinité	5	2 (3%)	38 (57%)	27 (40%)
Ste Marie	2	0	19 (86%)	3 (14%)
St Laurent	6	8 (9%)	79 (90%)	1 (1%)

Analysis of all words in the data with the potential to contain the [a:w] diphthong yielded the results displayed in table 6.11. In St Ouen, some variation was recorded between [o:] and [o:w], which, in practice, reflected the fact that some informants made exclusive use of the former, and others – notably around La Grève de Lecq (on the northern coast of the north-west corner of Jersey) – preferred the latter. Informants from St Jean, Ste Marie and St Laurent generally all made consistent use of [o:w]: indeed, the few realizations of [o:] noted for these parishes were all recorded in the phrase *i' faut* ('it is necessary that'). Since this form can only be used with a following infinitive, which usually takes the stress, it seems that, in this context, [o:w] may be frequently, though not systematically, reduced to [o:].

Of the three possible realizations, [a:w] was found to be losing most ground in modern Jèrriais. Unlike the case in the findings in the previous section, this diphthong was still heard frequently in the speech of informants from St Martin and Trinité. However, it was also clear that the western form [o:w] was encroaching upon the contexts in which [a:w] was traditionally used. Although some informants made exclusive use of [a:w], the speech of most people contained a certain amount of ([a:w]–[o:w]) 'mixing', without there being any noticeable lexical diffusion present. As with the other parishes (except St Ouen), the [o:] forms recorded in the speech of informants from Trinité and St Martin all occurred in the phrase *i' faut*.

6.4.3.4. *Realization of final [œ:]*

[œ:] can occur word-finally in WJ, although it is described as more open and less rounded than in standard French in the *parlers* of St Brélade and St Pierre (see section 3.3.1.1.a.). However, in EJ, the vowel may be replaced by [øy] after [r] or, more commonly, by [aj], although [æy] is also found in a narrow 'transition' zone between the eastern and western *parlers* (see section 3.3.1.1.a.). In NWJ (Les Landes), [œ:] unrounds and lowers to become [ɑ:] (see section 3.3.1.1.a.).

Unlike the other variables examined in this section, when words with the potential to contain final [œ:] were analysed, no indication of any deep-rooted dialect mixing was found. Informants who had lived all their lives in

Table 6.12 Realization of final [œ:]

Parish	Number of informants	[œ:]	[aj]	[ɑ]	[æy]
St Ouen	7	86 (67%)	0	42 (33%)	0
St Jean	3	102 (100%)	0	0	0
St Martin	6	21 (27%)	58 (73%)	0	0
Trinité	5	24 (37%)	36 (55%) (W Trin.)	0	5 (8%)
Ste Marie	2	60 (98%)	1 (2%)	0	0
St Laurent	6	29 (100%)	0	0	0

St Ouen showed no tendency to diphthongize, retaining a pure vowel in the word-final position, although, as table 6.12 demonstrates, the speech of some informants from this parish revealed evidence of the *landîn* pronunciation [ɑ:] (3.3.1.1.a.). This, when it occurred, tended to be used systematically to the exclusion of [œ:]. Interestingly, this pronunciation was found to occur in the speech of the elder of two brothers (who was aged 58 at the time of recording) both of whom had grown up and lived in the area, although it was completely absent from that of the younger sibling, who was a few years younger. Since Le Maistre states that in 1947, *lé landîn* was still spoken extensively, even by children (1947: 7), this finding may indicate that the decline in this linguistic pocket occurred quite soon after this date. The *landîn* pronunciation was also found in the speech of two informants who had moved away from the parish decades previously. It is possible, therefore, that, as was noted for [z] > [ð] substitution (in section 6.4.3.1. above), this feature is being retained as an indicator of identity.

Informants from St Jean, Ste Marie and St Laurent made consistent use of the pure vowel [œ:]. Although no evidence was found in St Laurent of the [æy] pronunciation, mentioned by Birt (1985: 10) as a feature of this area, a few instances of this diphthong were found in Trinité, the parish which also contained the highest degree of 'mixing'.[27] 'Mixing' was also found in St Martin, despite the fact that [aj] is the only pronunciation traditionally described for this *parler* (Birt 1985: 10). This confirms the findings made in section 6.4.3.2. regarding the decline of some of the localized features of St Martinnais.

6.4.3.5. *Diphthongization of [e]*

When word final, [e] often undergoes slight diphthongization in EJ, whereas in the WJ parishes of Ste Marie, St Pierre, St Brélade and St Ouen it is replaced by [ɛ]. In order to determine whether this regionally based opposition was being maintained, each of the first conjugation infinitives in the data was examined to see whether its ending was realized as [ɛ], [e] or [ej]. The results are displayed in table 6.13.[28]

As far as secondary diphthongization was concerned, the data revealed a

Table 6.13 Diphthongization of [eː]

Parish	Number of informants	[ɛ]	[e]	[ej]
St Ouen	7	67 (88%)	9 (12%)	0
St Jean	3	24 (71%)	10 (29%)	0
St Martin	6	2 (29%)	0	5 (71%)
Trinité	5	13 (52%)	11 (44%)	1 (4%)
Ste Marie	2	49 (98%)	1 (2%)	0
St Laurent	6	19 (79%)	2 (8%)	3 (13%)

distribution completely in line with that traditionally described for the dialect (Spence 1993: 44), namely that no secondary diphthongs appeared in the speech of informants from WJ and that the phenomenon was most prevalent in EJ, notably St Martinnais. Secondary diphthongization was also highly conspicuous in the speech of the two St Martinnais interviewed who no longer lived in the parish (and who were not, therefore, included in table 6.13). Diphthongization of [e] is, therefore, a regional feature of St Martinnais that is being retained to a greater extent than those described in sections 6.4.3.2. and 6.4.3.4. The reasons for this are, at present, unclear.

As regards the [e]–[ɛ] opposition, a certain amount of 'mixing' was found in the speech of many informants, with the different sounds occurring in free variation. Not surprisingly, this was most prevalent in the east–west 'boundary' parishes of St Jean and Trinité. However, some 'mixing' was also found to occur in St Ouen and (to a lesser extent) in St Laurent and Ste Marie.

6.4.3.6. *Summary*

Examination of the five variables discussed in this section revealed that, although some 'mixing' of localized features was discernible in modern Jèrriais, the phenomenon was by no means widespread in the speech of those who had remained within their native parish. Even in the throes of obsolescence, the speech of a St Jeannais remains distinct from that of a St Ouennais. There was certainly no evidence whatsoever of the emergence of an interdialect through any form of island-wide koinéization (Trudgill 1986: 62). However, analysis of the assibilation of intervocalic [r] seemed to suggest some presence of personal-pattern variant use, although further research will be needed in order to substantiate this finding.

As stated at the beginning of this section, the study did not analyse the speech of informants who had lived for some time outside their parish of origin. It is possible to speculate that the speech of these informants might contain a greater degree of dialect mixing than that recorded in the speech of people who had lived most of their lives in their native parish. However, it would not be prudent to make such an assumption blindly, as it was shown that in, for example, the case of intervocalic [z] (> [ð]; section 6.4.3.1.), a highly salient regional feature may be retained outside its historical territory. Clearly, the presence of 'mixing' is also contingent upon the part of the parish to which informants move, for, as seen in section 3.3., the geographical extension of these sub-dialect features does not coincide with parish boundaries and the speech of different parts of different parishes (for example St Jean or Trinité) may display different linguistic features.

6.5. CONCLUSION

This chapter has demonstrated that modern Jèrriais is undergoing a significant number of linguistic developments, which are discernible in all areas – phonology, morphosyntax and lexis – and which have resulted in a variety that shows marked differences from traditional descriptions of the dialect. All speech-varieties evolve and undergo change, and a variety whose speakers have frequent contact with another language will change faster than one whose speakers do not (Trudgill 1992: 196).

The linguistic developments highlighted in this chapter did not always admit a straightforward interpretation. Despite the temptation to identify changes such as those described in section 6.4.1. as purely contact-based, this course of action may enable us to see only half of a potentially complex picture, for, as has been demonstrated, it is possible for such change to have a complex motivation attributable to a number of mutually reinforcing tendencies. This results in a situation termed by Mougeon and Beniak 'ambiguous change' (1991: 218), and which Thomason and Kaufman (1988: 57) describe as multiple causation. One possible reason why several of these features appear to be in a state of flux (cf. variables 6.4.1.2., 6.4.1.4., 6.4.1.5., 6.4.1.6. and 6.4.1.7.) is suggested by Thomason's claim that replacement of one linguistic feature by another always requires at least two steps. Thomason argues that, at first, the new feature competes with a pre-existing one and then the old feature, which 'loses' the competition, gradually disappears (1997: 185). It is possible that the variation encountered in section 6.4.1., therefore, represents the first of these stages.[29] Furthermore, the types of change noted for Jèrriais are not, in themselves, extraordinary and are frequently attested in languages at no risk from obsolescence.[30] As was seen, although some of the changes described in section 6.4.1. were clearly attributable to the influence of English, others were not necessarily so. However, what is worthy of note is the number of changes shown to be occurring simultaneously in Jèrriais. This, coupled with the dialect's sociopolitical context of territorial contraction and decline in speaker numbers, makes the situation indicative of language obsolescence.

On the question of why Jèrriais should be undergoing change at all in the mouths of its native speakers, Sharwood Smith and Van Buren suggest that the L1 changes not because of a lack of use but 'because of a lack of confirming evidence that L1 is the way it is' (1991: 23). Mougeon and Beniak agree with such a scenario, arguing that, in a sociopolitical context such as that of Jèrriais, not even a high level of retention is a sufficient safeguard against influence from a dominant language (1991: 180) and that 'bilingual speakers need not be dominant in the majority language or experience restriction in the use of the minority language for interference-induced change to manifest itself' (1991: 219). It is also possible that grammatical deviances arising in the speech of more restricted speakers may pass to the speech of unrestricted speakers – or at least reinforce their tendency to use these (Mougeon and Beniak 1991: 180). It is unclear whether the speakers themselves are aware of these changes – as Schmidt points out, 'While linguistic analysis may reveal that widespread changes are occurring on many levels of a language system, speakers frequently perceive that their language is "healthy" . . . as long as certain formal markers of the language (be they lexical, morphological or phonological) are used' (1991: 122).

Obsolescent varieties may also be unpredictable. We expect to find complete breakdown and yet this does not always occur, the example *par excellence* being Dorian's description of East Sutherland Gaelic, which is said to be 'dying with its morphological boots on' (1978b: 608). In the case of a minority variety spoken on an island of some 45 square miles, and which displays a not inconsiderable amount of regional variation, one might assume that such variation would diminish, with possibly even the appearance of an Island-wide interdialect. Although the data analysed in section 6.4.3. revealed that some localized features of the *parlers* of Jèrriais were, in fact, being used outside their historical territory in the speech of some informants, despite the fact that they had been born and had lived most of their lives in the same parish, this phenomenon was far from widespread.

The persistence of the sub-dialect features in obsolescent Jèrriais has parallels with the situation of East Sutherland Gaelic. Dorian (p.c.) comments that, whereas older speakers of Embo Gaelic were highly conscious of the differences between their own Gaelic and that of Golspie (a nearby village), younger speakers in Embo were no longer aware of the nature of the Gaelic spoken in Golspie. She suggests that this might be attributable to a decline in cross-village social interaction between Embo and Golspie and an increase in interaction between the villagers of Embo and the English monolinguals in Dornoch, the royal burgh to which Embo is a satellite. In the case of Jersey, it is possible that, as rural pastimes diminished, occasions that used to draw largely agricultural people together across villages grew rare and trips to the more Anglicized St Hélier grew commoner. At this point, kin ties with one's original locality might have started to predominate in terms of Jèrriais-speaking contexts, and this might have acted to accentuate local differences rather than allowing them to recede.[31,32] This would also account for the retention of salient features by informants who had moved outside their locality.[33]

The fact that the first steps towards the standardization of Jèrriais were taken only in 1966 (with the publication of the DJF), by which time many of the informants interviewed in this survey had already become adults, means that the *parlers* of Jèrriais are not suffering the same fate as the dialects of Wales and Brittany, which are being gradually eradicated by the spread of a standard variety (Jones 1998a: 90–109, 188–208, 296–333). It remains to be seen what impact, if any, the introduction of Jèrriais in school will have on the situation.

From what has been said above, therefore, it would seem unlikely that regional variation in Jèrriais will be eliminated altogether. Indeed, if the variety dies in the relatively near future, with the demise of its last native speaker, it is unlikely to lose its regional variation until the very end, when only a handful of speakers remain as an isolated pocket in one parish – St Ouen, if we are to believe Le Maistre (1947: 4). If this scenario proves true, then the last speakers of Jèrriais are already alive and are, at least, middle-aged. However, they are in all likelihood distributed sufficiently between east and west Jersey to ensure that some regional variation will survive as long as they do. In this scenario, the only real 'losers' will be the so-called 'linguistic pockets' (see map 3), which, even in the heyday of Jèrriais, were comprised of a relatively small number of speakers.

There is, however, another – albeit at present rather unlikely – outcome. This would be the scenario whereby the embryonic revitalization campaign succeeds in its aim of creating a new cohort of fluent speakers who might then go on to produce a new generation of native speakers. Given that the present inter-generational chain of transmission has effectively ceased, the education system, in the form of school and evening classes, would need to play a pivotal role in this. For the school to be at all effective as a vehicle for teaching Jèrriais, there is a need to elaborate teaching materials in the dialect, and this necessitates the creation of a standard (Cuarón and Lastra 1991: 109). It was seen in section 3.4. that, as the DJF was written by a speaker of St Ouennais, this was the variety also used for the grammar/teaching manual *Lé Jèrriais pour tous* (Birt 1985), which has subsequently been adopted as a basis for learning the dialect both in evening classes and via autodidactic means. St Ouennais has, therefore, enjoyed a higher profile than the other *parlers* of Jèrriais and, if the dialect were to be taught systematically in school, it is likely that the availability of at least these two pedagogical resources would make St Ouennais a good candidate for diffusion throughout the Island as a sort of standard Jèrriais, to be taught to second-language speakers produced via the revitalization movement. Were this scenario to materialize, therefore, it is likely that regional variation would be eliminated, or at least lessened, in Jèrriais, as has been seen in, for example, Wales and Brittany (Jones 1998a), and that St Ouennais would become the sole surviving *parler*.

It may be, therefore, that regional variation proves to be the price that

Jèrriais pays for survival. This is, admittedly, a high price, but one which the dialect would not be alone in paying. Welsh, too, is undergoing revitalization at the cost of its dialects (Jones 1998a), and Ó Baoill writes of the situation in Eire: 'If Irish is to become a viable means of communication among the general population, I fear that much levelling will take place, and it is certain that many of the contrasts now existing in Irish will be lost' (1988: 125). However, he continues, 'If the revival of Irish were to succeed, then it might all be worthwhile', and this must surely apply equally to Jèrriais. At present, however, it is not certain whether even such a sacrifice as this will be able to halt the encroachment of obsolescence.

The lexical analysis undertaken in section 6.4.2. also revealed prolific amounts of change in progress, which were unambiguously attributable to influence from English. Although, in a situation of additive bilingualism, borrowing may be viewed positively, as a way of making full use of the increased lexical resources available, in situations of language obsolescence it may occur due to the progressive erosion of the lexis, as one variety loses ground to another and as speakers gradually have less opportunity and, perhaps, motivation to use it. Lexical loss, therefore, is an unambiguous sign of language shift. Although the presence of lexical erosion and loss in Jèrriais was detected in the analysis undertaken in section 6.4.2., the results were unable to provide much information about the extent of these phenomena in modern Jèrriais or whether they were more prevalent in some domains than in others. The next chapter, therefore, gives a systematic account of lexical erosion and loss in the contemporary dialect. As well as highlighting these areas, it seeks to determine whether the influence of the school and other language-planning measures seem to be precipitating any lexical growth.

7

LEXICAL EROSION IN
MODERN JÈRRIAIS

7.1. INTRODUCTION

In order to determine whether the fact that Jèrriais is no longer being used by many speakers as their sole – or even main – means of communication is having any repercussions on the vitality of different terms, ten semantic fields were identified and informants were questioned about terms selected in each field.[1] The reason for dividing words into separate semantic fields was in order to establish whether some domains were losing ground faster than others.[2] Admittedly, chance inevitably plays a part in a survey of this kind since a speaker's score depends on whether he or she is familiar with the forms included in the questionnaire. However, in an attempt to reduce the role of serendipity, the words chosen were common and in everyday usage and hence likely to be known to speakers who made regular use of Jèrriais in the domain in question.

In the case of a term not being known by an informant, the compensatory strategy resorted to was also of interest. For example, if a periphrasis was offered, its formation was analysed, or if a borrowing was suggested, the choice of donor-language (English, the Island's dominant variety, or standard French, traditionally the Island's official language) was noted. Finally, in the case of objects denoted by different terms in different parts of the Island (see section 3.3.2.), it was observed whether informants were using the word traditionally associated with their area, or whether some degree of dialect mixing was present.

As mentioned in section 4.2., the lexical survey formed the third part of the interview conducted with each informant. The informants in this part of the survey are, therefore, identical to those who supplied the data for chapters 4 and 6. Again, it is important to stress that, due to the size of the sample, the results in this chapter should be interpreted as a reflection of the tendencies that exist within the Jèrriais speech community rather than as an empirically exact picture of the contemporary situation.

7.2. RESULTS

Before embarking on a detailed discussion of the results obtained for each semantic field, it is useful to consider the broad trends evidenced by the survey, as illustrated in table 7.1.

Table 7.1 Lexical erosion in modern Jèrriais (summary)

Domain	Number of words	Average score
The weather	6	5.5 (91.7%)
The house	8	6.9 (86.25%)
The family	9	7.7 (85.5%)
The body	8	6.6 (82.5%)
Animals and insects	11	9.0 (81.8%)
Clothing	7	5.1 (72.9%)
Illnesses	4	2.7 (67.5%)
Flora	6	2.6 (43.3%)
Birds	4	1.6 (40.0%)
Technology	6	0.4 (6.7%)

The table reveals that the ten domains examined may be separated into four distinct groups. The first of these was comprised of semantic fields in which little lexical erosion was demonstrable in that the average scores obtained were above 80 per cent (namely, the weather, the house, the family, the body, and animals and insects). The fact that these categories are relatively well maintained is not in itself surprising, since they are all 'traditional' domains likely to be discussed in the home environment with family and friends. Indeed, such domains have often been demonstrated to represent the last stronghold of obsolescent varieties (Schlieben-Lange 1977: 102; Jones 1996: 54–9). The second group, featuring the next-best-maintained domains, was also comprised of traditional domains, namely clothing and illnesses. However, although the scores obtained for this group were also relatively high, these domains had lost more ground than those of group one and, in certain cases, terms were known to only a handful of informants.[3] The third group was comprised of the domains of flora and birds, both of which obtained scores of under 50 per cent,[4] and the fourth group was comprised of just one semantic field – technology – a 'modern' domain which recorded a very low score indeed. The results will be analysed on a domain-by-domain basis. Figures illustrating the results for individual words may be found in appendix 2. No figure has been produced for items obtaining maximum scores.

7.2.1. *The weather*

This proved to be the most stable of all domains (figures 7.1–7.6). The only terms that proved problematic were 'lightning' (*feu*) (figure 7.1) and, to a lesser extent, 'hail' (*grile*) (figure 7.6) and 'fog' (*bliâse*) (figure 7.3). In the case of the first of these, the terms *ecl'yaithe*, a Jèrriaization of the standard French term for 'lightning', *éclair*, was offered by four informants as an alternative to *feu*, the term given in the DJF (p. 238) and offered by thirty-one informants. *L'ôrage* ('thunder'), a term frequently associated with lightning in the expression *du feu et d'l'ôrage* ('thunder and lightning'), was suggested by twelve informants. This may indicate that, for this group of informants, the expression is no longer transparent and that *ôrage* was offered because 'lightning' is the second term in the English expression.

As with most of the other expressions in this domain, no informant had any difficulty in supplying a term for either 'it's boiling hot' (figure 7.5) or 'it's exceedingly windy' (figure 7.2). However, it is worth noting, that, in each case, only a small minority of informants produced the idiomatic phrases *i' fait eune arsion* (lit. 'it is burning') and *i' vente la pé du dgiâbl'ye* (lit. 'it's blowing the devil's skin'), preferring instead the more transparent *i' fait caud/tchi chaleu* ('it's hot'/'what heat') and *i' vente/i' vente dû* ('it's windy'/ 'it's blowing hard'), respectively. As idioms are unique to a particular speech-variety and are untranslatable, it is therefore likely that they will lose ground in a community in which the aforementioned variety is not used regularly. The apparent decrease in frequency in the use of these idioms seems to be a hallmark of obsolescence.

7.2.2. *The house*

In section 4.3.2.2., the family was seen to be one of the main settings in which Jèrriais was still used. This being so, it would seem logical to suppose that the house itself and its contents would represent one of the topics most frequently discussed in Jèrriais (figures 7.7–7.13). It was therefore not surprising to find that, as exemplified by figures 7.9 ('comb'), 7.11 ('spoon'), 7.12 ('fork') and 7.13 ('saucer'), most of the items in this section were known to the vast majority of informants (although 'kettle' was the only word to obtain a maximum score). It was also apparent, however, that not all informants used the same word for each item. For instance, in the case of the word for 'wardrobe' (figure 7.7), although most informants (thirty) suggested *grande armouaithe*, four also used *prêsse*. Similarly, thirty-two informants suggested *dêmêleux* ([de(j)melaj] or [demelœ:]) (see section 3.3.1.1.a.) for the word 'comb' (figure 7.9) whereas nine used *dêmêle*. This indicates that, despite the erosion seen in other domains, this one, at least, is stable enough to have retained some diversity within its vocabulary. More-over, the terms appear to be synonyms rather than examples of regional variation. In the case of the word for 'fork' (figure 7.12), both *fourchette* and *frouchette* (the latter a metathesized form) were widespread. However, the fact that 10 per cent of the sample suggested the word *frouque* ('garden fork') in this context also indicated some loss of semantic distinction between the terms.

The word for 'bedsheets' also yielded a variety of responses, although in this case only one, *lîncheurs*, was historically appropriate and, interestingly, more instances were recorded of the French borrowing *drap* (eight informants) than the English borrowing *sheet* (one informant) (figure 7.8). The other terms suggested represented a phenomenon whereby another term from the same field of reference was substituted for the unknown word (cf. Olshtain and Barzilay 1991: 142). Both *ântchies* ('pillowcases') and *couvèr-tuthes* ('blankets') were offered as equivalents for 'bedsheets', together with *ouvriers*, a term not listed in the DJF but which presumably has the meaning of 'a knitted blanket'. This substitution strategy was also found in sections 7.2.4. and 7.2.9. below.

Finally, the term for 'living room' (figure 7.10) proved problematic to many informants, who explained that many traditional Jersey farmhouses did not contain such a room. A variety of terms was suggested by individual informants, such as *grande salle* ('big room'), *salle à mangi* ('dining room') and *grand appartement* ('big room'). *Parleux* (pronounced as either [parlœ:] or [parlaj] (see section 3.3.1.1.a.) proved to be the most popular equivalent suggested (thirty-seven informants) followed by *grande tchuîsinne* ('big kitchen') (six informants).

7.2.3. *The family*

As this is one of the domains for which minority languages are most likely to be used (Timm 1980: 38), it was not surprising that it showed relatively few signs of lexical erosion (figures 7.14–7.21). Indeed, some terms, such as 'brother' (*fréthe*) (which obtained a maximum score) and 'grandmother' (*grand'méthe*) (figure 7.15), were known to almost all informants.[5] The words for 'son' (*fis*) (figure 7.14) and 'daughter' (*fil'ye*) (figure 7.20) also produced answers from everyone, although in a small minority of cases the standard French term was used.

Although what may be described as words designating 'core' family members were therefore found to be quite stable, those denoting less commonly encountered family members were not so well known. For example, although the Jèrriais word for 'grandmother' (*grand'méthe*) (figure 7.15) was familiar to all informants, the term for 'great-grandmother' (*grand-grand'méthe*, *grand'manman*) was not known to 12 per cent of informants (figure 7.16). In the same way, 'brother' (*fréthe*) obtained a maximum score, whilst only 34 per cent knew the term for 'stepbrother' (*fréthe emprunté/d'mié-fréthe*), with most of the remainder either venturing no term at all, or using an English borrowing (figure 7.19). Similarly, 98 per cent knew the term for 'daughter' (*fil'ye*) (figure 7.20) but only 86 per cent knew 'daughter-in-law' (*belle fil'ye*) (figure 7.21).

Some confusion was also found between 'non-core' male and female relations. For instance, the term *bieau fréthe* ('brother-in-law') was suggested by one informant as the equivalent of 'stepbrother' (figure 7.19), *belle soeur* ('sister-in-law') was suggested by three informants as the equivalent of 'daughter-in-law' (figure 7.21), and *grande soeur* ('big sister') was suggested for 'granddaughter' (*p'tite fil'ye*) (figure 7.17), and this despite the fact that, as figure 7.17 shows, the Jèrriais for the last of these was commonly known. The greatest amount of confusion existed with regard to the term 'second cousin' (figure 7.18): while 68 per cent offered *deuxième couôsîn*, the term listed in the DJF (p. 132) (itself clearly a calque on English), 10 per cent used the term *couôsîn gèrmain* ('first cousin') and 10 per cent said that in Jèrriais no distinction was made between first and second cousins and hence used the term *couôsîn* ('cousin') for both. One informant circumvented the problem by using the paraphrase *couôsîn dé man péthe* ('my father's cousin').[6]

7.2.4. *The body*

This was another quite stable domain (figures 7.22–7.26), with the Jèrriais terms for 'arm' (*bras*), 'face' (*fache*) and 'mouth' (*bouoche*) known to all informants.[7] However, as with the domain of 'the family', body parts which were referred to less commonly were not as well known. For example, only 28 per cent and 56 per cent of informants knew the Jèrriais for 'eyebrow' (*soucile*) (figure 7.25) and 'ankle' (*g'vil'ye*) (figure 7.23) respectively, with many people not being able to suggest any term at all and a few informants in both cases resorting to an English borrowing.

The results revealed that, when unsure of a particular word, speakers commonly resorted to two strategies. The first of these, already seen in section 7.2.2., was to substitute in its place another term from the same semantic field – in this case, *paûpil'ye* ('eyelash') for the unknown 'eyebrow' (figure 7.25) – and the second was to nativize a loan, which was then passed off as a native word. An example of the latter was seen in the case of the word *oncl'ye* (figure 7.23), which was suggested by eleven informants (22 per cent of the sample) as the Jèrriais equivalent of 'ankle' despite the fact that the only meaning listed for this term in the DJF is 'uncle'. *Oncl'ye*, therefore, may represent a Jèrriaization of English 'ankle' or it may even be possible to suggest that, when a term is unknown, informants may compensate by using a Jèrriais term that is phonetically similar to the English term. Although *oncl'ye* was mostly used by informants who came from St Ouen and/or who had lived most of their lives in that parish, it was by no means exclusive to these, and indeed it was not used by all such informants.

More than three-quarters of all informants knew the Jèrriais term for 'hip' (*hanque*) (figure 7.26). However, as with the case of 'eyebrow' above, words denoting contiguous body parts (*fêsse* ('buttock') and *tchiêsse* ('thigh')) were also suggested when informants were unable to recall the precise term.

7.2.5. *Animals and insects*

As was to be expected in a community largely dependent upon farming, terms for animals were widely known (figures 7.27–7.33), with the words for 'horse' (*j'va*), 'pig' (*couochon*), 'cow' (*vaque*) and 'hen' (*poule*) all obtaining maximum scores.[8] The term for a 'snail' (*colînmachon*) was also known to most informants (figure 7.30). In the case of 'horse' and 'pig', the names of both the male and female animal were solicited and it was found that, although the name of the male (which is also generally used as the generic term for the animal) was known to all informants, only 86 per cent and 88 per cent of the sample knew the Jèrriais for 'mare' (*jeunment*) (figure 7.27) and 'sow' (*trie*) (figure 7.28) respectively. In fact, in the case of the latter, one informant tried to feminize the masculine to *couochonne*, presumably on the model of the adjective *bouon–bouonne* ('good').[9] Most of the informants who claimed not to know the forms for the female animals stated that they would use the masculine terms for both: another possible indicator of obsolescence in that, although informants have lost this masculine–feminine distinction in their native language, further questioning revealed that they retained it in their second language, English.[10]

A considerable amount of variation was found with regard to words denoting the names of insects. The term for a 'housefly' (*moûque*) (figure 7.29) was known to most informants, although the phonetic realization of the latter varied according to area (see section 3.3.1.1.a. and table 6.10). Regional variation was also apparent in the case of the word for 'spider' (see section 3.3.2.), with *pêtre* being the form most widely used in St Ouen and *irangnie/ithangnie* elsewhere (figure 7.31) (see section 3.3.2.).[11] The most problematic terms in this category proved to be 'moth' (figure 7.33) and 'ladybird' (figure 7.32). In the case of the former, both terms listed in the DJF were found (*cahuche, papillon*), although many informants stated that they would only use *cahuche* to refer to a big moth. *Papillote* ('butterfly') was also cited (by three informants from East Jersey), confirming the assertion made in the DJF that 'Disons enfin que les gens ne distinguent quand même pas toujours très nettement entre papillotes et papillons' (p. 387).[12] However, half the informants questioned were unable to suggest any term whatsoever.

Although a variety of terms exist for 'ladybird' in Jèrriais (*bête du Bouôn Dgieu, démouaîselle, pâssecole, pâssequ'olle, paqu'nôte, pâqu'tholle, pâsserole, rouoge soudard, vaque du Bouôn Dgieu*: DJF, p. 566), only the first three of these were found in this survey and, in total, these were produced by a mere five informants. Twelve informants used borrowings (nine from English and three from French), whilst two-thirds of informants were unable to suggest any word at all. Both of these phenomena are, of course, indicative of the term's widespread erosion.

7.2.6. *Clothing*

The overall score obtained for this domain was somewhat lower than the domains, described above, despite the fact that several of the terms ('coat' (*câsaque*), 'shoe' (*soulié*)) were known by all informants (figures 7.34–7.38). Upon closer examination of the data, it emerged that the overall score had been brought down by the results obtained for two terms, namely 'cardigan' (figure 7.37) and 'slippers' (figure 7.36), neither of which was widely known. Most informants were quick to point out that 'slippers' were a modern concept and therefore doubted that an equivalent term existed in Jèrriais, hence they tended to refer to the object by borrowing from English, which was said to be logical since slippers had come to Jersey from England (figure 7.36). A solution used by some informants in the face of this apparent lack of terminology was to extend the frame of reference of *chavette* ('old shoe') to encompass that of 'slippers'. This clearly stemmed from the fact that many people see slippers as non-outdoor footwear worn casually around the house. Only two informants used the term *chapîn*, which is the term listed in the DJF (p. 96).

In the same vein, there emerged no widely recognized term for 'cardigan' (figure 7.37), with six possibilities suggested in addition to that of borrowing from French (four informants) and English (twenty-two informants). *Blianchet (d'oeuvre)* and *corset (d'oeuvre)*, both listed in the DJF (pp. 56, 127), were suggested by 8 per cent and 4 per cent of the sample respectively but *jersey* ('jersey'), *veste* ('waistcoat'), *jupet* (?) and the periphrasis *eune legethe câsaque* ('a light coat') were also suggested by one informant apiece.

The word for a 'dress', on the other hand, was known to all but one informant and it was clear that, of the two words that exist for this object in modern Jèrriais (*fro* < English 'frock' and *robe* < French 'robe'), the latter was far more frequently used than the former – possibly since it may be felt to be more 'French' (figure 7.34). Finally, in the case of the word for a 'suit', although two-thirds of informants preferred the indigenous term *fa* (DJF, p. 232), it was clear that the presence of the long-established English borrowing *suit* was also significant (figure 7.35). Three informants used the French borrowing *habit* for this item, while four were unable to suggest any term at all.

7.2.7. *Illnesses*

In order to investigate this domain, two 'everyday' ailments were chosen (toothache and the common cold) together with two less frequent, but still commonly known, illnesses, namely the measles and the mumps (figures 7.39–7.42). The Jèrriais term for 'a cold' (*suée d'fraid*) was known to all but one informant, who used an English borrowing (figure 7.41), and the word for 'a toothache' (*mal ès dents*) was also familiar, with only two informants failing to produce the term given in the DJF (p. 334) and using instead the standard French *mal aux dents* (figure 7.39). It was, however, plain that the two 'non-everyday' illnesses were less well known to informants. The term *ouothipieaux* ('mumps') was suggested by only 14 per cent of informants, with the English borrowing being used frequently in its stead (figure 7.42). *Ouothipieaux* was also offered as an equivalent for 'the

measles' (*rouogeule*), as were *vétheule* ('chicken pox') and *pépie*, described by
the DJF as 'la maladie des poules' (lit. 'the chicken illness') (p. 398)
(figure 7.40). This illustrates that, although 60 per cent of informants were
familiar with the appropriate term, the names of illnesses were often subject
to confusion – as, for example, in the case of the informant who suggested
ouothipieaux for 'measles' and then said that he did not know the Jèrriais
term for 'mumps'.

7.2.8. *Flora*

The responses obtained in this section (figures 7.43–7.48) indicated that the
names of some flowers, most notably 'snowdrop' and 'buttercup', were not
known to a significant number of the sample (66 per cent and 86 per cent
respectively). In the case of the former, only eight informants knew the term
listed in the DJF (p. 65) (*p'tite bouonnefemme*; lit. 'little woman'), but the
data revealed that a number of alternatives had been suggested (figure 7.45).
One informant offered *perche nè* ('snow piercer'), a calque on the French
term *perce-neige*; and *blianche femme* ('white lady'), *blianche fil'ye* ('white
girl') and *p'tite fil'ye* ('little girl') were also ventured – terms which, like *p'tite
bouonnefemme*, contain a female reference. None of the above is found in the
DJF. However, the last three terms seem to indicate that, although the
informants cannot recall the exact term, they may have a partial recollection
of its constituents and the words suggested may represent their search for the
right combination. The three informants who resorted to borrowing used
English as the donor-language.

In the case of 'buttercup' (*pipot*), only two informants knew the Jèrriais
term, although one did offer the formally similar *pipsol* (which actually
means 'primrose') (figure 7.43). This is another example of the correct term
being partially recollected: the informant knows that the term is '*pip-
something*' and so selects a form which he or she knows to exist that both
refers to a flower and begins with *pip-*. Clearly, this also reveals a degree of
uncertainty as to the meaning of *pipsol*. *Pipsol* was ventured as an equivalent
of 'daisy' too, the confusion arising, perhaps, because daisies and buttercups
are often seen, and therefore talked about, together.

The names of the other flowers on the lexical questionnaire were known to
a larger percentage of the sample, although only in the case of 'daffodil'
(*g'zette*) was the term recalled consistently, with a mere five 'don't knows'
(figure 7.48). It was interesting to observe that, although twenty-one
informants suggested *ierru* [jɛry] as the Jèrriais for 'ivy', ten also offered
the form *dgèrrue* [dʒɛry], in which the affricate derives from a development
of the partitive article *d'* before the yod (figure 7.47). Since the word is used
so often with this article, the phonetic sequence [dʒɛry] has been reinter-
preted by these speakers as the canonical form of the term for 'ivy', and
many spoke about *du dgèrrue*, featuring what are, etymologically, two

partitive articles. In fact, the DJF (p. 164) lists *dgèrrue* as a fully fledged word of Jèrriais, particularly common in St Ouen.

It was surprising that the names of the frequently found daisy (figure 7.44) and dandelion (figure 7.46) were not known by more informants, although it is possible that, in the case of the latter, the rather vulgar name (*pîssenliet*) ('wet the bed') may have discouraged informants from using it with me. In the case of the word for 'daisy' the French term, *marguerite*, was used by six informants in place of the Jèrriais *mèrgot* and, although this represented a higher degree of borrowing from French than was found with the other flower terms, use of the English borrowing was still more common than this (eight informants).

7.2.9. *Birds*

The names of birds were less familiar to informants that those of animals (figures 7.49–7.52), with the most commonly known being 'blackbird' (*meîl'ye*), which scored 50 per cent (figure 7.50). The word for 'owl' (*cahouain*), was known to 46 per cent of the sample (figure 7.49) and, at 34 per cent and 32 per cent respectively, the lowest-scoring terms in this section were 'sparrow' (*mouosson*) (figure 7.51) and 'thrush' (*grive*) (figure 7.52). Although the last two do not represent birds which would be as familiar as the blackbird or the owl, they are far from uncommon and their low scores suggest that the names of less frequently encountered birds, such as the wren or the starling, would be even less well known.

Borrowings were not as widespread in this section as they had been in others. It was, however, noteworthy that, on failing to recall the exact term, informants frequently suggested the name of another bird. Occasionally, this may have been due to confusion between the birds themselves (for example *corbîn* ('raven') was suggested for 'blackbird' (figure 7.50) and *mouosson* ('sparrow') for 'thrush' (figure 7.52)). However, this cannot possibly have been the case with the two informants who suggested *héthonde* ('swallow') for 'owl' (figure 7.49), as these two birds are extremely different physically. It is therefore suggested that, as seen in sections 7.2.2. and 7.2.4., this represents an instance of a term from the same semantic field being used due to an inability to recall the precise term being solicited.

In addition, it is worth highlighting the forms *grithe* and *grile*, which were also offered for the term 'thrush'. Unlike *mouosson*, which was also obtained for this term, neither *grithe* nor *grile* exists in Jèrriais to denote names of birds.[13] The fact that each of these forms was only obtained from one informant apiece suggests that they may be spontaneous lexical innovations, created due to their phonetic similarity to *grive*. In other words, although these informants have not succeeded in producing the appropriate term, they do seem able to recall its phonetic form partially (cf. section 7.2.8.). In the case of *grithe*, the voiced labio-dental fricative of *grive* has been replaced by a voiced dental fricative, which is not too dissimilar in sound. As far as the term *grile* is concerned, the fact that three of the four sounds in both words are identical, coupled with the fact that *grile* (= 'hail') may already exist in the informant's mental lexicon, may have led to its production in this context.

7.2.10. *Technology*

Although Jèrriais has never been used as a language of technology and might not, therefore, be expected to have any words to denote technological concepts, the fact that it is currently being introduced into the primary school has inevitably necessitated the creation of such vocabulary (see section 5.5.). Since the Jèrriais education initiative had already been envisaged at the time the fieldwork was being conducted, this section was included in order to see whether any such terminology had already started to be disseminated to the speech community at large.

The results showed that no Jèrriais term was known for any of the six words under study (figures 7.53–7.58) – with the exception of, perhaps, *un vidgeo* [vidʒoːw] ('video recorder'), which was suggested by one informant, and which features the affrication of [d] before a front vowel and final diphthongization which are characteristic of Jèrriais (figure 7.54).[14] Many informants expressed amusement when I asked about the terms in this section, stating that Jèrriais was not used to talk about such things. However, although this may have been true in the past, if the dialect is to have a future, and if it is to be seen (not least by schoolchildren) as a variety in its own right, then it must develop a vocabulary in this area – as has been done in recent years in the case of other obsolescent languages (see, for example, Thomson 1979: 20–5). Research has also demonstrated that such terms may be introduced successfully: in Wales, for instance, despite the fact that they are not known to a large percentage of the more elderly adult population, so-called technological terms now form part of the active vocabulary of all schoolchildren educated through the medium of Welsh (Jones unpublished).

Of those informants who said that they would use borrowings to denote the terms in this section, far more chose English than French as the donor-language, as indicated in table 7.2.

This reflects the findings in section 8.4.2.2.c., namely that for recent borrowings, especially in 'modern' domains such as technology, for most native speakers, English rather than French functions as the principal donor-language. Most individuals are therefore opting to borrow from their second 'everyday' language rather than from the Island's official language, despite the fact that, linguistically, the latter is far more similar to Jèrriais. Such a finding is not remarkable in itself in that borrowing is always likely to occur from a language which is readily accessible to the

Table 7.2 English and French borrowing in the lexical field of technology

Term	English borrowing: % of sample (number)	French borrowing: % of sample (number)
Computer (figure 7.53)	22% (11)	10% (5)
Video (figure 7.54)	22% (11)	8% (4)
Television (figure 7.55)	40% (20)	6% (3)
Projector (figure 7.56)	22% (11)	10% (5)
CD (figure 7.57)	22% (11)	10% (5)
Spaceship (figure 7.58)	20% (10)	12% (6)

individual, and English, after all, is Jersey's dominant language and one in which all informants were fluent. Nearly seven times more informants opted for an English than a French borrowing in the case of the word 'television', a term which would, presumably, be known well by informants in both standard French and English. This seems to indicate that, as yet, the puristic tendencies favouring own-family as opposed to other-family borrowing, seen in the case of Breton, where words borrowed from other Celtic languages are approved of but those borrowed from French are criticized (Jones 1995: 429), has not yet permeated the Jèrriais speech community. However, this is completely at odds with the strategy favoured by the language planners, who, as seen in section 5.5., used borrowings from standard French more than any other means of word creation in the Jèrriais coursebook *Lé neu c'mîn*, and tended to avoid 'wholesale' borrowings from English. It will be interesting to see whether, ultimately, it is the French or English borrowings which prevail.

7.3. CONCLUSION

The recall of isolated lexical items in an elicitation test such as this is clearly a difficult task. In an attempt to assess the degree to which these results reflected the speakers' natural production, the tape-recorded interview material was examined for the presence of any of the lexical items elicited for this chapter. As may be imagined, some common words, such as 'daughter' and 'son', and some farmyard animals, such as 'cow', 'horse' and 'pig', appeared frequently during descriptions of life on the Island.[15] However, words for flowers, parts of the body and birds rarely featured as part of the conversation. In view of this, it was not possible to make a systematic comparison between the informants' lexical recall 'on demand' and their natural production. Nevertheless, the following remarks are an attempt to highlight some points of interest.

In most cases, all the words used in the interviews, where they were recalled unproblematically, were also elicited unproblematically in the test. These are given in table 7.3.

There were only two instances when a discrepancy was revealed between the results obtained from the elicitation test and the taped conversations. The first of these was in the case of the word for 'owl' (*cahouain*), which was recalled by one informant in the phrase *ch'tait un malîn cahouain* ('he was a shrewd old bird'; lit. 'he was a shrewd owl') despite the fact that he had not managed to produce it 'on demand' as part of the elicitation test. Another informant recalled the word for 'second cousin' (*deuxième couôsîn*) unproblematically during the interview but displayed a certain amount of hesitation in the elicitation test.

It was also interesting to note that some informants produced one word in the elicitation test but another in the taped conversation. The most frequent instance of these occurred in the case of the word for 'son', where six

Table 7.3 'Elicitation test words' also used by informants in spontaneous conversation

Word in elicitation test	Number of informants who used the word in the taped conversation
'It's exceedingly windy'	2
'Fog'	2
'The weather is fine'	3
'Kettle'	1
'Wardrobe'	2
'Bedsheets'	1
'Spoon'	1
'Son'	25
'Grandmother'	5
'Granddaughter'	7
'Second cousin'	2
'Brother'	8
'Daughter'	31
'Daughter-in-law'	2
'Arm'	2
'Leg'	2
'Face'	1
'Finger'	1
'Horse'	17
'Pig'	7
'Hen'	5
'Cow'	19
'Housefly'	1
'Coat'	5
'Dress'	2
'Toothache'	1
'Owl'	1
'Computer'	1
'Television'	2

informants produced the form *fis* as part of the elicitation test despite having made exclusive use of *garçon* (which also means 'son') in the interviews. One informant also gave the form *grand'méthe* for 'grandmother' in the test but used *manman* (a synonym with more familiar overtones) in the interview. Two other informants gave the appropriate Jèrriais forms for 'cow' (*vaque*) and 'horse' (*j'va*) respectively in the elicitation test but used the standard French forms *vache* and *cheval* in the interviews. This indicates that actual usage may be slightly at variance with the results of the test. However, it is also clear that none of these represents a problematic form for the informants in question.

One of the main findings in this section is that, despite its dwindling number of speakers, lexical erosion in modern Jèrriais is not particularly advanced. Seven of the ten domains examined (the weather, the house, the family, the body, animals and insects, clothing, and illnesses) obtained relatively high scores, with those of the last two categories lowered only by the results obtained for a few isolated terms such as *ouothipieaux* ('mumps') or *blianchet* ('cardigan'), which were generally not as well known as others in the same domain. This reaffirms the comments made in the introduction, namely that on Jersey we are currently witnessing a type of obsolescence that differs from the 'gradual death' pattern that has been the subject of many case studies. As was seen in chapter 4, there seems to exist a situation where fluent speakers of Jèrriais abound in the generations aged 60 and above, but below the age of 40 only a handful are to be found. This chapter has demonstrated that the native speakers have a highly proficient knowledge of the lexis of Jèrriais but may not always be able to recall certain less common terms, due to the fact that opportunities for them to practise their native tongue are decreasing.[16] Since all the informants interviewed for this study were fluent speakers of Jèrriais, it was not therefore possible to look for any correlation between successful lexical recall and fluency in connected speech (the latter observed via the interviews analysed in chapter 6). However, when the number of 'don't knows' was compared with the age of informants, by means of a statistical f-test, it was found that age was positively correlated to successful lexical recall in the elicitation test at the 99.4 per cent level of significance, with the oldest speakers demonstrating the least problematic recall.

The cases of erosion that did occur were generally found to be less frequently used terms, whereas more 'core' items of vocabulary were usually known to all informants. For example, it was seen that, whereas *fil'ye* ('daughter') and *p'tite fil'ye* ('granddaughter') obtained high scores, that of *belle fil'ye* ('daughter-in-law') was much lower (section 7.2.3.). Similarly, in the domain of animals, the masculine form, which often doubled as the generic term, was often better known than the feminine (section 7.2.5.).

The study also revealed some of the strategies used by informants to compensate for not knowing a particular term. Borrowing was used regularly, with English proving a more frequent donor-language than French. More often than not, words were borrowed 'wholesale', although some loans had been nativized (for example *vidgeo*: section 7.2.10.). Occasionally, the phonetic resemblance between an existing English term and a Jèrriais 'false friend' may have encouraged the use of the Jèrriais term in an inappropriate context as in, for example, the case of 'ankle' (*oncl'ye*) (section 7.2.4.), and the partial resemblance of two terms of Jèrriais also seems to have led one to be substituted for the other (*grile* ('hail') for *grive* ('thrush'), section 7.2.9., and *pipsol* ('primrose') for *pipot* ('buttercup'), section 7.2.8.). Some phonetic 'near-misses' were also recorded – such as in the case of *grithe*, where it was clear that the word had been partially recalled (section 7.2.9.). The same phenomenon was apparent in the case of a word such as *p'tite bouonnefemme* ('snowdrop') where, from the other terms suggested (*blianche femme, blianche fil'ye, p'tite fil'ye*), it was plain that the informant had recalled that the indigenous term contained a female reference (section 7.2.8.). The use of a word from the same semantic field proved to be another widely used alternative, with, for example, *paûpil'ye* ('eyelash') being used for *soucile* ('eyebrow') (section 7.2.4.), *héthonde* ('swallow') for *cahouain* ('owl') (section 7.2.9.) and *ântchies* ('pillowcases') for *lîncheurs* ('bedsheets') (section 7.2.2.) (cf. Olshtain and Barzilay 1991: 142–5; Jones unpublished). Moreover, it was also not uncommon for a word's frame of reference to be extended, as with the use of *chavettes* ('old shoes') for 'slippers' (section 7.2.6.). Although informants are, therefore, sometimes unable to supply the indigenous term, many of the strategies discussed above suggest that they are often capable of partial recollection: a sign, perhaps, that they are becoming 'rusty' in their native variety.

The lexical survey also revealed instances where the phonetic form of a word was recalled but not its precise meaning. For example, it was seen that *ouothipieaux* ('mumps') was cited as the Jèrriais for 'measles' (*rouogeule*) by one informant, who then went on to say that he did not recall the word for 'mumps' (section 7.2.7.). This phenomenon was found to be particularly prevalent in the domain of illnesses (section 7.2.7.) and birds (section 7.2.9.), again possibly due to the fact that some of these terms are not used frequently on a day-to-day basis.

In the domain of the weather (section 7.2.1.), certain terms had been selected for the lexical questionnaire due to the fact that their equivalents in Jèrriais were highly idiomatic. However, it became clear that, although such idioms probably still formed part of the passive vocabulary of most informants, they were being replaced across the board in speech by more transparent equivalents. It will be interesting to observe whether the introduction of Jèrriais in the primary school will serve to revitalize such expressions.

The survey also highlighted the presence of several lexical gaps in Jèrriais.

This was most noticeable in the domain of so-called 'technological' terminology denoting 'modern' concepts (section 7.2.10.). However, the inability of informants to supply Jèrriais terms in this domain does not constitute lexical erosion, in that it is not a case of Jèrriais terms once having existed and subsequently having been forgotten. Rather, the words in this field have never existed in the dialect and, if they are coined and introduced successfully during the next few years as a corollary to the introduction of Jèrriais into the primary school (see section 5.5.), will represent an area of lexical growth. Technology is, of course, one of many domains which the dialect must penetrate if it is to have a realistic prospect of revitalization.

It is easy to see why Jèrriais should have no words for modern technological inventions. All objects investigated in this survey are relatively recent innovations and borrowing, rather than coining, a term to denote them has proved a convenient strategy, especially if 'the need for lexical elaboration is so high in persistent linguistic enclaves . . . confronted with the communicative demands of modern life, that there is no way for these communities to cope with this problem without importing massively, overburdened as they are by the sheer number of items to create' (Drapeau 1992: 3). However, the fact that, at the beginning of the twenty-first century, there exists no readily accessible Jèrriais term for such an everyday concept as a television indicates that the variety has failed to move with the times.[17] Some informants found it amusing that I should be asking about the Jèrriais equivalent for 'modern' terms, which clearly did not fit their mental picture of what the dialect represented. However, just as life on Jersey is changing, so a variety attached to the farmyard and fishing boat will not survive and it is, therefore, necessary for that mental picture to change.

The survey also highlighted lexical gaps in the case of three other words, namely 'cardigan', 'slippers' and 'living room' (sections 7.2.6., 7.2.6. and 7.2.2. respectively). This result initially seemed surprising in view of the 'everyday' nature of the items concerned but, in fact, it emerged that the reason these terms posed so many problems for informants was that they do not 'fit' the traditional Jèrriais way of life. As discussed in section 7.2.6., I was told that slippers were a relatively modern concept, 'imported' from the mainland and not traditionally worn around a farm, where a pair of old shoes would generally be used as indoor footwear. Similarly, although a traditional farmhouse might have a parlour or a 'best' room, it would rarely have anything more akin to a living room than a big kitchen. When such concepts were introduced into Jersey, therefore, the English term was borrowed alongside them. This highlights how important it is for researchers not to assume that their reality will necessarily be that of their informants. The case of 'cardigan' is different in that this item of clothing was frequently worn by Jersey people, and although *blianchet*, the Jèrriais term listed in the DJF (p. 56), does not correspond exactly to a 'cardigan', Le Maistre writes 'ce qu'on appelle en Anglais [*sic*] de nos jours un "cardigan" se rapproche de notre *blianchet* et nombreux sont ceux qui appellent le vêtement anglais, maintenant bien connu à Jersey, par ce nom de blianchet' (1966: 56).[18] Perhaps this word, then, represents a prime example of lexical erosion.

To end this chapter on a positive note, it was plain that, despite the decrease in speaker numbers, regional variation was still visible in the lexis of Jèrriais, in terms of variation in both pronunciation — for example the [œː]– [aj] opposition (section 3.3.1.1.a.), as seen in *dêmêleux* ('comb') and *parleux* ('living room'), or the [oːw]–[aːw] opposition (section 3.3.1.1.a.), as seen in the word *moûque* ('housefly')[19] – and lexis: for example the term for 'spider', *pêtre* (WJ)–*ithangnie* (EJ) (section 3.3.2.). However, some regional terms were also found outside their historical territory: for example *pâssecole* ('ladybird'), described by Spence (1993: 21) as a WJ variant, was used by an informant who had always lived in St Martin. Moreover, it emerged that, in fact, the term most consistently used by WJ informants to refer to a ladybird was *démouaîselle* (section 7.2.5.) and not any of the localized WJ variants listed by Spence (1993: 23). Similarly, the term *papillon* ('moth'), described as occurring mainly in EJ (Spence 1993: 23), was used by several WJ informants, whereas *papillote*, the western variant (of the term for 'butter-fly') according to Spence, was used by three informants whose home and families were in Eastern Jersey. This indicates the presence of dialect mixing on Jersey, although, as with the phonological variables described in section 6.4.3., its presence was not particularly widespread.[20] As a final point, the fact that non-regionally based synonyms were still prevalent, as with the case of, for example, *grande armouaithe–prêsse* ('wardrobe') and *dêmêle–dêmêleux* ('comb') (section 7.2.2.), was an indication that Jèrriais was still showing some signs of vitality.

8

CROSS-LINGUISTIC INFLUENCE ON JERSEY

8.1. Introduction

It is a well-known fact that varieties in contact influence one another (Weinreich 1953). As was discussed in chapter 2, the historical circumstances of Jersey have led to a situation whereby three different varieties are present on the Island: Jèrriais, the indigenous dialect, standard French, the official language of Jersey, and English, which, by today, is the Island's dominant language and which was introduced over several centuries as a by-product of Jersey's political attachment to Great Britain. The linguistic influence that English has exerted on Jèrriais has been examined in detail in chapters 6 and 7. This chapter now seeks to consider three other types of linguistic influence discernible on Jersey. The first two sections examine the substrate effect of Jèrriais on the languages that have been subsequently introduced onto the Island, by demonstrating the ways in which insular English and French differ from the corresponding mainland varieties. The third section forms a parallel of sorts with chapters 6 and 7 in that, once again, developments in the linguistic system of Jèrriais are examined, the difference being that, this time, the influence comes from standard French.

8.2. The influence of Jèrriais on the standard French spoken on Jersey

8.2.1. *Preliminary remarks*

Although standard French is not a variety native to Jersey, the fact that it is well known on the Island is attested by Brasseur, who, in 1977, stated that 'Tous les patoisants comprennent parfaitement le français et sont capables de le parler' (1977: 99).[1] As outlined in chapter 2, until relatively recently, French performed the function of an H variety in relation to Jèrriais in a diglossic situation, being used, until the late nineteenth century, for all legal, financial and juridical administration. In 1912, a law was passed stating that French should be taught in all the Island's schools for an hour per day and, although Brasseur has claimed that this time allowance is 'appliqué rarement' ('rarely applied') (1977: 98), the language is introduced to pupils at the age of 7 in all primary schools – four years before its introduction in the United Kingdom.

The term 'regional French' has been given to the intermediary variety that exists 'between' local dialects on the one hand and standard French on the other. Its creation is attributed to speakers transferring features associated with their native tongue into the variety that they are acquiring (standard French). The regional French of Jersey has been studied extensively by Hublart (1979) through tape-recordings made of four individuals whose mother tongue was Jèrriais. Hublart's study documents the idiosyncratic features of the regional French of Jersey (hereafter RFJ) in detail, but he does not always make clear which of the features have arisen due to influence from English and which are attributable to the Jèrriais substrate. This section, therefore, attempts to review and discuss further the features found in Hublart's data which show the influence of Jèrriais in the creation of RFJ.

8.2.2. Linguistic features

8.2.2.1. Morphosyntax

a. *Position of adjectives* (Hublart 1979: 97)

In RFJ, attributive adjectives are frequently preposed. This is especially common in the case of colour adjectives:

(1) *On n'en voulait pas de **blancs** chevals*
     'We didn't want any white horses'

but also occurs with other adjectives:

(2) *Dans les **dernières** trois ans*
     'During the last three years'

As seen in section 6.4.1.7., many attributive adjectives are also preposed in Jèrriais (Birt 1985: 43–4). Given that such adjectives in English too precede the noun they qualify, the position of the adjective in RFJ might possibly be interpreted as transference from English, perhaps via Jèrriais. However, the fact that Mainland Norman displays this tendency with regard to colour adjectives and also 'short' adjectives (UPN 1995: 36–7) suggests that the preposing of these adjectives in RFJ is likely to represent transference from Norman rather than an anglicism, although it is also possible that the tendency has arisen due to a combination of both these factors.

b. *Pronouns* (Hublart 1979: 102)

The third person plural pronoun of Jèrriais is invariable as to gender (Spence 1993: 32), with *i'/il'/li's* being used to refer to both the masculine and feminine.[2] This lack of a distinction has led to the generalization of the masculine 3pl. pronoun in RFJ in contexts where the feminine pronoun would be used in standard French, for example:

(3) **Ils** *[les îles] n'étaient pas défendues*
'They [m.] (the Islands [n.f.]) were not defended'

c. *The verb*

(i) *Morphology*

(1) *Reflexive verbs* (Hublart 1979: 102)
Récupérer ('to get better') is used reflexively in RFJ despite the fact that, in standard French, it is not a reflexive verb. This seems to be attributable to a form of syntactic calquing from Jèrriais in that all the Jèrriais equivalents of *récupérer*, namely *s'èrfaithe*, *s'èrgraie*, *s'èrhaler*, *s'ramener*, *s'rafistoler*, *s'rapiploter*, *s'rêtablyi* and *s'èrdgéthi*, are reflexive verbs.

(2) *Choice of auxiliary* (Hublart 1979: 111)
Avoir ('to have') is often used as an auxiliary in RFJ to form the perfect (and pluperfect) tense of many intransitive verbs, such as:

(4) *On **a** rentré en France*
'We went back to France'

where standard French would use the auxiliary *être* ('to be'). This is due to the fact that in Jèrriais, as in mainland varieties of Norman (UPN 1995: 160–1), *être* is only consistently used as an auxiliary with reflexive verbs and with a few verbs of motion, such as *aller* (see section 6.4.1.4.).

(ii) *Tenses*

(1) *The past historic* (Hublart 1979: 107)
Although the past historic is not used in standard spoken French, the fact that this tense is widespread in spoken Jèrriais (Birt 1985: 104) has led to its use in RFJ, where it denotes actions which have been completed at a specific time in the past. Moreover, the Jèrriais verb form also frequently replaces the standard French verb form, for example:

(5) a. *Mon père **allit***
         'My father went'

rather than

     b. *Mon père **alla***
        'My father went' (standard French)

(2) *The present continuous* (Hublart 1979: 110)
The present continuous of Jèrriais is expressed by a construction composed of *être* ('to be') + *à* + infinitive (Birt 1985: 28–9), for example:

(6) *Jé **sis à liéthe** la gâzette du sé*
     'I am reading the evening newspaper'

Both Hublart (1979: 110) and Brasseur (1977: 101) state that, in RFJ, this construction is used to the exclusion of *être en train de* + infinitive ('to be doing something'), which is used to convey the present and past continuous in standard French:

(7) *Il **est à manger***
     'He is eating'

(8) *J'**étais à écouter** mon radio*
     'I was listening to my radio'

(iii) *Mood*

(1) *The subjunctive* (Hublart 1979: 109)
As seen in section 6.4.1.8., the use of the subjunctive is in decline in modern Jèrriais and, in many contexts, it is being replaced by the indicative. Hublart found many examples of the non-use of the subjunctive in RFJ in contexts in which the mood would be required historically in standard French, for example:

(9) *Faudrait qu ch'**est** le patois*
     'It has to be the *patois*' (cf. standard French *il faudrait que ce **soit** le patois*)

(10) *Je regrette que je ne **peux** pas le faire*
     'I'm sorry that I can't do it' (cf. standard French *je regrette que je ne **puisse** pas le faire*)

It is worth reiterating, however, that such non-use of the subjunctive is not exclusive to RFJ, and has been discussed by, for example, Gadet (1992) in relation to *français populaire*.

(2) *The conditional* (Hublart 1979: 109)
The discussion in section 6.4.1.8. also demonstrated that, in Jèrriais, the conditional was often substituted for the subjunctive in a number of contexts by which the latter would be triggered historically. This was found to be especially prevalent when the matrix verb was in the conditional or the conditional perfect. Hublart indicates that this substitution was also apparent in RFJ:

(11) *J'aurais bien voulu que les enfants **auraient** parlé le patois*
     'I would have liked the children to have spoken patois' (cf. standard French *j'aurais bien voulu que les enfants **aient** parlé le patois*)

Again, this usage is not exclusive to RFJ. Grevisse describes the use of the conditional in expressions such as:

(12) *Je voudrais qu'il **viendrait***
'I wanted him to come'

and

(13) *Il aurait fallu qu'on **aurait chanté***
'We would have to have sung'

as 'fréquent dans l'usage populaire de diverses provinces et du Canada'[3] (1988: §869; cf. §865e). This indicates that conditional substitution is quite a widespread tendency in the French-speaking world and that influence from Jèrriais might therefore not be the only possible motivation behind this development in RFJ.

(iv) *Agreement* (Hublart 1979: 113)
The third person plural presentative form of standard French (*ce sont*) is absent from RFJ, where it is replaced by the third person singular presentative *c'est*, for example:

(14) ***C'est** mes cousins*
'It's my cousins'

This is undoubtedly due to the lack of a corresponding third person plural presentative form in Jèrriais, where the singular pronoun in used, even with a plural subject:

(15) ***Ch'est** mes couôsîns*

This construction may occur on the pattern of English, where the pronoun 'it' + singular verb are used in the context of both the singular and the plural.

d. *Adverbs*

(i) *Presence of 'que'* (Hublart 1979: 118)
Many of the adverbs of standard French take on an additional *que* in RFJ, for example, *combien que* ('how many?'), *où que* ('where?'), *comment que* ('how?'), *quand que* ('when?'). This represents transference from Jèrriais, where the adverbs corresponding to standard French *combien* ('how many?'), *où* ('where?'), *comment* ('how?'), *quand* ('when?') and *pourquoi* ('why?') are commonly found with a following *qué*: *coumbein qué, où est qu', comme est qu', quand tchi qué, pour tch'est qué*. This phenomenon is also attested in *français populaire*, where forms are found such as:

(16) *On restait jusqu'à **quand que** la gare elle ferme*
'We stayed until the station had shut' (Gadet 1992: 98–9)

Coume que ('how?') and *coumbyin que* ('how many?') are also attested for Mainland Norman (UPN 1995: 139).

(ii) *Calques* (Hublart 1979: 116)

RFJ also contains many adverbial phrases, unknown to standard French, which are used frequently in Jèrriais but which themselves represent calques of English phrases, for example:

(17) *Et puis,* **tout soudainement,** *une figure à la vitrine*
      'And then, suddenly, a face appeared at the window'

(18) *De voir* **combien grand** *était le pays*
      'To see how big the country was'

These, therefore, represent transference from English via Jèrriais.

e. *Prepositions*

Hublart's data also contain many examples of standard French prepositions which are used in constructions of RFJ which would be meaningless to a speaker of Mainland French. This is because these prepositions represent calques of English usage. However, such examples may also be interpreted as influence from Jèrriais due to the fact that, in most cases, the calqued preposition is in common usage in the equivalent expression in Jèrriais, where it usually represents the only means by which the desired meaning may be expressed. This, therefore, is another widespread instance of transference from English into RFJ via Jèrriais.

(i) *De* (Hublart 1979: 122)

(19) *Le Don Balleine est* **supposé d'** *les faire*
      'The Don Balleine is supposed to do it' (in Jèrriais, 'to be supposed to' is rendered as *supposé dé* (cf. standard French *être censé de*))

(ii) *Environ de* (Hublart 1979: 122)

Although in standard French *environ* ('about') does not require a preposition, the reason that it is used with *de* in RFJ may be attributable to the fact that *dé* is found as part of the corresponding preposition in Jèrriais – *à l'entou dé*. In other words, similarity of meaning may have precipitated an increased similarity of form:

(20) *Ils gagnent* **environ de** *60 livres*
      'They earn about sixty pounds'

(iii) *Dates* (Hublart 1979: 122)

In standard French, dates are expressed as *le* + cardinal numeral + month. However, in RFJ the preposition *de* is frequently inserted, for example:

(21) *Le 23* **de** *novembre*
      'The twenty-third of November',

which is the construction also found in Jèrriais (*lé vîngt-trais d'novembre*) and which may have entered the dialect as a syntactic calque of the English expression.

(iv) *Dans* (Hublart 1979: 121)
This preposition has a widespread currency in RFJ, replacing those of standard French in phrases such as:

(22) *Tous les services étaient en français **dans** le temps de mes grands-parents*
'When my grandparents were alive, all the services were in French' (where *au* ('at the') would be the preposition historically required in this context by standard French)

(23) *Elle est interéssée **dans** tout ça*
'She is interested in all that' (where *par* ('by') is the preposition historically required in this context by standard French)

In Jèrriais, *dans* ('in') is the preposition traditionally found in these contexts (DJF, pp. 305 and 509 respectively).

(v) *Par* (Hublart 1979: 124)
This preposition is often used in RFJ to convey a meaning akin to English 'by', whereas standard French would traditionally use different prepositions according to context, for example:

(24) *On a été **par** le bateau*
'We went by boat' (the expression *en bateau* would traditionally be used in standard French)

(25) *À St Martin, **par** deux heures, on va savoir*
'We'll know by two o'clock in St Martin's' (the preposition *avant* ('before') would traditionally be used in standard French)

Although neither of these uses of *par* is mentioned in the DJF, my data suggested that the preposition was used at least with the latter function in Jèrriais:

(26) *I' faut être à la maîson **par** trais heuthes*
'We have to be at home by three o'clock'

(vi) *Pour* (Hublart 1979: 124–5)
Pour was also used in contexts where it would not traditionally be found in standard French and where its meaning appeared to be similar to the English preposition 'for':

(27) *Pouvez-vous changer un chèque **pour** dix livres?*
'Can you cash a cheque for ten pounds?' (*de* ('of') would traditionally be used in standard French)

(28) **Pour** *trois cent ans*
'For three hundred years' (*pendant* ('during') would traditionally be used in standard French)

The use of *pour* in such contexts is widespread in Jèrriais:

(29) *J'fus prisonnyi dé dgèrre* **pour** *trais ans*
'I was a prisoner of war for three years'

(30) *I'tait responsabl'ye* **pour** *lyi*
'He was responsible for her'

It is worth mentioning, however, that in her work on 'everyday' spoken French (*français ordinaire*) Gadet (1989: 177) found that since *pour* is a preposition that has little meaning of its own, it could be used extensively in several historically inappropriate contexts, where its 'fuzziness' made the resultant phrase acceptable to the listener. It is possible, therefore, that Hublart's RFJ data reflect this tendency.

(vii) *Sur* (Hublart 1979: 125–6)
The preposition *sur* was found in a variety of contexts in RFJ, none of which would be considered grammatically correct in standard French but all of which would admit *sus* in Jèrriais, probably as a calque of the English preposition 'on', for example:

(31) *Tchi programme qu'y a* **sur** *la télévision?*
'What programme is on the television?' (*à* ('at') would be used in standard French)

(32) *C'est un jeu* **sur** *mots*
'It's a play on words' (*de* ('of') would be used in standard French)

(33) *Y'a beaucoup de gens qui dépendent* **sur** *les touristes*
'There are many people who depend on the tourists' (*de* ('of') would be used in standard French)[4]

(34) *On n'est bien que* **sur** *les fermes*
'Life is only good on the farm' (*dans* ('in') would be used in standard French)

(viii) *Creation of new prepositions*
Hublart (1979: 127, 128) also recorded the use of two compound prepositions in RFJ that do not exist in standard French, namely *en devant de* ('in front of') and *à cause que* ('since/because'):

(35) *Il était assis* **en devant de** *moi dans le théâtre*
'He was sitting in front of me at the theatre'

(36)   . . . *à cause qu'on à des ouvriers français*
      '. . . since we've got French workers'

These are clearly borrowings from Jèrriais, where the aforementioned prepositions are in common use (DJF, pp. 180 and 91 respectively).

8.2.2.2. *Lexis*

Jèrriais influence was widespread in the lexis of RFJ and manifested itself in a number of ways.

a. *'Archaisms'* (Hublart 1979: 129–32)

The terms listed by Hublart as examples of 'archaisms' in RFJ are words which once formed part of standard French but which have since become obsolescent – either due to the object they denote having become obsolete or due to their replacement by another term. Examples of such terms include *vergée* (a unit of land measurement no longer used in standard French), *ouïr* ('to hear', *entendre* in standard French), *septante* ('seventy', *soixante-dix* in standard French) and *sieur* ('mister', *monsieur* in standard French). However, since these words are still actively used in Jèrriais, it may be more appropriate to consider them as borrowings from the dialect, which it may be convenient to class together in that they also all once formed part of the lexicon of standard French. Given that all of Hublart's informants could also speak Jèrriais, borrowing from the dialect seems a more convincing explanation of the presence of such terms in RFJ than suggesting that they have somehow survived in this variety after disappearing from the standard French of the mainland. However, it is also possible that the fact that speakers would be using such terms frequently when they spoke Jèrriais may have encouraged their retention in RFJ. Since both Jèrriais borrowings into RFJ and French words which would have remained in RFJ as archaisms would be likely to be pronounced according to the phonotactics of French, in this case it is not possible to draw on phonology as a source of evidence to distinguish whether these words represent ancient French survivals or more recent borrowings from Jèrriais.

b. *Same form – different meaning* (Hublart 1979: 141–7)

As *langue d'oïl* varieties, Jèrriais and standard French have many words in common, which share an identical form and meaning. However, in some cases, although the same form may be found in both varieties, the meanings may not be identical. For example, the word *bois* [bwa] is found in both standard French and Jèrriais (realized as *bouais* [bwe] in the latter) and can mean 'wood' in both varieties: however, in Jèrriais *bouais* also functions as the generic term for a 'tree' (*arbre* in standard French). When speaking RFJ, Hublart's informants frequently used such terms with their Jèrriais meaning – yielding phrases which would not be readily understood by a speaker of Mainland French. Examples of such terms include:

(i)   *monde* ('people'; used with a plural verb in a phrase such as *le monde disent que* ('people say that'): cf. DJF, p. 356). The word *gens* ('people') is used in this context by standard French, where *monde* can only be used with a singular verb to mean 'people', and in phrases such as *tout le monde* ('everyone') and *il y a du monde* ('there are some people').

(ii) *terrain* ('the interior of a country', *intérieur du pays* in standard French: cf. DJF, p. 510). In standard French, *terrain* means 'ground'/'terrain'.

(iii) *vitrine* ('window pane': DJF, p. 546). *Carreau* is used to convey the meaning of 'window pane' in standard French, where *vitrine* means 'shop window'.

c. *Figurative expressions* (Hublart 1979: 148)

RFJ also contains several idiomatic phrases which have their origins in Jèrriais, for example *ne pas avoir tous ses boutons* ('to be stupid');[5] *gaver de l'oeil* ('to stare at'); *gaûfrer* ('to repair').[6] None of these expressions would be readily understood by a speaker of standard French.

d. *Lexical creations* (Hublart 1979: 149)

In certain cases, a term may be used in RFJ which exists neither in standard French nor in Jèrriais and may be considered as a lexical creation specific to the variety. However, the influence of Jèrriais is often plain:

(i)   *aréoport* ('airport): cf. standard French *aéroport*. The RFJ term displays metathesis, a phenomenon commonly found in Jèrriais (Spence 1990: 215–20) (cf. section 6.4.2.1.).

(ii) *rentendre* ('to hear again') < *entendre*: cf. standard French *entendre encore une fois*. This term has probably been created due to the influence of the numerous verbs beginning in *ren-* in Jèrriais, for example *renv'yer* ('to send back'), *reunfreunmer* ('to enclose'), *renchiéthi* ('to become more expensive'), *rendormi* ('to go back to sleep'), *renseigni* ('to inform') and so forth (DJF, pp. 449–50).

e. *Gallicized English words* (Hublart 1979: 154–61)

Some of the words which form part of the lexicon of RFJ are standard French in form but their actual usage is influenced by English, for example *union* ('trade union') (in standard French, *union* = 'union' in its literal sense; 'trade union' is expressed by the term *syndicat*); *papier* ('newspaper') (in standard French, *papier* = 'paper' and 'newspaper' is expressed by the term *journal*); *actuellement* ('actually') (in standard French, *actuellement* = 'at the present time' and 'actually' is expressed by the phrase *en fait*). In some cases, the terms used represent calques of English phrases (*donner un discours*, 'to give a speech' (cf. standard French *prononcer un discours*)) and *le livre des téléphones* ('the telephone book' (cf. standard French *l'annuaire*)), and other terms, despite their 'French' appearance, do not form part of the lexicon of standard French: *queuer* ('to queue' (cf. standard

French *faire la queue*)), *allouer* ('to allow' (cf. standard French *permettre*)), *désappointant* ('disappointing' (cf. standard French *décevant*)). It is, of course, possible that such terms may have entered RFJ via Jèrriais, where centuries of contact with English have left their mark on the dialect's lexicon: for example *allouer* (meaning 'to allow') and *actuellement* (meaning 'actually') are both commonly used words of Jèrriais (DJF, pp. 15 and 6 respectively).

8.2.3. *Concluding remarks*

This section has attempted to extend Hublart's analysis of what he terms the regional French of Jersey by demonstrating which of the features listed in his work may be attributed to influence from Jèrriais. The list is not exhaustive – for example, Hublart does not mention the phonetic characteristics of RFJ, where it is also possible to isolate instances of Jèrriais influence, such as in the use of dental [r] and nasal [i].

Hublart concludes that 'le français régional de Jersey se présente comme un langage fortement contaminé'[7] (1979: 163), due to the fact that he found 432 morphosyntactic and 232 lexical features that differed from standard French in 205 minutes of recordings. Although many of them were contact-based, not all the features noted had arisen due to the influence of Jèrriais. Work such as that of Gadet (1989, 1992) and Sauvageot (1962, 1972) have shown clearly that our view of what constitutes standard French is often a narrow, prescriptive one and that the French spoken by the average French person may frequently differ considerably from the established norm. It is therefore possible that, in the case of those features of RFJ which differ from standard French, but where a similar divergence is also found in *français populaire* or other varieties of regional French, contact with Jèrriais may not be the sole – or indeed even the main – motivation, and internal simplification may also have had a role to play.

Many of the features outlined by Hublart as characteristic of RFJ were clearly attributable to English, which, despite being the second language of all of Hublart's informants, would, as the Island's dominant variety, feature widely in their everyday lives. These features have not been discussed in this section. It is, of course, possible that, as Hublart notes, some of the features in the survey were idiolectal rather than typical of RFJ (1979: 163). This would seem especially likely in the case of lexical features such as calques or borrowings.

On the basis of the work done by Hublart, it is possible to conclude that the standard French spoken by native speakers of Jèrriais differs significantly from the prescriptive norm. Hublart calls the resultant variety the regional French of Jersey, a term which, for the sake of convenience, has also been adopted in this section, although, as will be discussed in the conclusion, when used in the context of Jersey, this term has a slightly different meaning from when it is used in conjunction with the varieties spoken on the French mainland. Due to constraints of resources and time, it has not been possible to present a systematic analysis of RFJ in this section. However, by re-examining Hublart's data, this section has, nevertheless, been able to demonstrate that, although the presence of some of the features examined admit more than one possible explanation, Jèrriais can still be shown to have played a significant role in the creation of RFJ.

8.3. The influence of Jèrriais on the English spoken on Jersey

8.3.1. *Preliminary remarks*

Although Jersey traditionally forms part of the francophone world, there can be no doubt that, in the twenty-first century, English is the Island's dominant variety. As demonstrated in chapter 2, although the Channel Islands underwent political separation from the Duchy of Normandy in 1204, after electing to continue their allegiance to the English crown, Anglicization was far from immediate and, despite the fact that the subsequent centuries brought the Islanders into limited contact with English, it was not until the twentieth century that the latter came to predominate.

Like the standard French of Jersey, the English spoken on the Island has been heavily influenced by the Jèrriais substrate, to the extent that it is possible to describe it as a separate regional variety of English. Unlike Guernsey English, however, which has been analysed in detail by Ramisch (1989) and Barbé (1995), the English of Jersey has not been the subject of any systematic study. This section represents a provisional attempt to remedy the situation by examining the features of Jersey English which seem to be attributable to a Jèrriais substrate. Although no systematic data collection was undertaken for this part of the study, the section is based on extensive notes and observations made during field trips to Jersey between 1996 and 2000.

As not all the inhabitants of the Island are Jersey-born or even from families indigenous to Jersey, not all the features listed in this section are to be found in the English of every Islander. Moreover, the fact that such features are frequently stigmatized has also led many Islanders to eliminate them consciously from their speech, a practice often instigated by the education system, which encouraged children to adopt a more standardized English. The features listed below are, however, quite prominent in the speech of many older Jersey-born Islanders, especially those who also speak Jèrriais.

8.3.2. *Linguistic features*

8.3.2.1. *Morphosyntax*

a. *'There's' + time reference*

In standard English, the present perfect followed by the preposition *for* and a reference to the time involved are required in an expression such as:

(37) *I've been a farmer for ten years*

In Jersey English, however, the construction *there's* + time reference + present tense is used:

(38) *There's ten years I'm a farmer*

This is clearly due to transference from Jèrriais, where the equivalent phrase would be *Y'a dgiex ans qué j'sis fermyi*. The sentence in (38) is therefore a syntactic calque. This construction is commonly found in Jersey English:

(39) *There's a year now that I'm drawing my pension*

(40) *Is there a while you haven't seen your sister?*

The same construction is also found in Guernsey English:

(41) *There's nearly a thousand years we are British* (Ramisch 1989: 150)

b. *'There's' + plural subject*

Unlike in standard English, the presentative *there's* may be used in Jersey English with a plural subject. This seems to be attributable to the fact that, in Jèrriais, the most commonly used presentative, *y'a*, contains a singular verb.

(42) *There's two castles on Jersey*
      (cf. Jèrriais *Y' a deux chatés en Jèrri*; standard English 'There are two castles on Jersey')

The same lack of agreement is apparent in Guernsey English (Ramisch 1989: 92–6) but, as Ramisch states, this may also be observed in many varieties of non-standard English (Miller and Brown 1982: 16; Petyt 1985: 237). Indeed, in American English, the use of *there's* in such a construction is so dominant a form as not to be considered non-standard, at least in the spoken language.

c. *The particle 'eh'*

This is possibly the feature of Jersey English of which its speakers are most conscious. In informal speech, the particle *eh* is extremely frequent and occurs as both a tag at the end of a question, with a meaning akin to English 'isn't it?'/'aren't they?'/'don't you think?', for example:

(43) *That's the one, eh?*

and as a phatic particle used to maintain the connection between speaker and hearer. In the latter context, it may be used so frequently by some speakers that it could almost be seen as a marker of the end of a clause:

(44)   *You used to get all little shops, **eh**. I mean you get towns in England that have changed too, **eh**. No more little shops. Well, it's like that in Jersey now too, **eh**.*

The particle is considered in detail with reference to Guernsey English by Ramisch, who points to transference from Norman (Guernésiais) as a likely explanation. It would be impossible to conclude anything different for Jersey English, especially given the fact that the contexts involved are identical (Ramisch 1989: 111). Moreover, such usage is also found in standard French, where the particle involved is *hein?* (Hublart 1979: 48):

(45)   *Qu'est-ce que tu fais, **hein**?*
       'What are you doing, eh?'

(46)   *Tu ne penses pas, **hein**?*
       'You don't think so, do you?'

d. *Emphatic use of personal pronouns*

Another widespread feature of Jersey English is the use of the accusative form of the personal subject pronouns *me, you, him, her, us* and *them* as emphatic forms at the beginning or end of an utterance, thus:

(47)   ***Me**, I'm from St Ouen's / I'm from St Ouen's, **me*** (cf. Hublart 1979: 48)

This is clearly parallel to the emphatic use of such pronouns in Jèrriais:

(48)   *Oulle a tréjous 'te d'même, **lyi***
       lit. 'She's always been the same, her'

(49)   *Jé n'veurs pon y aller, **mé***
       'I don't want to go, me' (Birt 1985: 238)

This use of pronouns is mentioned by Ramisch (1989: 124–9) and Tomlinson (1981: 19) for Guernsey English. That this feature is considered to be a hallmark of Guernsey English may be seen in the fact that Le Pelley chose the title 'I am Guernsey – me!' for his 1975 article.[8]

e. *Stress*

In the case of polysyllabic words, the main stress of Jersey English often falls on a different syllable from that of standard English, hence: ['təumatəuz] ('tomatoes'; standard English [təu'matəuz]), [grin'haʊs] ('greenhouse'; standard English ['grinhaʊs]). Although it is not possible to demonstrate Jèrriais influence in each instance, it is noteworthy that, where a word of English and Jèrriais share a similar form but a different stress placement, usually due to the fact that the Jèrriais form is a borrowing from English which has been modified according to the phonotactics of Jèrriais, Jèrriais stress placement is often used for the form in question in a sentence of Jersey English (cf. Hublart 1979: 47; Ramisch 1989: 164 n.1). For example, the English word 'gravy' (['gɹajvi]) is borrowed into Jèrriais as *grevîn* in a sentence such as:

(50) *Soulais faithe du grevîn*
      'I used to make gravy'

In Jèrriais, however, the pronunciation is [grɛ'vĩ]. When used in a sentence of Jersey English, therefore, the word *gravy* may be given a different stress pattern from that of standard English, hence:

(51) *I used to make [gɹaj'vi]*

f. The definite article

As in Guernsey English, non-standard use is made of the definite article in Jersey English in the following contexts:

(i) Names of languages:

(52) *My son speaks **the** Good French and I speak **the** Jersey French*
      (cf. 'Mon fis pâle lé bouon français et jé pâle lé Jèrriais')

(53) *Now everyone speaks **the** English*
      (cf. 'À ch't heu tout l'monde pâle l'Angliais')

(ii) Before a plural noun with generic reference:

(54) ***The** Jersey people are quite stubborn, you know*
      (cf. 'Les Jèrriais sont un mio têtus, dis')

Again, the Jèrriais phrases indicate that (52), (53) and (54) are syntactic calques.

Ramisch (1989: 113) also mentions several other non-standard uses of the direct article in Guernsey English that are likely to be attributable to transference from Guernésiais, namely with adverbials of direction, adverbials of time expressing a regular repetition, before the noun *school* and in the idiomatic expression *to go by bus* (1989: 113–24):

(55) *Only if you want to, well, do extra shopping then you'd better go into **the** town to do it*
      (cf. standard English '. . . then you'd better go into town to do it')

(56) *He gives the news out on the wireless in h'm in patois on **the** Friday*
      (cf. standard English 'He gives the news out on the wireless in patois every Friday')

(57) *But I mean that [Guernsey French] wasn't taught in **the** school, you see*
(cf. standard English '[. . .] 'wasn't taught in school')

(58) *It was always by **the** bus we went, because h'm . . .*
(cf. standard English 'We always went by bus . . .')

Although such usage was not heard in Jersey English, as stated above, my remarks are not based on systematic observation and it is possible that a more comprehensive study of the variety might also yield similar examples.

g. *'Isn't it?' as a tag question*

The form *isn't it?* is used in Jersey English as a universal tag question, for example,

(59) *She did well, **isn't it**?*

(60) *Ian Botham's got a house on Alderney, **isn't it**?*

This feature is highlighted by Brasseur as common to all varieties of Channel Island English (1977: 101), and its use in the English of both Jersey and Guernsey has been attested previously by Hublart (1979: 48) and Ramisch (1989: 149). Although *isn't it?* also functions as a tag question in other varieties of regional English (Ramisch 1989: 149–50), it is possible that transference from Jèrriais may account for the presence of this invariable form in Jersey English, where it could represent a calque of the Jèrriais invariable tag *n'est-che pon?* ('isn't it?'):

(61) *Oulle est hardi belle, not' fil'ye, **n'est-che pon**?* (Birt 1985: 237)
lit. 'She's very pretty, our daughter, isn't it?'

h. *'But yes'*

The expression *but yes* is used in Jersey English as an emphatic form of the affirmative with a meaning akin to standard English 'yes indeed' or 'yes of course', for example:

(62) *Did your parents speak Jèrriais? - **But yes***

The presence of this form in Jersey English is also described by Hublart (1979: 48), and Ramisch (1989: 154) mentions it in conjunction with Guernsey English. It is clearly due to transference from Jèrriais, representing a calque of the expression *mais oui* ('but yes'), which may be used in the dialect as an emphatic form of the affirmative.

i. *Pronominal apposition*

Linked to point 8.3.2.1.d. above (emphatic use of personal pronouns) is the emphatic use of a personal pronoun immediately after its antecedent, for example:

(63)   . . . *and the teacher,* **she** *was angry, eh*

Although this feature, termed pronominal apposition by Ramisch, who describes its usage in Guernsey English (1989: 156–7), is also widespread in colloquial English, in this context it may reflect transference of a widely used device in Jèrriais:

(64)   *Les p'tites fermes,* **i'** *sont toutes hortes*
       lit. 'The little farms, they are all out', meaning 'the small farms are all gone'

(65)   *Et la p'tite fil'ye,* **oulle** *est bouonne*
       lit. 'And the little girl, she is good'

j. *The conditional*

Conditional clauses of Jersey English are frequently formed without the word *if*, which would be necessary in standard usage, for example:

(66)   *You'd have seen that, you'd never have thought there was any news in it.*

This is clearly formed on the basis of a construction such as:

(67)   *J'éthais l'temps, j'pouôrrais l'vaie aniet*
       lit. 'I'd have had the time, I would be able to see him today', meaning 'If I'd have had the time, I would have been able to see him today'

which is commonly found in Jèrriais – and in spoken standard French (Price 1993: §423). Although common in Jersey English, this construction is not mentioned by Ramisch for Guernsey English.

k. *Prepositions*

Prepositions used in Jersey English often differ from those which would be used in the same contexts in standard English, for example:

(68)   *He wrote a letter* **for** *thank me.*

This is plainly due to the fact that, in Jèrriais, the preposition used in this context is *pouor* ('for'). Compare:

(69)   *Il êcrit eune lettre* **pouor** *m'èrmèrcier*

which would be the Jèrriais translation of (68).
    Another common example is the use of the preposition *on* in a phrase such as:

(70)   *That was* **on** *the 'Evening Post'*

where standard English would use the preposition *in*. Again, transference from Jèrriais is clear. Compare:

(71)   *Ch'tait **sus** l' 'Evening Post'*

1. *Object pronouns*

English and Jèrriais differ in terms of the pronouns used to refer to objects. In English, the gender-neutral *it* is used unless the object has an obvious gender, hence:

(72)   ***She**'s a girl*

but

(73)   ***It**'s a dog*

Since all nouns carry a grammatical gender in Jèrriais, the pronoun used to refer to them is also marked for gender. For example, when talking about a chair, which is feminine in Jèrriais, a speaker might say:

(74)   *Est-**alle** grande?*
       'Is it (lit. 'she') big?'

whereas in English *it* would be used in this context.

Under the influence of Jèrriais, a masculine or feminine pronoun may often be used in Jersey English to refer to inanimate objects, hence:

(75)   ***He**'s a Jersey cart*
       (the Jèrriais for 'cart', *hèrnais*, is masculine)

(76)   *Mind that, **she**'s hot, eh!* (i.e. the plate)
       (the Jèrriais for 'plate', *assiette*, is feminine)

8.3.2.2. *Lexis*

a. *Lexical borrowing*

Instances of Jèrriais borrowings in Jersey English are too numerous to list and often occur spontaneously in an *ad hoc* fashion, when a native speaker of Jèrriais is unable to recall the exact English term, for example:

(77)   *Go to the shed and get me the **batchu*** ('whipple-tree')

(78)   *That's the **faûcheuse*** ('mowing machine')

Many of the established Jèrriais borrowings in the English of Jersey are from the vocabulary of administration – *connétabl'ye* ('constable', the municipal head of the parish) – or the land – *vergée* (a unit of measurement).[9] These are also used in conjunction with borrowings from standard French such as *Jurat* (one of twelve members of the Royal Court) and *Greffe* (office of the Clerk to the States). Such borrowings are, therefore, further examples of 'folklore' usage (Dressler 1991: 102–3).

8.3.3. *Concluding remarks*

Although based on casual observation rather than systematic study, the findings in this section reveal that Jèrriais has exerted a strong influence on the English of Jersey, which has served to distinguish it from the varieties spoken on the British mainland. The focus of this book has meant that the only features of Jersey English that have been discussed are those which can be linked to a Jèrriais substrate. However, it is likely that, as Ramisch found in his study of the English spoken on Guernsey (1989: 191–2), Jersey English also contains non-standard features attributable to influence from other varieties of British English, brought to the Island by traders or immigrants. It is hoped to make a comprehensive and systematic survey of the regional English of Jersey the subject of a future study. Such a survey would not only serve to examine the different linguistic influences that characterize the variety but would also furnish data that would allow a detailed comparison to be made with the English of the other Channel Islands.

The findings in this section indicate that many of the non-standard morphosyntactic features noted for Jersey English were also found in the English spoken on Guernsey. On the face of it, this is not surprising, given their common Norman substrate. However, it would be interesting to determine the extent of this similarity and also whether any difference in provenance on the part of immigrants settling in the respective islands has led to a different 'colouring' in each case. In other words, is it appropriate to consider Jersey English as a distinct variety from Guernsey English, or does there exist a relatively homogeneous Channel Island variety?

It would also be desirable to compare the English spoken by Islanders from inside and outside the Jèrriais speech community. This would make it possible to determine the extent to which features originally attributable to the Jèrriais substrate persist even when speakers have no knowledge of the substrate language, and grow up speaking English as their native tongue (cf. Dorian 1997: 209–10 on this phenomenon in East Sutherland English). It would be interesting to establish whether this colouring was affected by age as well as knowledge of Jèrriais and whether younger people, divorced from Jèrriais by several generations, still preserve traces of the dialect in their English.[10]

8.4. The influence of standard French on Jèrriais

8.4.1. *Preliminary remarks*

Although Jersey has not been governed politically by France since 1204, it is not surprising that such a geographically close and economically important neighbour would have exerted some linguistic influence on the Island. As seen in chapter 2, the inhabitants of Jersey have been in contact with standard French for many centuries via trade with mainland France, French immigrants and political refugees. The facts that Jèrriais is a northern French dialect, that much of the Island's toponymy and even the names of the Islanders themselves are French, and that standard French was, until recently, used for all official administration and is still the official language foster strong feelings of allegiance with France among the Islanders. As standard French is taught in all primary schools on the Island (see section 8.2.1.), most natives of Jersey have some knowledge of standard French and traditionally take pride in their francophone heritage.

Despite the fact that they do not use it as an everyday language, most speakers of Jèrriais are reasonably fluent in standard French. Moreover, during the course of the interviews undertaken to obtain data for chapters 6 and 7, it was found that the Jèrriais of several informants showed signs of interference from the standard variety. Although some of this interference occurred unsystematically, the present section illustrates some instances which occurred frequently and in the speech of a number of informants and were therefore felt to warrant further comment.[11] Given that both standard French and Jèrriais are *langue d'oïl* varieties and that, consequently, any features of standard French occurring in a speaker's Jèrriais would be likely to be understood by their interlocutor, the presence of standard French features is not altogether inexplicable. However, the fact that any such interference is occurring in a speaker's L1 is surely indicative of the reduced opportunities available to native speakers to practise the dialect.

8.4.2. *Linguistic features*

8.4.2.1. *Morphosyntax*

a. *The third person plural subject pronoun*

As seen in section 8.2.2.1.b., the third person plural subject pronoun of Jèrriais is *i'* (*il'* before a vowel). It is derived from the Old French plural pronoun *il* (< Latin ĪLLI) which, in standard French, was replaced by *ils* as final -*s* became generalized as a plural marker. Although the form *il'* [il] is frequently heard before a vowel in modern Jèrriais, analysis of the corpus revealed that, in 15 per cent of contexts (82/543 tokens), *i's* [iz] was being used as the prevocalic pronoun. This form is not mentioned in Birt (1985), although DJF (p. 299) does mention that 'certains diront i's ont'.[12] [iz] is clearly a borrowing from standard French, which has the third person plural prevocalic pronoun *ils* [ilz]. In casual speech, this standard French form frequently reduces to [iz].

b. *Other subject pronouns*

The corpus also contained examples of the standard French subject pronouns *on* [ɔ̃] (impersonal), *nous* [nu] (1pl.) and *vous* [vu] (2pl.), which

were substituted for the equivalent Jèrriais forms *nou* [nu], *jé* [ʒə] and *ou* [u].
Although this occurred more often in the speech of some individuals than
others, the substitution was too common to be considered merely as an
idiolectal feature, although neither could it be described as systematic – even
in the speech of a single individual. It is therefore probable that, as in section
8.4.2.1.a. above, the phenomenon also represents a form of lexical borrowing rather than a morphosyntactic change under way in the pronominal
system of Jèrriais and may arise due to confusion regarding formal similarity
between some of the pronouns of Jèrriais and of French, which do, nevertheless, have different functions. For example, the phonetic sequence [nu]
exists in Jèrriais as an impersonal pronoun and in standard French as the
first person plural pronoun.[13] That confusion between these forms already
exists can be seen from the fact that the *nou* which functions as the
impersonal pronoun of Jèrriais has a liaison form in [z] ([nuz]), which
cannot be etymological. It is likely that the common tendency in Jèrriais to
use the impersonal pronoun to refer to the first person plural (as also occurs
in standard French, Price 1993: §302), together with the fact that the
impersonal pronoun is phonetically similar to the standard French first
person plural pronoun, has led to the increase in use of *nou* in this context.[14]
Furthermore, the use of *nou* as a first person plural pronoun may be
precipitating the replacement of *nou* as the Jèrriais impersonal pronoun by
on, the corresponding pronoun of standard French.

   The substitution of standard French *vous* [vu] for Jèrriais *ou* [u] as the
second person plural subject pronoun is probably also due to confusion
arising between an existing form of Jèrriais and a pronoun of standard
French. In Jèrriais, *vous* [vu] functions as the disjunctive form of the second
person plural (*ou* is the conjunctive form). Since *vous* is also the second
person plural subject pronoun of standard French (both conjunctive and
disjunctive), this may be leading to its use being extended to include this
function in Jèrriais. Substitution may also be encouraged by the fact that it
results in an increase in economy, with Jèrriais using the same pronoun for
both conjunctive and disjunctive functions, as opposed to having two
distinct forms.

8.4.2.2. *Lexis*

As mentioned in section 3.2., Jèrriais, like Mainland Norman, has been
subject to both phonetic and lexical influence from standard French for
many centuries. The aim of this section is not to provide a comprehensive list
of all the borrowed forms that occur in modern Jèrriais, as these may easily
be obtained from a perusal of the DJF. Rather, a few examples of some
typical borrowings found in contemporary Jèrriais will be selected and
discussed. All the borrowings mentioned in this section are fully integrated
into Jèrriais and may be considered part of the dialect's vocabulary. These
are, therefore, distinct from words that are borrowed by individuals in an

apparently *ad hoc* fashion, often due to a momentary lapse of memory, and which lead to the appearance of phrases such as:

(79) *I' fîtent* **beaucoup** *d'effort*
'They made a lot of effort'

(80) *J'sis* **très** *heureux*
'I am very happy'

(81) *Ou'tait* **paresseuse**
'She was lazy'

(In each case the standard French term is in bold.)

a. *Numerals*

Like many dialects and regional varieties of French, the numerical system of Jèrriais does not traditionally change from base-ten to base-twenty between seventy and one hundred. Unlike the system of standard French, which has *soixante-dix* (lit. 'sixty-ten' for 'seventy'), *quatre-vingts* (lit. 'four-twenties' for 'eighty') and *quatre-vingt-dix* (lit. 'four-twenties-ten' for 'ninety'), Jèrriais makes use of the base-ten forms *septante* ('seventy'), *huiptante* ('eighty') and *nénante* ('ninety').

However, when the corpus was analysed for the use of *huiptante*, the form was found to occur in only 6 per cent of all possible contexts (fifty-two tokens), with the borrowing *quatre-vingts* used by people from all parishes. The only informants who used the traditional form *huiptante* came from St Ouen – but it was not used by all informants from this parish. It is unclear why the numeral *quatre-vingts* alone should have been borrowed – especially since base-ten *huiptante* mirrors usage in the English counting system. Moreover, the use of *septante* and *nénante* was not found to be affected.

b. *Other borrowings*

(i) In terms of the lexis, nowhere do established borrowings from standard French into Jèrriais abound more than in the field of local administration. This, of course, is due to the fact that, as mentioned in chapter 2 and in section 8.4.1., given its role as Jersey's official language, until recently all legal, fiscal and judicial administrative matters were conducted in standard French. Thus, terms such as the following are commonly found in Jèrriais:

Billet d'Etat (the written records of the proceedings in the States of Jersey)
Député (the representative of a parish)
Senateur (a member of the States legislative body)
Greffe (the office of the clerk to the States)
Jurat (one of twelve members of the Royal Court)
Projet de loi (the draft of a bill brought before the States by one of its committees)

Procès-verbal (the minutes of a meeting)
La Chambre (the Chamber of the States)

(ii) Since all conveyancing and official buying and selling are done in standard French, borrowings are also found in the field of land administration, for example *contrat* ('title deed'). Loan-words also occur in the domain of religion – *abbaye* ('abbey'), *diocèse* ('diocese'), *chapelle* ('chapel'), *evêque* ('bishop'), *liturgie* ('liturgy'), *le Saint Sacrément* ('the Holy Sacrament'), *le jour du Jugement* ('Judgement Day') – and for the names of professions: *journaliste* ('journalist'), *capitaliste* ('capitalist'), *clerc* ('clerk'), *professeur* ('teacher'), *prédicateur* ('preacher'), *gouverneur* ('governor'), *docteur* ('doctor'), *garagiste* ('garage mechanic'). As with the English borrowings discussed in section 6.4.2.1., some of these terms are adopted 'wholesale' and others, such as *secrétaithe* ('secretary'), *êtudgiant* ('student') and *homme d'affaithes* ('business man'), are adapted to the phonotactics of Jèrriais.

c. *Borrowings in 'modern' domains*

As seen in section 7.2.10., the increasing dominance of English on Jersey during the twentieth century has led to it replacing French as the main donor-language for borrowings. Thus, English borrowings far outnumber French ones in domains denoting 'modern' concepts, such as new technology, motor transport and the media. As seen in section 5.5., however, the introduction of Jèrriais in the primary school is leading to some of these being replaced by borrowings from standard French. It remains to be seen whether such language-planning measures will ultimately succeed in reducing the number of English borrowings in 'modern' domains.

8.4.2.3. *Phonetic influence*

The most noticeable phonetic influence of standard French on modern Jèrriais is in the decrease of secondary palatalization of a stop after a front vowel. Not all words containing secondary palatalization are affected – for example, the word *dgèrre* ([dʒɛr]) ('war') was not pronounced [gɛR], as in standard French, in any of the fifty-six instances in which it appeared in the corpus (likewise, *dgiex* ([dʒi]) ('ten') always retained its palatalization (fifty-four tokens), as did *tranchille* [trãtʃil] ('quiet') (twenty-eight tokens) and *tchitter* [tʃite] ('to leave') (thirty-seven tokens)). However, analysis of all tokens in the corpus of the word *êtudgiant* ('student') (pronounced [etʃydʒã] in traditional Jèrriais) yielded sixteen cases (30 per cent) where palatalization was present and thirty-eight cases (70 per cent) where it was absent (fifty-four tokens in total). Similarly, the relative pronoun *tchi* [tʃi] ('whom, which'), with initial palatalization, was extremely uncommon and most informants now used the unpalatalized form *qui* [ki]. Indeed, the only context in which the *tchi* form was still commonly used was in a 'frozen' set expression referring to time, such as *l'année tchi veint* ('next year'). The non-palatalization of this relative pronoun also has repercussions for the form *tch'est tchi* [tʃɛstʃi] (corresponding to the standard French interrogative particle *qu'est-ce que*), which has largely been replaced by *tch'est qué* ([tʃɛskə]) or even *qu'est-ce qué* ([kɛskə]). This widespread decrease in secondary palatalization is mentioned in the DJF, which refers to the 'forte tendance' ('strong tendency') to produce the non-palatalized forms (p. 434).[15]

8.4.3. *Concluding remarks*

This section has demonstrated that although standard French does seem to have exerted some influence on Jèrriais, this influence has been relatively limited and is of a primarily lexical nature, with many of the borrowed terms discussed in section 8.4.2.2. apparently remaining as vestiges of the use of standard French as the official language of Jersey. Moreover, it is possible to suggest that the morphosyntactic and phonetic developments highlighted above may also be attributable to borrowing, although this may not always be the only interpretation.

8.5. CONCLUSION

This chapter has attempted to complete the linguistic portrait of Jersey begun in chapters 6 and 7. It has highlighted the fact that the presence of standard French on the Island has left its mark on Jèrriais, although to a far lesser extent than English (cf. chapters 6 and 7), but that the dialect has also influenced the English and standard French spoken on Jersey and has contributed to the emergence of distinctive regional varieties that are readily distinguishable from those of, respectively, mainland Britain and France. As mentioned above, it would be desirable to extend some of the work begun in this chapter in order to determine whether it is possible to distinguish between both the regional varieties of French and the regional varieties of English spoken on the different Channel Islands. It would also be desirable to show whether these forms can be shown to be largely homogeneous and to compare the varieties of native dialect speakers with those of the indigenous non-dialect-speaking speech communities.

If the future of Jèrriais appears bleak, then what of that of RJF and Jersey English? Hublart is convinced that the future of RFJ remains inextricably linked to that of Jèrriais and that it, like the dialect, is 'en voie de disparition' ('on the road to extinction') (1979: 164). The reason for this is, undoubtedly, the ineluctable encroachment of English, whose growing dominance means that standard French is becoming increasingly irrelevant to the Islanders, despite its status as the Island's official language. Given that the native speakers of Jèrriais are also most likely to be those who constitute its RFJ speech community and are probably those for whom Norman and French culture have most significance, it seems reasonable to assume that the disappearance of the dialect will not be without consequence for the survival of RFJ.

Of course, the fact that standard French is taught in all Jersey's primary schools as a compulsory subject from the age of 7 means that the disappearance of Jèrriais would not herald the total demise of the official language on the Island. However, in the absence of native dialect speakers, it is doubtful whether any French that continued to be spoken on Jersey would bear many of the Jèrriais-influenced characteristics of RFJ. Indeed, if standard French survives the disappearance of Jèrriais on Jersey it will, in all likelihood, become relegated to the position of a foreign language, divorced from any indigenous cultural context – a situation akin to that of standard French in a country such as the United Kingdom. In such circumstances, any remaining presence in the Island's legislature or in its toponymy would amount to little more than ultimately meaningless ceremonial usage.

As for the regional variety of English spoken on Jersey, that the effect of a substrate can persist long after a speech variety itself has ceased to be spoken can be seen as close to home as the United Kingdom, where, in some Anglicized areas, non-standard constructions in the Regional English of Wales, Ireland and Scotland remain as the only vestiges of their Celtic past, for example:

(82)   *He's under the doctor* (Welsh English)
       (cf. standard English 'He's in the care of the doctor')

(83)   *She's after telling him the news* (Irish English; Bliss 1984: 147)
       (cf. standard English 'She has told him the news')

(84)   *I'm a widower for six years* (Scottish English; Shuken 1984: 155)
       (cf. standard English 'I have been a widower for six years')

Although, unlike that of standard French, the future of English on Jersey is assured, it remains to be seen whether Jersey English will be preserved by the Island's inhabitants as a mark of identity, serving to distinguish them from the remainder of the British Isles (cf. Appel and Muysken 1993: 132–3).[16]

9

CONCLUSION

The aim of this study has been to give a comprehensive account of the situation of Jèrriais at the beginning of the twenty-first century. To this end, the study has examined both internal features of the dialect and its external sociolinguistic situation, thereby complying with Devitt's claim that 'Any historical study should consider the social context of a linguistic change' (1989: 8).

After centuries of being spoken throughout Jersey, Jèrriais is now under-going territorial contraction and speaker reduction characteristic of language obsolescence. Its internal structure is also displaying a considerable amount of linguistic change, which, in this context, may be considered as a further manifestation of the same phenomenon. However, as mentioned in the introduction, the sociolinguistic history of Jèrriais differs from that of many documented case studies of obsolescent languages in that, rather than decreasing gradually from one generation to the next, the decline in speaker numbers has taken place over a relatively short time span. In 1989, 45 per cent of self-declared speakers of Jèrriais were aged 65 and over. This percentage remains more or less constant (44 per cent) for the next youngest age-group (those aged between 40 and 64). However, when the statistics for the two youngest age-groups are examined, we see that, of all the speakers of Jèrriais living on Jersey in 1989, only 10 per cent were aged between 15 and 39 and under 1 per cent were less than 15 years old. This makes the linguistic 'tip' (Dorian 1981: 51) quite easily locatable as the late 1940s and early 1950s: in other words, the decade immediately following the Second World War, when, as discussed in the introduction, the considerable and atypical amount of population movement had serious repercussions for the dialect. This corroborates the remarks made in the same chapter about the case of Jèrriais representing a mixture of both gradual and radical death (Campbell and Muntzel 1989: 183–4).

As radical death is a relatively little documented sub-type of language death, the unique sociopolitical circumstances of Jèrriais make it of particular interest to the field. Moreover, unlike radical death 'proper', on Jersey political repression is only indirectly responsible for the loss of the variety. Unlike in El Salvador, where repression made people stop using their native tongue through fear for their lives, on Jersey, although the German Occupa-tion had the by-product of increasing the use of Jèrriais on the Island due to the practice of exclusionary speaking, it also drove away a considerable proportion of the native speech community, who subsequently either lost the habit of speaking Jèrriais or returned to the Island with the desire to promote a new self-image in which there was little room for their native tongue.

It would, however, be mistaken to attribute any language shift on Jersey solely to the German Occupation. As shown in chapter 2, the presence of English on the Island had increased steadily since the nineteenth century and, even if the Occupation had not taken place, it is probable that, by today, there would remain few, if any, monoglot speakers of the dialect and that numbers of bilingual speakers would have diminished, albeit maybe less dramatically. Although in some cases, such as Tasmania, it is possible to isolate one reason as the cause of language shift, this is usually the exception rather than the rule and, in practice, the phenomenon is caused by a plethora of interrelated and interacting factors. Giles, Bourhis and Taylor (1977: 308–18) distinguish three main categories of such factors which can, ultimately, have some bearing on whether or not a variety will continue to be used in a community, namely status, demographic factors and institutional support. These will now be discussed in relation to Jèrriais.

As mentioned in chapter 5, economic status is a powerful incentive to use a speech-variety. From the nineteenth century especially, the importance of commercial links with mainland Britain caused many of Jersey's traders to be disadvantaged if they had no knowledge of English, whereas knowledge of Jèrriais could offer no such advantages. This was exacerbated by the growth in the tourist and finance industries. Its greater economic clout also gave English more social status within the community, and its perceived superiority vis-à-vis Jèrriais is reflected in the fact that borrowing between the two varieties is mostly unidirectional (English to Jèrriais) (cf. section 6.4.2.1.). As a world language, English also has high status outside Jersey and its acquisition is both desirable and necessary for most international communication. English therefore enjoys a high reputation world-wide whereas, by comparison, Jèrriais, when it is known at all, is seen as no more than a little-spoken Norman dialect, with no relevance outside the Island.

As seen in Eire, granting a variety official status in no way guarantees its survival, but the prestige associated with such status considerably enhances a variety's standing both inside and outside the speech community. Although, in practice, this may have no tangible linguistic effect on the variety in question, psychologically, the difference is huge: people will be ready to support a variety which they perceive to be a symbol of the State but are less likely to attach importance to the maintenance of a patois. Undoubtedly, part of the reason for the decline of Jèrriais is that throughout the two thousand or so years that a form of Romance has been spoken on Jersey, it has never been recognized as an official variety. English and French have exerted varying degrees of influence with respect to one another, but with Jèrriais almost always at the bottom of the linguistic heap. Giving Jèrriais an official status would enhance its position not only in the eyes of its speakers but, crucially, also in those of the dominant speech community. Even though they may not speak Jèrriais themselves, the attitude of this group will inevitably have a bearing on the fate of the dialect, since the very fact that non-Jèrriais speakers represent at least 93 per cent of the current population of Jersey means that, in practice, their consent must necessarily be attained before any large-scale financial support may be obtained from the States. The non-Jèrriais speakers are unlikely to accede to substantial financial support being given to a group with which they have no links and, at worst, from which they feel alienated. There is, therefore, need for the revitalizers to conceive of their movement on an Island-wide basis.

The future of English as Jersey's dominant variety now seems assured. Standard French may continue to be used for ceremonial purposes but, with hardly any native speakers resident on the Island and no one calling for its retention, it seems destined to become, if it is not already, no more than a widely taught foreign language, with a status on a par with that which it currently enjoys in a country such as the United Kingdom.

Turning now to consider demographic factors, on a world-wide scale, there is clearly no comparison between speaker numbers of Jèrriais and of English. However, in recent decades, numerical superiority has increasingly been on the side of English even within the Island itself. The gradually reducing size of the Jèrriais speech community and the growth of its English counterpart undoubtedly facilitate the influence of the latter on the former (cf. Hovdhaugen 1992). Once the English population becomes sufficiently large to penetrate communities where the dialect is spoken widely, the established communication patterns of these communities will become disrupted and, instead of being used as the 'default' variety of daily interaction with friends and neighbours, Jèrriais will be used only in contexts from which English speakers are completely absent.

The third category, institutional support, has, until very recently, been entirely lacking in the context of Jèrriais. As seen in chapter 2, the dialect had never been used in any H-type domains, hence its concomitant lowly status, and, moreover, for many years, speaking it was a punishable offence at school. Thus, not only was Jèrriais not given institutional support but institutions were actively engaged in discouraging its use.

Although some of these intertwining factors may prove more influential than others, it is clear that they all contribute cumulatively to the process of obsolescence. Ultimately, though, for a speech community to give up its language and to adopt that of another there must also exist some desire to become integrated with the latter. In the case of Jèrriais, the aforementioned considerations were coupled to the fact that, since 1204, Jersey had been united politically with Great Britain, which had made France the enemy. To the inhabitants of the Island, therefore, English did not merely represent some arbitrary foreign language: it had already been a focus of their political loyalties for many centuries and, just as the Hundred Years War contributed to the demise of Norman French on the British mainland, centuries of allegiance with England – much of it against France – were bound to leave their mark on the Channel Islands. After the Second World War especially, there must have been a strong desire to identify with the 'winning side', the liberators, as opposed to the liberated. These reasons, coupled with those outlined above, all led speakers of Jèrriais to consider English as a more viable variety than their own native tongue. It is therefore likely that, even without the Occupation, which, as it turned out, was to be a rather large nail in its coffin, Jèrriais would today still be treading the path of obsolescence.

Just as the sociolinguistic situation of Jèrriais departs from the more conventional language-death scenario, so too are differences to be found vis-à-vis other documented cases of language death in terms of its internal structure. Although both lexical borrowing and simplification are often found in 'healthy' languages as well as obsolescent ones – indeed, it was shown that similar developments have been attested in both regional and low-register French – and in spite of the fact that the sheer amount of change under way made the Jèrriais situation more characteristic of an obsolescent than a 'healthy' language, it was significant that, for the most part, the developments observed were less advanced than those noted in other varieties undergoing the same phenomenon (Jones 1998a). Jèrriais may be obsolescent but, in chapter 6, it was seen that many of its linguistic features are still relatively intact (cf. Dorian 1978b).

It is, of course, interesting that the dialect should be changing at all in the mouths of its native speakers, who might be thought to maintain a constant level of proficiency throughout their adult lives. In fact, the data obtained from Jersey support the findings made in the case of other obsolescent languages, namely that, in such circumstances, L1 speakers may gradually move away from the conservative norm (Dorian 1997: 225), hence their designation as 'rusty speakers' in the language-obsolescence literature (Sasse 1992b: 61). This is probably attributable to the fact that merely passive familiarity with a historically inappropriate feature can increase the likelihood of its use, even among highly proficient speakers (Thomason 1997: 198). Such 'deviant' features may have their origins in the (involuntary) accommodation of fluent speakers to the speech of semi-speakers, but can also arise through a process which Thomason labels negotiation (1997: 199), whereby, in the interests of facilitating communication, incomplete bilinguals may change their own pattern of speech to approximate that which they perceive as the patterns of another language. Should such features subsequently become ingrained in the speech of bilingual L1 speakers of Jèrriais who do not, however, use the dialect on a daily basis, it is not inconceivable that they might get passed on to following generations. An alternative explanation, of course, is that, as English comes to dominate on Jersey, lack of opportunity to speak Jèrriais may lead to precisely this type of bilingual speaker being faced with, to quote Sharwood Smith and Van Buren again, insufficient 'confirming evidence' of the nature of the L1 (1991: 23). It is possible to argue that, in the face of such a situation, an L1 speaker may resort to L2 rules in order to confirm the grammaticality of an utterance via what Seliger calls 'indirect positive evidence' (1991: 231).

The fact that very little levelling is occurring among the *parlers* of contemporary Jèrriais further confirms the remarks made above about the dialect dying 'intact'. As all the *parlers* are by-and-large mutually intelligible, there is no need for an interdialect form to exist for purposes of inter-regional communication (this function is, in any case, already fulfilled by English). Moreover, as suggested in section 6.5., it is also likely that such differences are being preserved due to the changed pattern of socialization in Jèrriais, with kinship ties, which, by definition, tend to be situated in one's own locality, coming to predominate over inter-village interaction.

Although it is impossible to predict how long Jèrriais will survive, the extensive regional variation currently witnessed on Jersey is almost certain to disappear in the not-too-distant future. As demonstrated in chapter 6, despite the paucity of speakers that exists for certain *parlers*, this variation is, at present, still reasonably intact. Moreover, given the fact that the 1989 Census figures show native speakers of comparable ages to be distributed throughout the Island, regional variation will undoubtedly survive for their lifetimes. However, it seems likely that, with their demise, this variation will disappear more or less simultaneously from all parts of Jersey, persisting a few years longer, perhaps, in parishes such as St Ouen, Ste Marie, St Jean and Trinité, where, according to the 1989 Census, the highest concentrations of speakers are to be found (see table 3.2). As discussed in chapter 5, even if Jèrriais underwent a complete reversal of fortunes via recent initiatives in the education system – a scenario which, at present, seems very unlikely – and began to acquire new fluent speakers, given that, for practical and financial reasons, one variety must predominate in the classroom, it seems that the only *parler* with even the most tentative chance of survival must be St Ouennais. Whether even this variety survives at all, and for how long, must, however, remain a matter for speculation – after all, as mentioned above, there is no guarantee that even a variety such as Irish will survive, despite being made an official language in Eire and being given both extensive financial and institutional backing from the Irish state. Further-more, there is no guarantee that any surviving St Ouennais variety would remain identifiable with its present form. As seen in chapter 5, Bentahila and Davies (1993) point out that revitalization is more likely to transform varieties than restore them to their old selves, and insufficient support is being given to the schools to enable a substantial cohort of new reasonably fluent speakers to grow up and use Jèrriais while there are enough native speakers still alive to communicate with, a situation also seen in contem-porary Brittany (Jones 1998a: ch. 5). In all likelihood, even if, against all odds, it survives that long, any Jèrriais spoken in the late twenty-first century would be a xenolect, a slightly foreignized variety spoken natively (Holm

1988: 10).[1] In the absence of native-speaker monitoring, it is inevitable that L2 speakers would carry some syntactic influence from English into their Jèrriais. This phenomenon has been witnessed in many situations of L2 learning (Harley, Cummins, Swain and Allen 1990: 19–21; Maguire 1991: 218–28). Whereas attempts to eliminate this influence often involve learners spending time in immersion contexts, where contact with native speakers is intended to lessen the presence of L1 influence (Maguire 1991: 45; McDonald 1989: 168–71), this course of action could not prove possible in the case of Jèrriais unless a new generation of reasonably fluent speakers was produced before the death of the last native speakers, who, as mentioned in section 6.5., are already at least middle-aged. As all languages develop over time, there is nothing intrinsically problematic about an English-influenced Jèrriais being the variety that survives. Nevertheless, given the reluctance of the States of Jersey to back revitalization measures while Jèrriais is still spoken natively in some households, where it still represents the 'default' variety, it is highly unlikely that any support would be given to a variety which no longer represented a reality of Island life.

At present, there is still a point to learning Jèrriais. However, unless transmission is restored before the demise of the last native speaker Jèrriais will, in the not-too-distant future, be facing a situation where, as in Cornwall, all its speakers are L2 learners who are already fluent in English. At this point, practical reasons for speaking the dialect will be replaced by symbolic ones. From the point of view of communication, there will be no need for the dialect to exist. The only hope for Jèrriais is if it can survive as a symbol of Island identity, for this is one function that English cannot perform. The problem is that this function is not as easily promoted on Jersey as in other such contexts, since, as the result of immigration, 47.3 per cent (in 1996) of the Island's total resident population were born outside Jersey and so, for the most part, presumably have no particular allegiance with the Island in terms of identity. For these reasons, therefore, the role of economic motivation for language learning of the kind mentioned in chapter 5 becomes increasingly important.

Although very little action was taken in support of Jèrriais for many decades after the decline of the dialect was recognized, the past few years have witnessed a number of language-planning initiatives, which are detailed in chapter 5. As a semi-independent country, all control of language decisions rests with the States of Jersey. At the moment, the main problem in the area of language planning is one of motivation – the revitalizers need to convince their representatives that Jèrriais is worth supporting and, for the reasons given in chapter 5, any support forthcoming must be of a financial nature. Moreover, although a standard form of Jèrriais is now readily available to all who wish to use it, its mere existence does not in any way guarantee that it will be used. At present, the only real access to the standard variety, other than by autodidactic means, is via evening classes for adult learners or the weekly extra-curricular lessons given to some primary school pupils. Consequently, it is extremely unlikely that the standard variety will be used by native speakers from parishes other than St Ouen, whose *parler* is virtually synonymous with standard Jèrriais. Certainly, there is no question yet of standard Jèrriais being used alongside a speaker's native *parler* in a diglossic relationship.

It is, nevertheless, true to say that the language-planning measures described in chapter 5 have had the net effect of reducing the state of diglossia that had hitherto existed in the community between Jèrriais and English. However, as discussed in that chapter, in fact, the situation of Jèrriais sounds better on paper than it is in practice. This is well exemplified by considering the case of the education system. Admittedly, the presence of Jèrriais in the Island's primary schools represents a major breakthrough for the revitalizers, but the fact remains that current provision is far from anything like sufficient to ensure the dialect's survival. To be sure, the Manx revival started from a far worse position than Jèrriais in that there remained no native speakers, but the greater amount of resources allocated to the maintenance of Manx has meant that it has been possible to engage full-time teachers, which has allowed tuition to be provided on a more frequent basis and for a greater number of pupils in both the secondary and primary sectors,[2] and has enabled the formal lessons to be supplemented with extra-curricular activities such as Manx-speaking weekends (Stowell 1996: 217). Moreover, even with such relatively enhanced provision, Stowell still describes the position of Manx as 'precarious' (1996: 215).

Although L2 classes that use L1 as the medium of instruction may be successful in imparting a considerable amount of knowledge of the L2 to their target audiences, it is necessary to question their usefulness in the context of revitalization. Jacobs (1998) describes how even fifteen minutes of Mohawk language instruction per day (i.e. more than double the time currently received by pupils on Jersey – and on a far more regular basis) was found to be unsatisfactory, and states that, in practice, immersion schooling backed up by active parental participation in attendant activities represented the only realistic way that children could be taught to communicate in Mohawk. The mere fact that in the United Kingdom (and on Jersey) children who study a foreign language up to school-leaving standard are not expected to be fluent shows how unrealistic it is to pin any hopes for revitalization on the current provision for Jèrriais at primary level.

It is also worth pausing to consider the position of Jèrriais in the media. Although provision has recently increased by a few minutes each week, this still remains insufficient to contribute meaningfully to the creation of a Jèrriais climate in the community, and, in the case of television broadcasting, it is nothing more than derisory. Admittedly, the lobbying undertaken in this area by the revitalizers has had some success (see section 5.3.2.); however, such a course of action has finite limitations beyond which there is need for the kind of financial backing that only the States can offer.

Although, then, in terms of prestige, the introduction of Jèrriais into 'new' domains may be seen as a positive step forward for the dialect, in practice, Jèrriais is entering these domains in only an extremely measured way. Moreover, the dialect's presence in each of these domains seems, to all intents and purposes, to be operating in isolation: at present, at least, one domain is not reinforcing another. An obvious example of this may be seen in the lack of interface between the domains of media and education. Given the proven ability of the media to reinforce work undertaken in the classroom, it would seem desirable for the Jèrriais presence on the radio to take account of this new potential audience. At present, however, no such strategy has been adopted. Enhanced social prestige is not, finally, sufficient to stem erosion (Puga 1996: 65), and it is very often a variety's entrenchment rather than its prestige which, ultimately, accounts for its maintenance (Cobarrubias 1983: 55): indeed, in the long run, this may even prove to be of more importance to the future of a variety than are numbers of speakers. The importance of community-based socialization in the acquired language is beyond question, and increasing the opportunity for learners to use Jèrriais outside the classroom would also bring native speakers into the heart of the revitalization campaign, giving them a role which they are best equipped to fulfil (Spolsky 1989: 91). In fact, unless these individuals have received specialist training in methods of second-language teaching, this socialization role may often prove to be more valuable than any formal pedagogical function they can fulfil in the classroom, for, as Dauenhauer and Dauenhauer discuss, native fluency alone does not make someone proficient to teach a variety as a second language (1998: 84).

Despite the efforts of the revitalizers, therefore, it is clear that the survival of Jèrriais is by no means assured. Nevertheless, the movement may draw some comfort from the fact that, even if Jèrriais ceases to be spoken in the near future, its presence will continue on Jersey via the imprint it has left on the other languages spoken on the Island as a result of centuries of contact.

To take the case of French first, Brasseur (1977) argues that, in terms of the lexis, the influence of the Norman dialects is so marked in the French spoken by the inhabitants of the Channel Islands that it may even be possible to claim the existence of a variety of regional French peculiar to the archipelago. Nevertheless, although, as was seen in chapter 8, the variety of French recorded by Hublart (1979) on Jersey contains the unequivocal hallmark of Jèrriais, it seems desirable to resist describing it as a type of regional French. Although the origins of both varieties are undoubtedly similar – with dialect speakers who were acquiring standard French, usually at school, transferring into it elements of their native variety, a situation often seen in such contexts (Hamers and Blanc 1989: 22) – in the case of the regional French of France, the resulting variety was usually passed to the next generation via the transmission chain, especially after the local dialect became less frequently used as the normal means of communication within that community. However, the diffusion of French on Jersey forms part of a completely different process. By the twentieth century (the period in which Hublart's informants grew up), the first contact most children had with standard French was via the education system, where it was then, as now, learnt as a foreign language.[3] Although contact with French tourists and Jersey's proximity to France undoubtedly made French a useful language to speak, it was never passed on to one's offspring and consequently was – and still is – generally relearnt at school by each new generation. To speak, therefore, of the existence of a regional variety of French particular to Jersey would be somewhat misleading. Although individuals who had Jèrriais as their native tongue were all likely to carry into it similar L1 features, with the result that the variety of French they spoke was, in all probability, similar, and may even have been regionally identifiable, it was not a regional variety of French in the sense that the term is used today in studies such as that of Wolf (1993).

It is the influence of Jèrriais on the English spoken on Jersey that has resulted in the production of a true regional variety. As discussed in section 8.3.1., although not all the features described are necessarily present in the speech of all the Island's inhabitants, it is clear that they probably arose in the speech of bilinguals using Jèrriais on a daily basis due to interlingual interference. As English has become increasingly dominant on the Island, such features may even be found in the speech of monolingual speakers of English whose families are native to Jersey.[4,5] Moreover, it was seen in section 8.3. that, by drawing on studies such as Ramisch (1989) and Barbé (1995), it is possible to establish that many of the Norman-influenced features noted in the English of Jersey are also to be found in the variety of English spoken on Guernsey. Although, as Ramisch has pointed out, the linguistic features characterizing Guernsey English are not all exclusively due to the Norman substrate (1989: 191–7), it appears that enough common developments can be found in the English of these two islands to posit the existence of a Channel Island variety of English.

An investigation of the different varieties of English spoken in the Channel Islands represents a fruitful avenue for further enquiry. In the first instance, it would be interesting to examine the features of Jersey English which are not attributable to the Jèrriais substrate, and to determine their similarity, or otherwise, to the non-Norman-influenced features found in the English of Guernsey. This would allow us to determine whether any 'superordinate' pan-Channel Islands variety of English that might exist was, in fact, more homo- or heterogeneous than suggested in section 8.3. Moreover, it would be interesting to establish whether, in practice, it would be more appropriate to consider this posited pan-Channel Islands English not as a spoken variety but, rather, as a 'common core' of features attributable to Norman influence which is to be found in the English of all the Islands and which may be 'transformed' into the Regional English of a specific Island by the addition of certain other features peculiar to that Island. For such a hypothesis to be explored, it would also be necessary to study the English spoken on Sark and Alderney, varieties which, in addition to providing evidence in support of or against the existence of the proposed pan-Channel Islands English, would make worthy objects of study in their own right. In the first place, it would be interesting to see whether the fact that Sark was colonized by people from Jersey has made Sark English similar to the English of Jersey, or whether the geographical proximity of Guernsey to Sark has acted as a counter-influence here. Moreover, the case of Alderney may offer a glimpse into future developments on the other Islands. As seen in section 3.2., Auregnais, the Norman dialect of Alderney, is now extinct. It would therefore be interesting to see whether traces of its influence are still to be found in the English of Alderney, or whether the fact that the dialect has already been lost for many decades, coupled with the subsequent influx of immigrants born outside the Island, has resulted in the disappearance of any variety bearing identifiable hallmarks of Channel Islands English.

The fate of Alderney English may give some indication as to the future of the Regional English of Jersey. At present, we can do little more than speculate that it is unlikely that people born outside the Island would adopt what is widely perceived to be a substandard speech form. Moreover, evidence from Guernsey also suggests that the Norman French colouring of the English spoken on the Channel Islands may not survive by much the loss of the local dialect, even in the mouths of the native inhabitants, since Ramisch's survey found that the presence of some features of Guernsey English differed markedly between the speech of Guernésiais speakers and younger monolingual speakers of English who were indigenous to the Island and who had lived there all their lives.[6] This does not mean that the varieties of English spoken on the different Channel Islands will necessarily lose their distinctive regional character, but it does suggest that the Norman substrate might no longer have a major part in their formation.

If a regional variety of a language is indeed describable as 'ce qui reste du dialecte quand le dialecte a disparu'[7] (Tuaillon 1974: 576), then, if things continue as present, the definitive departure of Jèrriais from Jersey will occur not with the death of the dialect but, rather, via the elimination of Norman influence from the variety of Regional English spoken on the Island. It may be, however, that the revitalization campaign will provoke a change in the expected outcome, for the complete reversal of language shift on Jersey via the language-planning measures described in chapter 5, though extremely unlikely at present, would, in all probability, produce a cohort of new (bilingual) fluent speakers of Jèrriais whose English revealed little trace of the dialect. Such are the vagaries of language death.

APPENDIX 1 LIST OF INFORMANTS ACCORDING TO PARISH OF ORIGIN

St Ouen
O1   F; 70+
O2   M; 70+
O3   M; 40–59
O4   M; 60–9
O5   M; 40–59
O6   M; 60–9
O7   M; 60–9
O8   M; 40–59
O9   M; 70+
O10   F; 20–39
O11   M; 40–59
O12   M; 40–59

St Jean
J1   F; 40–59
J2   F; 70+
J3   M; 70+
J4   M; 40–59
J5   M; 40–59
J6   F; 60–9

St Martin
Mt1   M; 70+
Mt2   F; 40–59
Mt3   M; 60–9
Mt4   M; 40–59
Mt5   F; 70+
Mt6   F; 60–9
Mt7   M; 60–9
Mt8   M; 70+

Trinité
T1   F; 70+
T2   M; 70+
T3   M; 70+
T4   F; 60–9
T5   M; 70+
T6   F; 60–9
T7   M; 60–9
T8   F; 40–59
T9   M; 60–9
T10   F; 70+

Ste Marie
Ma1   M; 60–9
Ma2   M; 60–9
Ma3   F; 60–9
Ma4   F; 70+

St Laurent
L1   F; 70+
L2   M; 60–9
L3   F; 70+
L4   F; 70+
L5   F; 60–9
L6   M; 60–9
L7   M; 40–59

Grouville
G1   M; 70+

St Hélier
H1   M; 60–9

St Brélade
B1   F; 70+

APPENDIX 2 FIGURES ILLUSTRATING RESULTS DISCUSSED IN CHAPTER 7

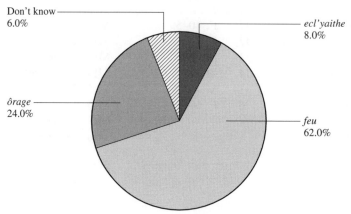

Figure 7.1 'Lightning'

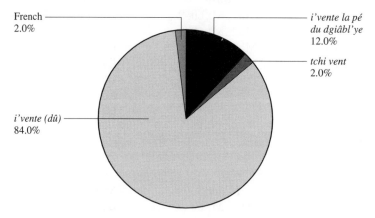

Figure 7.2 'It's exceedingly windy'

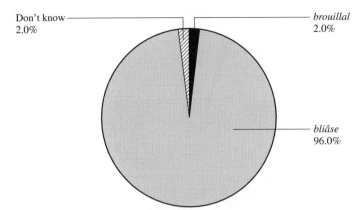

Figure 7.3 'Fog'

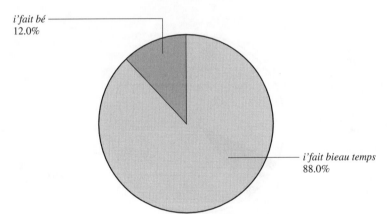

Figure 7.4 'The weather is fine'

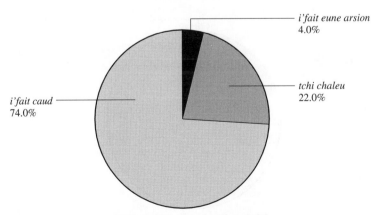

Figure 7.5 'It's boiling hot'

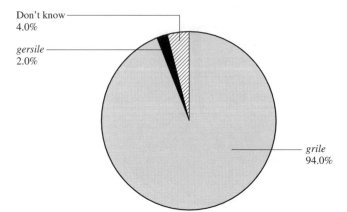

Figure 7.6 'Hail'

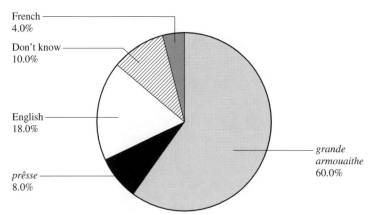

Figure 7.7 'Wardrobe'

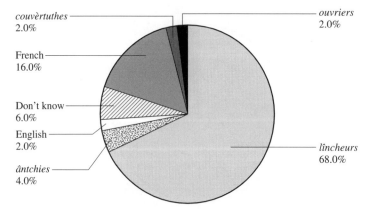

Figure 7.8 'Bedsheets'

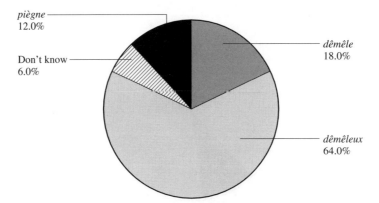

Figure 7.9 'Comb'

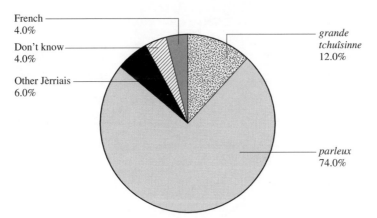

Figure 7.10 'Living room'

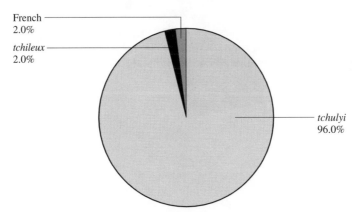

Figure 7.11 'Spoon'

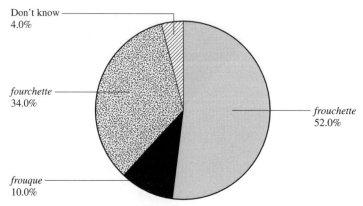

Figure 7.12 'Fork'

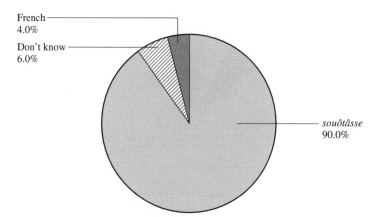

Figure 7.13 'Saucer'

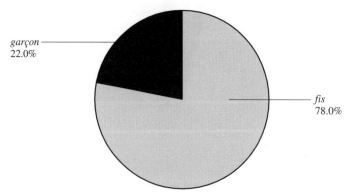

Figure 7.14 'Son'

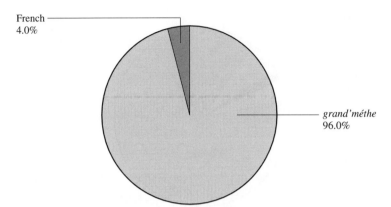

Figure 7.15 'Grandmother'

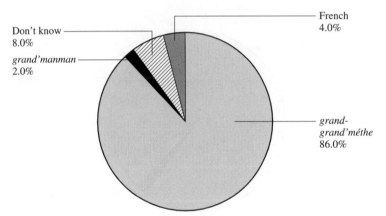

Figure 7.16 'Great-grandmother'

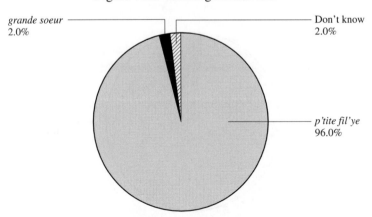

Figure 7.17 'Granddaughter'

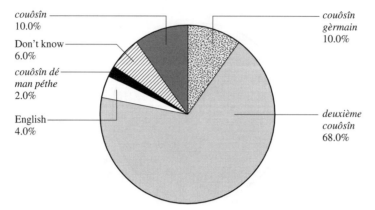

Figure 7.18 'Second cousin'

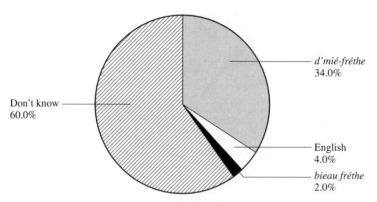

Figure 7.19 'Stepbrother'

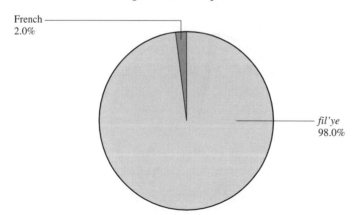

Figure 7.20 'Daughter'

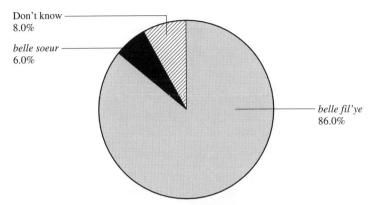

Figure 7.21 'Daughter-in-law'

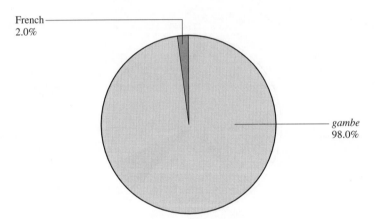

Figure 7.22 'Leg'

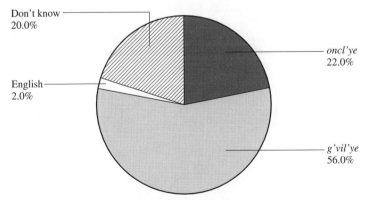

Figure 7.23 'Ankle'

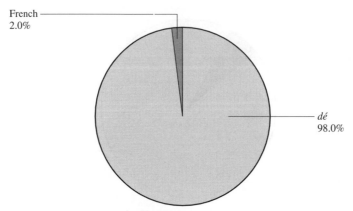

Figure 7.24 'Finger'

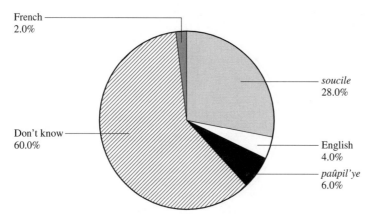

Figure 7.25 'Eyebrow'

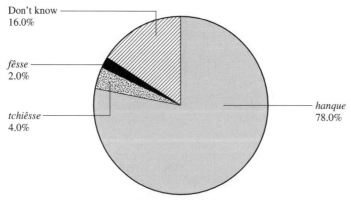

Figure 7.26 'Hip'

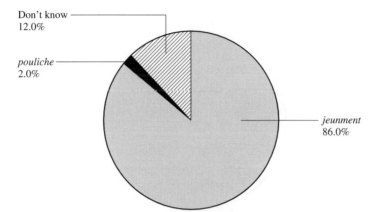

Don't know
12.0%

pouliche
2.0%

jeunment
86.0%

Figure 7.27 'Mare'

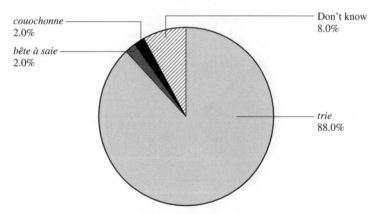

couochonne
2.0%

bête à saie
2.0%

Don't know
8.0%

trie
88.0%

Figure 7.28 'Sow'

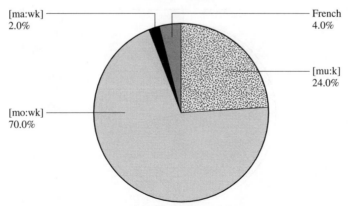

[ma:wk]
2.0%

French
4.0%

[mu:k]
24.0%

[mo:wk]
70.0%

Figure 7.29 'Housefly'

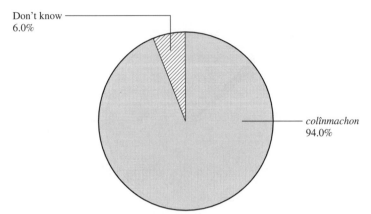

Figure 7.30 'Snail'

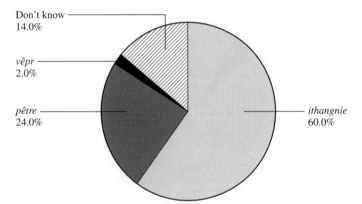

Figure 7.31 'Spider'

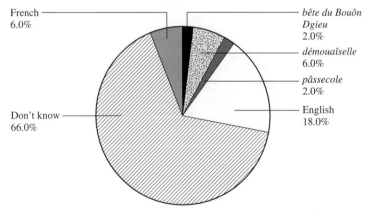

Figure 7.32 'Ladybird'

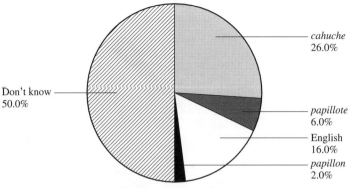

Figure 7.33 'Moth'

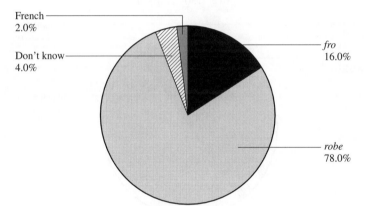

Figure 7.34 'Dress'

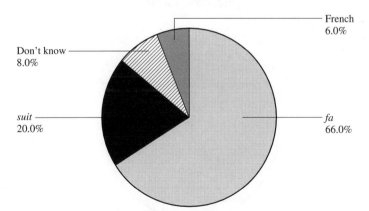

Figure 7.35 'Suit'

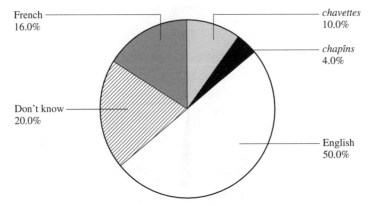

Figure 7.36 'Slippers'

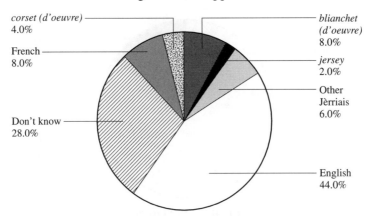

Figure 7.37 'Cardigan'

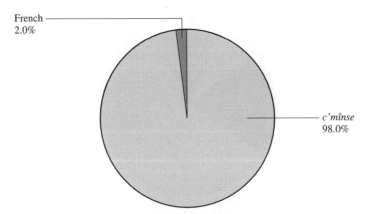

Figure 7.38 'Shirt'

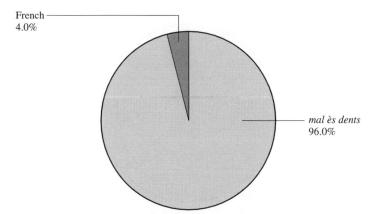

Figure 7.39 'Toothache'

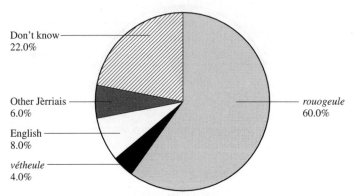

Figure 7.40 'Measles'

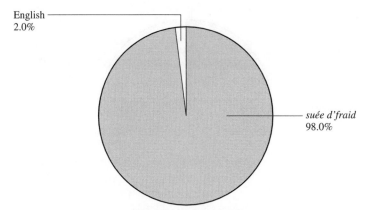

Figure 7.41 'A cold'

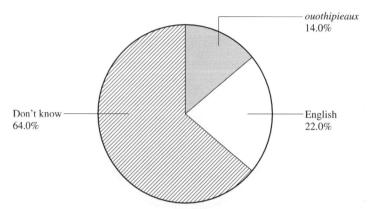

Figure 7.42 'Mumps'

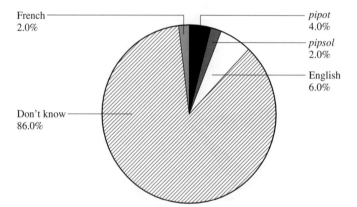

Figure 7.43 'Buttercup'

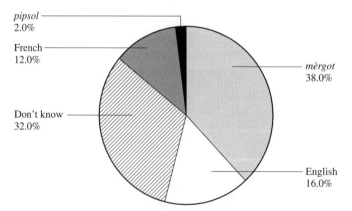

Figure 7.44 'Daisy'

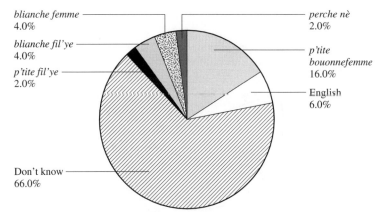

Figure 7.45 'Snowdrop'

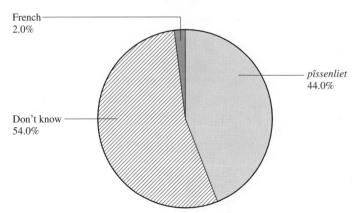

Figure 7.46 'Dandelion'

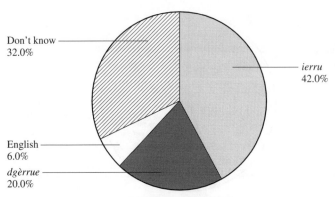

Figure 7.47 'Ivy'

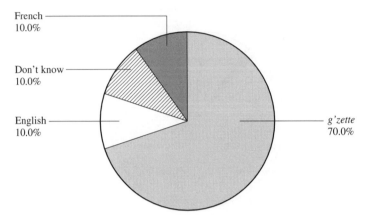

Figure 7.48 'Daffodil'

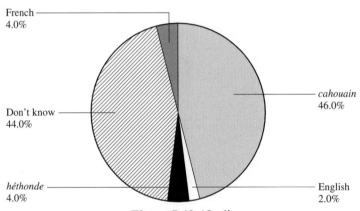

Figure 7.49 'Owl'

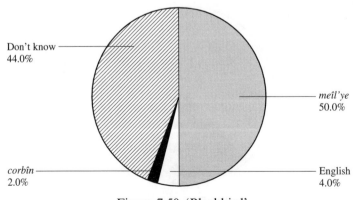

Figure 7.50 'Blackbird'

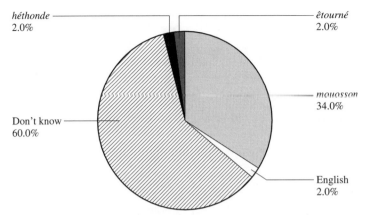

Figure 7.51 'Sparrow'

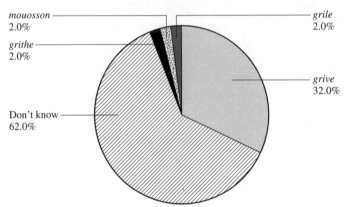

Figure 7.52 'Thrush'

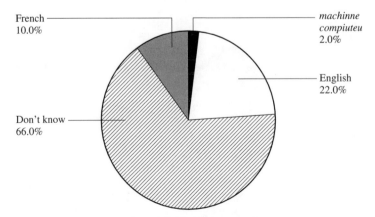

Figure 7.53 'Computer'

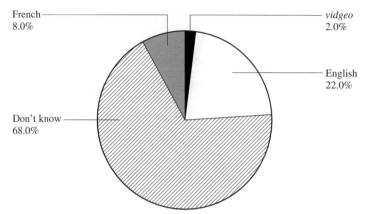

Figure 7.54 'Video'

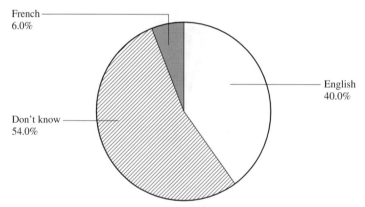

Figure 7.55 'Television'

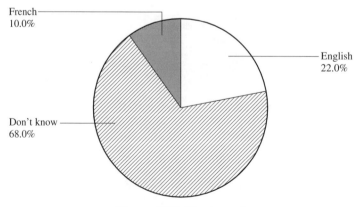

Figure 7.56 'Projector'

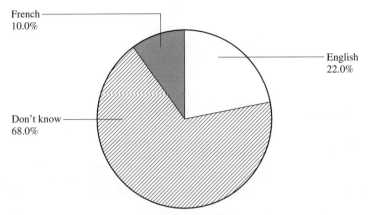

Figure 7.57 'CD'

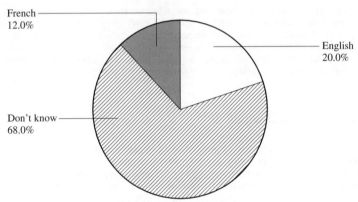

Figure 7.58 'Spaceship'

NOTES

1 Introduction

1 An exception to this is classical Arabic, which, although no longer spoken, acts as a unifying force within the Islamic world.

2 Point (vi) of Bauman's classification seems to be somewhat open to question. Yiddish, for example, is clearly obsolescent despite having a tradition of widespread literacy, and other endangered languages, such as Irish, Scots Gaelic and Nahuatl, have long literary traditions.

3 Tucano has only 4,500 speakers but is not deemed to be obsolescent (Aikhenvald 1996: 81).

4 It is, however, increasingly apparent that there do not seem to exist any 'typical' language-death scenarios.

5 Campbell and Muntzel note, however, that this case study does not constitute a perfect illustration of bottom-to-top death as a limited proficiency continuum was found here, making the situation reminiscent of the more common gradual death (1989: 186).

6 As mentioned above, in this context the term 'language death' is intended as a reflection of the territorial contraction and speaker reduction of Jèrriais rather than as a prediction of the ultimate fate of this variety.

2 The sociohistorical setting

1 The 1996 Census of Jersey put its total resident population at 85,150.

2 It has been claimed on the basis of the Antoine Itinerary (c.284), which lists the islands in the sea between Gaul and Britain, that the Romans gave Jersey the name Caesarea. However, it is also possible that the name may refer to one of the Scilly Isles.

3 For an accessible account of the Norse element in Jèrriais, see Spence (1993: 17–18).

4 This occurred during the reigns of William I, Henry I, Henry II, Richard I and, briefly, King John.

5 'I say and will say again that I am Wace, from the Isle of Jersey.'

6 However, the additional supra-regional characteristics present in these texts make it impossible to claim that what Wace was writing was Jèrriais.

7 This is, clearly, a rather simplistic account of the demise of Norman French from the British mainland. For a more detailed account, see Baugh and Cable (1993: chapter 6).

8 Three years later, this was altered to the diocese of Winchester.

9 The Prayer Book of 1552 was also translated into French and sent to Jersey in the spring of 1553. However, with the succession of the Catholic queen Mary I after the death of Edward VI, Latin services were restored in Jersey, although the Island did not convert to Catholicism. With the succession of Elizabeth I, Protestantism was restored in Britain but, for linguistic convenience, the Channel Islands adopted the model favoured by the French Huguenots (Calvinism) rather than embracing the episcopal model of the Church of England, with the queen as its head.

10 The names of the parishes of Jersey have been given in French throughout. This has been done in order to highlight the francophone nature of Jersey's toponymy. For ease of comprehension by non-speakers of the dialect, the Jèrriais spelling has not been used.

11 The first of these was *Le Magasin de l'Île de Jersey* (October 1784), published by Mathieu Alexandre, who, in the same year, started a weekly *Gazette de l'Île de Jersey* (Hublart 1979: 38).

12 L'Estourbeillon de la Garnache (1886) states that as many as 3,000 priests came to Jersey during this period.
13 In the nineteenth century, there were further emigrations of French people to Jersey, as politicians, revolutionairies and exiles alike came as refugees after the 1851 coup d'état of Louis Napoléon.
14 'It is from this period, after 1815, that the English language started to become more widespread and to be spoken regularly in the Islands, a state of affairs that had not existed until then.'
15 In 1794, a regular postal service between the Channel Islands and Weymouth had also been established (Lemprière 1974: 135–6).
16 'Times change; after having been a source of prosperity for the archipelago, steam ships could also be the source of their ruin. These islands are henceforth too close to London; the English element is becoming implanted rapidly, and too many interested voices chatter about this little world.'
17 'The English, masters of this island for more than eight hundred years, are going to great lengths to Anglicize it. The official and commercial world are increasingly English, but the indigenous population has preserved the native tongue and speaks a Norman patois.'
18 'The archipelago of the English Channel speaks French, with a few variants as one sees with words such as "paroisse" (parish), which is pronounced "paresse".' (Other Channel Island French variants are listed for several words). 'The legal and juridical language also has a Norman aftertaste' (some examples of these are also listed).
19 'too precious a heritage to be disavowed or changed'.
20 The emergency legislation put in place during the Second World War was all drafted in English due to a shortage of staff and the fact that a growing number of members of the States knew no French.
21 By way of comparison, in 1989, the total resident population of Jersey was 82,809.
22 In the mid-1990s, Jersey's finance industry generated 55 per cent of the Island's national income (Syvret and Stevens 1998: 285). In 1996, it employed 20 per cent of the Island's workforce and comprised 78 deposit-taking institutions (Syvret and Stevens 1998: 287).
23 Moves in 1982 to adopt English were resisted by the legal profession.
24 Given that the question on the Census form simply asked whether the respondent could speak Jèrriais without specifying any degree of proficiency, it is likely that the figure is only approximate and the native-speaker population making everyday use of the dialect may be somewhat lower, since it is possible that the figure includes some over-reporting for political reasons, as is common in situations of language obsolescence (Jones 1998a: 120). Furthermore, since 89 per cent of all speakers of Jèrriais were aged over 40 in 1989, by today this number is likely to have decreased through natural wastage.

3 The Jèrriais dialect

1 Standard French (St. Fr.) evolved from Francien, a central French dialect. Note, however, that the name 'Francien' is a nineteenth-century invention.
2 Here, the symbol [E] is used to denote an 'e-type sound' without specifying whether it is open or close.
3 As in the case of the other Channel Islands, the Norman dialect of Alderney was dealt a heavy blow during the German Occupation of the Second World War. On Alderney, evacuation preceding the invasion had been far more comprehensive than on the other Islands – all but eighteen of its residents left the Island in the first wave and even some of these later left for Guernsey (Bunting 1996: 13). Although some Islanders did return after the war, the construction on Alderney of Helgoland, Sylt and Norderney slave-labour camps (the names are also those of Frisian islands and should not be confused with them) where thousands of Slavs and French Jews were beaten or worked to death, a situation which Bunting describes as 'the greatest mass murder which has ever occurred on British soil' (1996: 289), meant that, after the German surrender, Alderney was desolate and full of concrete bunkers. Consequently, Islanders were unable to resettle there immediately and

could only return as and when houses were available for them. The community that had existed before the war was lost forever and the dialect was quick to follow.

4 Fleury argues that the Channel Islands form part of what he calls the *haguais* dialect area, termed as such 'parce qu'il paraît avoir son plus caractéristique développement à la Hague' (1886: 4) ('because its most characteristic development seems to occur in la Hague'). He also outlines six characteristics that unite the *haguais* area, and distinguishes *haguais* not only from standard French but also from other Norman dialects (1886: 29).

5 The part of the isoglosses that crosses Normandy was named the Ligne Joret in Joret's honour by Fernand Lechanteur, in his article 'Quelques traits essentiels des parlers de la Basse-Normandie et plus particulièrement du département de la Manche' (1968).

6 Lepelley uses the term 'Delta' to refer to the region between the two isoglosses – i.e. where the 'Norman' development occurs with [k] after [a] but not with [k] after a front vowel (1999: 61).

7 Dorian (1981: 92) comments on how attitudes towards speech-forms may affect one's ability to understand them, an opinion also shared by Hindley (1990: 218).

8 Brasseur (1978a, 1978b) examined only one variety of Mainland Norman, namely the dialect of Magneville, spoken in the canton of Briquebec, Manche. It is possible that the examination of a different variety might have yielded a slightly different result.

9 Spence (1984: 350–1) also outlines some ways in which Guernésiais differs from Jèrriais and Serquiais and discusses differences between Jèrriais and the dialects of Mainland Norman (1957a: 85–9). See also Collas (1934: 218–21) for a detailed exposition of three differences between Jèrriais and Guernésiais.

10 The dialect of Sark is now relatively homogeneous but, in former times, the island of Little Sark had its own distinct variety.

11 Intervocalic [r] becomes [z] (3.3.1.2(ii)).

12 The [a:w] diphthong is used here, ([o:w] elsewhere on the Island (3.3.1.1.a.)).

13 [e] opens to [ɛ] (3.3.1.1.a.).

14 [u] becomes the triphthong [wow] (3.3.1.3.c(i)).

15 [e] opens to [ɛ] (3.3.1.1.a.).

16 Interestingly, the territory described for some of the features does not correspond with other findings. Most notably, assibilation of [r] is described for St Laurent, despite the fact that Le Maistre states that this development does not occur there (1979a: 14). However, Spence's map for the assibilation of [r] (1957b: 272–3) does indicate one informant from St Laurent whose speech displayed the phenomenon quite regularly.

17 This section relies heavily on Spence (1960) and (1985).

18 Long vowels are often represented in orthography by a circumflex: *hître* [i:tr] ('oyster'), *gâche* [gɑːʃ] ('cake'). However, this representation is not systematic: *fis* [fi:] ('son').

19 It will therefore be seen that the Jèrriais orthographic symbol *é* does not necessarily denote the same sound as standard French *é*.

20 This development is also found in parts of mainland Normandy (Northern Manche and Seine Inférieure) and in parts of central France and the Franco-Provençal area (Bloch 1927). However, Jèrriais is the only insular variety of Norman to display this feature.

21 For details of this further development, occurring where the elision of [ə] has brought [r] into contact with a velar ([k], [g]) or a labial ([p], [b]), see Spence (1993: 53).

22 Spence (1957a: 86 n.3) mentions, however, that the substitution of orthographic *dg* for intervocalic *r* in some words of Serquiais may indicate some weakening of intervocalic [r] here also – for example *m'dgouque* ('stinking may-weed') < Vulgar Latin *AMARUSCA. Compare Jèrriais *m'sôque, m'souque*.

23 The function of the apostrophe between an orthographical double consonant here is to indicate that the consonant is repeated in pronunciation. The apostrophe is commonly found in the future and conditional tenses and in verbal nouns.

24 See verse four, line one, of Langlois' poem in section 3.3. above.

25 Spence does note, however, that he heard tell of an old couple at Anne Port (St Martin) whose speech allegedly included this feature (1957b: 275 n.8). Moreover, the orthographic symbol *z* was found to replace intervocalic *r* consistently in the stories written by Jan du Valon and C. du Mont in the *Almanach de la Chronique de Jersey* at the end of the nineteenth and beginning of the twentieth centuries.

26 'We have found a few traces of a development to [l] . . . this feature seems destined to disappear.'

27 The orthographic combination -l'ye at the end of a word represents the sound [λ], which, when prevocalic, often depalatalizes to [l] in parishes other than St Ouen. When preconsonantal, this sound is often reduced to [ç], or not pronounced at all, hence:

meubl'ye [mœbç] / [mœb] ('furniture')
oncl'ye [ɔ̃kç] / [ɔ̃k] ('uncle')
pôssibl'ye [pɔsibç] / [pɔsib] ('possible')

28 'Jèrriais will survive for a while in the old parish of St Ouen when the rest of the Island has forgotten it . . . it's there [in St Ouen] that the funeral rites of Jèrriais will take place.'

29 As table 3.2 demonstrates, in 1989 there were 477 recorded speakers in St Ouen as opposed to 324 in St Jean and 193 in Ste Marie.

30 The *parler* of La Moie.

31 The *parler* of Les Landes.

32 As Edwards points out, such attitudes may be associated with the social prestige and power of the speakers of these varieties (1985: 21).

33 See, among other publications, the *Almanach de la Chronique de Jersey*.

34 Its long political attachment to Britain means that the inhabitants of Jersey (the Jèrriais) may, to a certain extent, identify with the United Kingdom. However, few Jersey-born people would put British allegiances above those due to Jersey.

35 On Jersey, standard French has been traditionally regarded as Jèrriais' 'standard'.

36 Haugen's schema is, however, not the only way by means of which a language can be standardized. Jones (1998a) gives details of an alternative method of standardization, which resulted in the creation of standard Welsh.

4   A sociolinguistic profile of the Jèrriais speech community

1 A comparable survey of the non-Jèrriais speech community would, in itself, represent an interesting project for, as Fishman notes, positive attitudes towards a minority language on the part of the speakers of the dominant variety can have an influence on its revitalization (1991: 174).

2 In all the tables in this chapter, the results are expressed as a percentage of the total sample or, as in the case of, for example, table 4.4, 4.6 and 4.7, the percentage of the sample eligible to respond to the question. In all cases, the actual numbers represented by those percentages are given in brackets.

3 Note that in this and in figures 4.2, 4.3, 4.5, 4.6, 4.8, 4.9 and 4.10, the percentages involved are expressed in terms of the variables on the y axis and not of those on the x axis. For instance, in the case of figure 4.1, they indicate the percentage of informants who answered 'Always', 'Often' and 'Never' within the respective age-groups.

4 The 1989 Census records that 10 per cent of the Jèrriais speech community at that time were aged between 15 and 39.

5 The 1989 Census records that 44 per cent of the Jèrriais speech community at that time were aged between 40 and 64.

6 Cf. Jones (1996: 50), where it was found that only 45 per cent of the population of Plougastel-Daoulas were able to read Breton proficiently.

7 This could, of course, be attributable to the nature of the particular social networks I happened to break into in St Laurent and may not be a typical reflection of the parish as a whole.

8 The fact that Jèrriais spelling was not standardized until 1966 means that most of those interviewed had reached adulthood by the time that the standard spelling system emerged. Moreover, they will never have been presented with many opportunities to write Jèrriais, much less its standardized form.

9 Of course, as seen in the introduction, even when both partners spoke Jèrriais they did not always choose to pass the dialect on to their offspring, believing instead that they would do their children a greater service by speaking to them in English – a situation which is

extremely common in language obsolescence (Mackinnon 1982: 53; Hindley 1990: 179, 195; Winter 1992: 224).

10 Lecturer at the Centre de Recherche Celtique et Bretonne at the Université de Bretagne Occidentale (Research Centre for Celtic and Breton Studies, University of West Brittany).

11 As mentioned in chapter 3, n.7, there is extensive evidence in the literature on language obsolescence which suggests that speakers' attitudes towards speech-forms may affect the speakers' ability to understand them (Dorian 1981: 92; Hindley 1990: 218).

12 The age-gradation in the Jèrriais speech community differs significantly from the pattern found in Brittany and in Wales. Whereas a clear proficiency continuum was found with both the latter (Jones 1996: 51–3, 1998a: 80, 183), the 1989 Census of Jersey revealed that most of the Jèrriais speech community were aged over 40. If trends in my sample are indicative of the population as a whole, it is likely that the members of the 40+ age-group were in the older, rather than the younger, part of this group.

13 However, positive attitudes alone may not always be enough to revitalize an obsolescent variety (Jones 1996: 71).

14 Cf. Maguire (1991) on the situation in Northern Ireland.

15 Fear that the minority language would hinder children's progress in other subjects at school was also found by Zepeda and Hill (1991: 141) during the course of their research on native American languages in the United States.

16 It should not be forgotten, however, that all the informants were native speakers of Jèrriais and that the opinion of non-Jèrriais speakers might be different. This being said, research in Plougastel-Daoulas, as mentioned above, demonstrated that in fact more non-Breton speakers than Breton speakers were in favour of teaching the minority language at school (Jones 1996: 65).

17 The provision for Jèrriais radio broadcasts is slightly better (see section 5.4.2.2.).

18 An H domain refers to the presence within a community of a diglossic situation, which is when two or more languages exist throughout that community, with each having a different role to play. One language is termed H, or the 'High' language, and is used for official functions, and the other, termed L, or the 'Low' language, is used for more familiar functions. For a definition and explanation of this concept, see Ferguson (1959: 325–40). For a subsequent important modification to the concept, see Fishman (1972: 92).

19 Jèrriais is, however, by no means alone in facing this prospect. Dauenhauer and Dauenhauer (1998: 79) report that the varieties of Tlingit, Haida and Tsimshian in south-east Alaska represent just one such instance of varieties which have ceased to be spoken in the home but whose revitalization is being discussed, and there is no doubt that this scenario could be repeated a hundred-fold throughout the modern world.

20 For further details of the revival of Cornish, see Jones (1998a: 338–44). An outline of the Manx revival may be found in Stowell (1996).

5 Language planning on Jersey

1 See, for example, Cooper (1989: chapter 2), which discusses twelve definitions from the literature.

2 Cooper also sees the processes as interdependent (1989: 32–3).

3 Nyati-Ramahobo also discusses acquisition planning in relation to language maintenance (1998: 55).

4 See also Rabin (1983: 53), Gorter (1981: 180), Spolsky (1989: 92), Daoust-Blois (1983: 212) and Rubin (1983: 331) for examples of official language-planning bodies in, respectively, Israel, Friesland, New Zealand, Canada and Finland.

5 'the conservation of the Jersey language by all means possible . . . Anyone interested in the objectives of the Assembliée can be a member.'

6 As mentioned in section 3.4., the fact that it was not fashionable to write in local languages until some 200 years ago has meant that there exists no established literary tradition for Jèrriais before this time. The first texts written in Jèrriais date from the late eighteenth century, and although these increased in number in the nineteenth and early twentieth centuries, the fact that these were mostly poems or short stories published as pamphlets or

in English- or French-language newspapers and almanachs – rather than as separate volumes, or books in their own right – has meant that by today they are not easily accessible to the would-be reader. By publishing work written in Jèrriais, the *Don Balleine* Trust is, therefore, ensuring the presentation of material, as well as increasing its dissemination and availability throughout the Jèrriais speech community. An overview of the main Jèrriais writers is given in Lebarbenchon (1988).

7   An annual fête in which traditional products are sold and local crafts are exhibited.
8   An evening of singing, recitation and acting competitions in Jèrriais based on the Welsh model and brought to Jersey in 1908 by the Reverend Samuel Falle.
9   *Crapaud* ('toad') is the nickname given to the inhabitants of Jersey by other Channel Islanders.
10 The speech of 'exiled' speakers of minority languages may often be more conservative than that of people of the same age who have spoken it all their life in a speech community which has experienced major changes in the position of that variety (Dorian 1997: 227).
11 The words discussed below are taken from the Section de la Langue Jèrriaise's website (see section 5.3.2.).
12 A comprehensive list of reasons why words are borrowed may be found in Appel and Muysken (1993: 165–6).
13 Hovdhaugen (1992: 62), however, also mentions a type of case where speakers do not always recognize lexical borrowings as such.
14 This term also undergoes phonetic modification in different parts of Jersey. In NWJ (St Ouen), the suffix is pronounced [œ:], a realization not very different from that of English. However, in EJ, it would be realized as [aj] (Spence 1993: 20) (cf. section 3.3.1.1.a.).
15 For a definition of calques, see section 5.5.2. below.
16 French has the English borrowing *le Web*, so clearly the calque has been adopted to avoid using this – cf. *la c'mînse-T* (for 'T-shirt') (in the *Lé neu c'mîn* textbook), where French has the English borrowing *le T-shirt*.
17 Except in the case of words which have a common form in both English and standard French.
18 The term used in standard French is *un accro de la télé*.
19 Payton also points out that, in 1981, despite the fact that there were at least 1,000 people alive who had attended some kind of Cornish class, only some forty of these were able to speak the language fluently (1996: 116).
20 Fishman describes how pilot testing of proposed neologisms is even being undertaken in 'healthy' languages such as Swedish in order to prevent such a situation (1991: 347–8).
21 It is possible to argue that, by introducing new terminology and, in some cases, ironing out irregularities, corpus planning also transforms the obsolescent variety into a new entity.
22 Fishman notes, however, that even this stage is not unproblematic, as issues may arise regarding political autonomy and linguistic pluralism within the region in question (1991: 107–9).
23 As mentioned in section 5.4.2., this applies more to radio than to television.
24 However, as seen in section 5.4.1. and in the conclusion, in the case of Manx, revival is not an impossible task (Stowell 1996), although, admittedly, Manx enjoys far more resources than Jèrriais does at present.

6   Linguistic developments in modern Jèrriais

1   This is a process described by Trudgill as 'the levelling out of minority and other marked speech forms and . . . simplification, which involves . . . a reduction in irregularities' (1986: 107), which can give rise to a new, stable variety, containing elements of the different dialects that went into the mixture, or even interdialect forms that were not present in any of the original speech varieties.
2   As mentioned in sections 3.4. and 5.3.3., St Ouennais is the variety used in the *Lé Jèrriais pour tous* grammar/teaching manual (Birt 1985) and the DJF.
3   In Mainland Norman, *v'nîn* takes the auxiliary *avaer* ('to have') but *allaer* ('to go') takes *être* ('to be') (UPN 1995: 205).
4   Adjectives of more than one syllable and past participles used adjectivally are normally postposed in Mainland Norman (UPN 1995: 36–7).

5 As Dressler shows (1991: 105–6), not all instances of the loss of an opposition can be attributed directly to interference from the dominant language. Dorleijn (1996: 2) also indicates that, whereas language contact may be easily pinpointed as the cause of lexical borrowing, the causes of other types of change, such as syntactic change, are less easy to identify.

6 These remarks also apply to the variation in patterns of usage noted in the case of gender in adjectives (see section 6.4.1.3.a.) and conditional substitution (see section 6.4.1.8.).

7 Example (21) is an exception to this, as the elided form of the definite article means that gender is not marked explicitly anywhere in the sentence.

8 This differs from the situation in some obsolescent languages, such as Dahalo (Tosco 1992: 148).

9 A low functional load was found to facilitate the loss of the 3sg./3pl. distinction in Ontarian French (Mougeon and Beniak 1991: 109).

10 Note that table 6.3(a) represents traditional usage of auxiliaries for Jèrriais. This may differ from those used in standard French. For example, whereas *sorti* ('to go out') is traditionally conjugated with the reflexive *aver* ('to have') in Jèrriais, in standard French, the same verb, *sortir*, is traditionally conjugated with the auxiliary *être* ('to be').

11 *V'nîn* was also used exclusively with *être* in HGJ and in JJ.

12 Canale, Mougeon and Belanger (1978) describe the tendency towards the elimination of the auxiliary *être* in favour of *avoir* in the French of Canada. Sauvageot (1962: 139) also comments on the generalization of *avoir* for *être* in uneducated French.

13 The conservative influence of standard French and its role in maintaining the *avoir/être* auxiliary distinction is demonstrated by Esch (forthcoming) with regard to the regional French of Nancy.

14 Despite the fact that the *Chanson de Roland* was not written in Normandy, the fact that it was copied by an Anglo-Norman scribe means that it does provide some idea of the characteristics of this dialect.

15 The use of the subjunctive after constructions of the type *ch'est* + adjective + *qué* was far more common in the written language.

16 Silvá-Corvalán demonstrates that the imperfect and pluperfect subjunctive also tended to disappear in the language of children in Los Angeles born to Spanish-speaking families (1991: 161).

17 'people tend to replace it [the subjunctive] by a verb in the indicative'.

18 Spence (1993: 14–18) discusses in detail the words of Germanic, Celtic and Norse origin that have made their way into the dialect's lexis.

19 For a discussion of borrowing in Jèrriais as a means of word creation, see section 5.5.1.

20 These geographic regions are not, however, to be equated with the Island's parishes (see section 3.3.).

21 A high rate of substitution was also recorded in La Moie (St Brélade), although this has not been included in table 6.9 as I was only able to record one informant from this area (probably the last remaining speaker) (see section 3.3.3.).

22 This group of informants differs slightly from that of table 6.9 in that it includes both informants who had been born and had lived most of their lives in St Ouen and those born there but who had subsequently moved to another parish.

23 It should be pointed out, however, that the speakers of St Ouennais are conscious of the presence of [z] > [ð] substitution in their speech, whereas Labov suggests that centralized diphthongs are not salient for most Vineyard speakers, who 'are not aware of it nor are they able to control it consciously' (1985: 9).

24 According to the 1989 Census, at 9.2 per cent, the parish of St Martin formed part of the 'middle tier' of Jèrriais-speaking parishes (see table 3.2). However, in terms of actual speaker numbers, at 300, St Martin now surpasses only Ste Marie and Grouville.

25 Spence (1985: 160) also mentions the existence of the forms [mzuk] (WJ) and [mzo:wk] (EJ). No examples of these forms were found in my data.

26 This is also seen in some Norman dialects in Manche, Calvados and Orne (Spence 1985: 153 n.7).

27 Given its geographical location as an east–west 'boundary' parish, the presence of 'mixing' in Trinité parish is not surprising. As mentioned in section 3.3., although on the Island it is commonly assumed that sub-dialect and parish boundaries coincide, in practice this is not

the case, as may be illustrated by linguistic maps such as that reproduced in the same section (map 3).

28   Table 6.13 illustrates only the broad trends involved here, as, in rapid speech, a following sound may reduce diphthongization.

29   However, as noted in section 6.4.1.2., it is likely that any further change that does occur in the case of these variables will be in the speech of fluent speakers who, nevertheless, make more use of English than Jèrriais in the course of their daily lives, rather than in that of proficient speakers who make frequent daily use of Jèrriais. Further research will, however, be needed before any specific claims can be made in this area.

30   Cf. Dorleijn (1996: 151), who mentions that most of the changes observed in the Kurmanci of speakers in close contact with Turkish could also, in an incipient stage, be observed in the Kurmanci of speakers with hardly any or no contact with Turkish.

31   I am grateful to Professor Nancy Dorian for bringing this point to my attention.

32   The accentuation of local differences via kin ties does not, of course, preclude the existence of personal-pattern variant use as an additional, and unrelated, development.

33   This theory provides a plausible explanation for the retention of sub-dialect features in the speech of informants whose family is native to one area of Jersey. However, there is also a need to take account of observations such as those of Le Maistre (1979a: 14), who indicated that speakers whose parents were not both natives of the same part of the Island usually had a 'mixed form' of speech and that such a phenomenon was much more frequent than in former times. Although his comments are wholly impressionistic and not substantiated by any data, it would not be surprising to find 'mixing' in such cases, and the increased frequency of the phenomenon is undoubtedly a consequence of the Islanders' increased mobility, which has led to more contact with people from different parishes and has put an end to the norm of marrying within one's parish (cf. Schmidt 1991: 114–15).

7   Lexical erosion in modern Jèrriais

1   Informants were not allowed to see the questionnaire containing the English words. In each case they were given a description of the item in question and their response was noted at the side of the English equivalent.

2   To this effect, it was assumed that if a term was not widely known then it was unlikely to be used frequently.

3   As will be demonstrated in section 7.2.7., in the case of illnesses, the overall result is due to some terms being better known than others.

4   The reason that the names of animals are far better known than those of birds is probably that many informants had been farmers, or were the children of farmers.

5   Cf. Schmidt (1991: 119), who describes 'human classification' as a stable zone resistant to erosion in Dyirbal.

6   Olshtain and Barzilay (1991: 142) mention paraphrase as one of the three possible strategies used by speakers when they are unable to recall words.

7   Body parts were also well known in obsolescent Dyirbal (Schmidt 1991: 119).

8   'Well-known animates' was also described as a resistant domain in obsolescent Dyirbal (Schmidt 1991: 119).

9   The form *couoche* for 'sow' exists in Jèrriais but not *couochonne*.

10   Admittedly, this conclusion can only be tentative, as it is made on the basis of only two words. However, it would be interesting to pursue further this line of enquiry in order to gauge how widespread this tendency is in modern Jèrriais.

11   *Vêpr* ('wasp') was also suggested in this context by one St Ouennais informant.

12   'Let's just say that people don't distinguish very clearly between *papillotes* and *papillons*.'

13   As seen in section 7.2.1., *grile* exists in Jèrriais with the meaning 'hail', but I do not believe that this is the intended meaning in this context.

14   Final diphthongization is not characteristic of St Ouennais, which forms the basis of standard Jèrriais. It is therefore interesting that this feature should be incorporated in the borrowing.

15   The frequency of farmyard animals in the data is explained by the fact that as Jersey was,

and still is to some degree, a farming community, many informants either owned farms themselves or had been brought up on one.

16 Olshtain and Barzilay claim that 'the most susceptible items to suffer from language attrition are infrequent, specific nouns' (1991: 140).

17 As discussed in section 5.5., this situation is being remedied by the Section de la Langue Jèrriaise of the Société Jersiaise and other language planners involved with the Jèrriais education initiative. However, at present there exists no ready mechanism for neologisms to penetrate the wider speech community.

18 'That which we call today a "cardigan" in English approximates to our *blianchet* and many people refer to the English garment, which by now is well known on Jersey, by the term "blianchet".'

19 Both of these phonetic oppositions were found to remain constant for all informants between the results obtained in the elicitation test and the interviews, indicating that personal-pattern variant use may not be very prominent in these contexts.

20 Of course, such usage could also be attributable to personal-pattern variant use.

8   Cross-linguistic influence on Jersey

1 'All the patois-speakers understand French perfectly and are able to speak it.'

2 Before a vowel *il'* is used, which derives from the Old French 3pl. pronoun *il* (< Latin ĪLLI). In recent times, *i's* has also been used in this context. The latter is clearly a borrowing from standard French and will be discussed in section 8.4.2.1.a.

3 'common in the popular usage of different provinces and of Canada'.

4 The DJF does not mention the use of the Jèrriais preposition *sus* with *dépendre*, citing *dé* as the form used with this verb (p. 156). However, the data recorded in my survey revealed many instances of *sus* (and no instances of *dé*) in this context, for example *tout chenna dépend sus l'temps* ('all that depends on the weather').

5 Cf. DJF: 68, 'Celui qui n'a pas "touos ses boutons" est un niais' (lit. 'He who hasn't got "all his buttons" is a fool').

6 In standard French, *gaufrer* means 'to emboss'.

7 'the regional French of Jersey is a highly contaminated language'.

8 Citing Shorrocks (1981: 542), Ramisch observes that the emphatic use of personal pronouns may be also be observed in the variety of English spoken in parts of Greater Manchester county. However, while it is impossible to discount influence from this variety, since there is no intrinsic demographic connection between Jersey and Greater Manchester county it seems far more likely that, as explained above, the presence of this feature in the English of Jersey is attributable to a Jèrriais substrate.

9 As the term *vergée* was once used in standard French, it might be possible to claim that its presence in Jersey English was due to borrowing from standard French (or indeeed RFJ) rather than Jèrriais. However, since the term has been obsolete in standard French for many centuries, as discussed in section 8.2.2.2., this seems unlikely.

10 Schmidt (1991: 121) states that Jambun English, spoken by aborigines who are losing their Dyirbal, is characterized by a high intrusion of Dyirbal forms and remains for them an important vehicle of identity. It would be interesting to see whether similar considerations applied in the case of Jersey English.

11 It is possible that my presence as a non-Islander, and therefore someone to whom it would not be usual to speak Jèrriais, might have had some bearing on these results, although, as mentioned in section 6.2., 'spot-checks' on the data did not reveal any evidence of any significant influence.

12 'Some people say *i's ont* ("they have").'

13 Despite the phonetic similarity of these forms, their etymologies are different. *Nous* is a reflex of the Latin 1pl. personal pronoun NOS, whereas, according to Lepelley (1999: 88), *nou* is derived from the impersonal pronoun *l'on* (see section 3.2.).

14 An alternative explanation, of course, is that it simply represents a case of lexical borrowing.

15 Although the replacement of palatalized by non-palatalized forms may be considered as an example of the phonetic influence of standard French on modern Jèrriais, since such

substitution does not occur systematically and is, at present, restricted lexically, it may also be possible to interpret this phenomenon as a further instance of lexical borrowing.
16 Mithun (1992: 114) poses the same question for the English of Central Pomo communities in California.

9 Conclusion

1 For further discussion of this concept, see Jones (1998a: 322–4).
2 In the first school year of Manx teaching there was a total of 1,179 pupils (1,027 primary and 152 secondary) (Stowell 1996: 214).
3 The few French families resident on the Island do, of course, form an exception to this.
4 The features described in section 8.3. are not generally found in the English of more recent immigrants, since they will usually have little contact with Jèrriais.
5 The influence of the native substrate in the production of regionally identifiable varieties of English is widespread and has been demonstrated in, amongst other studies, Thomas (1984) and Cheshire (1991).
6 Cf. for instance, the use of the definite article (Ramisch 1989: 123); prepositions in/to (Ramisch 1989: 139); present for perfect with time reference (Ramisch 1989: 150–2); deletion of 's in the local genitive (Ramisch 1989: 152–3); *there's* used with time reference (1989: 97–8).
7 'what is left of the dialect when the dialect has disappeared'.

REFERENCES

1990. *Report of the Census for 1989.* Jersey: States' Greffe.

Abalain, H., 1989. *Destin des langues celtiques.* Paris-Gap: Editions Ophrys.

Aikhenvald, A. Y., 1996. Areal diffusion in northwest Amazonia: the case of Tariana. *Anthropological Linguistics* **38/1**, 73–116.

Anstead, D. T and Latham, R. G., 1865. *The Channel Islands.* London: W. H. Allen.

Appel, R. and Muysken, P., 1993. *Language contact and bilingualism.* London, New York, Melbourne and Auckland: Arnold.

Ball, M. J. and Müller, N., 1992. *Mutation in Welsh.* London: Routledge.

Ballart, J., 1996. Language planning in Catalonia. In M. Nic Craith (ed.), *Watching one's tongue: aspects of Romance and Celtic languages* (Liverpool Studies in European Regional Cultures 5). Liverpool: Liverpool University Press, 7–19.

Barbé, P., 1995. Guernsey English: my mother tongue. *Report and Transactions of La Société Guernesiaise* **23/4** (1994), 700–23.

Baugh, A. C. and Cable, T., 1993. *A history of the English language*, 4th ed. London: Routledge and Kegan Paul.

Bauman, J. A., 1980. *A guide to issues in Indian language retention.* Washington, D.C.: Center for Applied Linguistics.

Bentahila, A. and Davies, E., 1993. Language revival: restoration or transformation? *Journal of Multilingual and Multicultural Development* **14/5**, 355–73.

Birt, P., 1985. *Lé Jèrriais pour tous. A complete course on the Jersey language.* Jersey: Don Balleine.

Bliss, A., 1984. English in the South of Ireland. In P. Trudgill (ed.), *Language in the British Isles.* Cambridge: Cambridge University Press, 135–51.

Bloch, O., 1927. L'assibilation d'r dans les parlers Gallo-Romans. *Revue de Linguistique Romane* **3**, 92–157.

Bois, F. de L., 1976. The disappearance of official French. *Jersey Evening Post*, 9 January, 9.

Boretzky, N., 1994. Interdialectal interference in Romani. In Y. Matras (ed.), *Romani in Contact.* Amsterdam and Philadelphia: John Benjamins, 69–94.

Bouchard, D., 1982. Les constructions relatives en français vernaculaire et en français standard: étude d'un paramètre. In C. Lefebvre (ed.), *La syntaxe comparée du français standard et populaire: approches formelle et fonctionelle.* Quebec: Office de la Langue Française, 103–34. (Cited in Appel and Muysken 1993: 160–1.)

Boyd, S., 1985. *Language survival: a study of language contact, language shift and language choice in Sweden.* University of Gothenberg: Dept of Linguistics.

Brasseur, P., 1977. Le français dans les îles anglo-normandes. *Travaux de Linguistique et de Littérature* **16**, 97–104.

Brasseur, P., 1978a. Les principales caractéristiques phonétiques des parlers normands de Jersey, Sercq, Guernesey et Magneville (canton de Bricquebec, Manche), première partie. *Annales de Normandie* **25/1**, 49–64.

Brasseur, P., 1978b. Les principales caractéristiques phonétiques des parlers normands de Jersey, Sercq, Guernesey et Magneville (canton de Bricquebec, Manche), deuxième partie. *Annales de Normandie* **25/3**, 275–306.

Broudic, F., 1991. Ar brezoneg hag ar vrezonegerien e 1991. *Brud Nevez* **143**, 20–60

Brunot, F. and Bruneau, C., 1969. *Précis de grammaire historique de l'ancien français.* Paris: Masson.

Bunting, M., 1996. *The model occupation. The Channel Islands under German rule 1940–1945.* London: HarperCollins.

Campbell, C., 1992. Cymdeithasu yn y Gymraeg ymhlith oedolion ifanc: ydy'r peuoedd Cymraeg wedi cael eu chips? In B. Jones (ed.), *Hyrwyddo a chadw'r defnydd o'r Gymraeg ymhlith pobl ifanc.* Aberystwyth: CYD, 33–45.

Campbell, L. and Muntzel, M. C., 1989. The structural consequences of language death. In N. C. Dorian (ed.), *Investigating obsolescence*. Cambridge: Cambridge University Press, 181–96.

Canale, M., Mougeon, R. and Belanger, M., 1978. Analogical levelling of the auxiliary *être* in French. In M. Suñer (ed.), *Contemporary studies in Romance linguistics*. Washington, D.C.: Georgetown University Press, 41–61.

Carruthers, J., 1999. A problem in sociolinguistic methodology: investigating a rare syntactic form. *Journal of French Language Studies* **9/1**, 1–24.

Cheshire, J. (ed.), 1991. *English around the world: sociolinguistic perspectives*. Cambridge: Cambridge University Press.

Cobarrubias, J., 1983. Ethical issues in status planning. In J. Cobarrubias and J. A. Fishman (eds), *Progress in language planning*. Berlin, New York and Amsterdam: Mouton, 41–84.

Cohen, M., 1965. *Le subjonctif en français contemporain*, 2nd ed. Paris: SEDES.

Collas, J. P., 1934. Some aspects of the Norman dialect in the Channel Islands, with special reference to Guernsey. *Report and Transactions of La Société Guernesiaise* **12**, 213–25.

Cooper, R. L., 1989. *Language planning and social change*. Cambridge: Cambridge University Press.

Crystal, D., 1999. Death sentence. *Guardian*, 25 October, 2–3.

Cuarón, B. G. and Lastra, Y., 1991. Endangered languages in Mexico. In E. M. Uhlenbeck and R. H. Robins (eds), *Endangered languages*. Oxford: Berg, 93–134.

Cummins, J. and Genesee, F., 1985. Bilingual education programmes in Wales and Canada. In C. J. Dodson (ed.), *Bilingual education: evaluation, assessment and methodology*. Cardiff: University of Wales Press, 37–49.

Daoust-Blois, D., 1983. Corpus and status planning in Quebec. In J. Cobarrubias and J. A. Fishman (eds), *Progress in language planning*. Berlin, New York and Amsterdam: Mouton, 207–34.

Dauby, J., 1979. *Le livre du 'Rouchi', parler picard de Valenciennes*, 2nd ed. Amiens: Musée de Picardie.

Dauenhauer, N. M. and Dauenhauer, R., 1998. Technical, emotional and ideological issues in reversing language shift: examples from Southeast Alaska. In L. A. Grenoble and L. J. Whaley (eds), *Endangered languages: current issues and future prospects*. Cambridge: Cambridge University Press, 57–98.

De Garis, M., 1983. Guernésiais: a grammatical survey. *Report and Transactions of La Société Guernesiaise* **21**, 319–53.

De Guérin, T. W. M., 1905. The English garrison of Guernsey from early times. *Transactions of the Guernsey Society of Natural Science and Local Research* **5**, 66–81.

Devitt, A. J., 1989. *Standardizing written English. Diffusion in the case of Scotland 1520–1659*. Cambridge: Cambridge University Press.

Dickès, J.-P., 1992. *Le patois boulonnais*. Boulogne-sur-Mer: La Société d'Impression du Boulonnais.

Dimmendaal, G., 1992. Reduction in Kore reconsidered. In M. Brenzinger (ed.), *Language death. Factual and theoretical explorations with special reference to East Africa*. Berlin and New York: Mouton de Gruyter, 117–35.

Dorian, N. C., 1978a. The dying dialect and the role of the schools: East Sutherland Gaelic and Pennsylvanian Dutch. In J. E. Alatis (ed.), *International dimensions of bilingual education*. Washington, D.C.: Georgetown University Press, 646–56.

Dorian, N. C., 1978b. The fate of morphological complexity in language death: evidence from ESG. *Language* **54**, 590–609.

Dorian, N. C., 1981. *Language death: the life cycle of a Scottish Gaelic dialect*. Philadelphia: University of Pennsylvania Press.

Dorian, N. C., 1987. The value of language-maintenance efforts which are unlikely to succeed. *International Journal of the Sociology of Language* **68**, 57–61.

Dorian, N. C. (ed.), 1989. *Investigating obsolescence*. Cambridge: Cambridge University Press.

Dorian, N. C., 1994a. Purism vs. compromise in language revitalization and language revival. *Language in Society* **23**, 479–94.

Dorian, N. C., 1994b. Varieties of variation in a very small place: social homogeneity, prestige norms, and linguistic variation. *Language* **70/4**, 631–96.

Dorian, N. C., 1997. A convergence-resistant feature in a convergence-prone setting: the East

Sutherland vocative case. In S. Eliasson and E. Håkon Jahr (eds), *Language and its ecology: essays in memory of Einar Haugen*. Berlin and New York: Mouton de Gruyter, 209–33.

Dorian, N. C., 1998. Western language ideologies and small-language prospects. In L. A. Grenoble and L. J. Whaley (eds), *Endangered languages: current issues and future prospects*. Cambridge: Cambridge University Press, 3–21.

Dorleijn, M., 1996. *The decay of ergativity in Kurmanci*. Tilburg University Press.

Drapeau, L., 1992. Language birth: an alternative to language death. Paper presented at the 15th International Congress of Linguists, Quebec. (Cited in Dorian 1994a: 492.)

Dressler, W. U., 1981. Language shift and language death – a protean challenge for the linguist. *Folia Linguistica* **15**, 5–28.

Dressler, W. U., 1991. The sociolinguistic and patholinguistic attrition of Breton phonology, morphology, and morphophonology. In H. W. Seliger and R. M. Vago (eds), *First language attrition*. Cambridge: Cambridge University Press, 99–112.

Edwards, D. G., 1984. Welsh-medium education. *Journal of Multilingual and Multicultural Development* **5**, 249–57.

Edwards, J., 1985. *Language, society and identity*. Oxford: Blackwell.

Elcock, W. D., 1975. *The Romance languages*, rev. ed. London: Faber and Faber.

Ellis, P. B. and Mac A 'Ghobhainn, S., 1971. *The problem of language revival*. Inverness: Club Leabhar.

Esch, E., forthcoming. My Dad's auxiliaries. In M. C. Jones and E. Esch (eds), *Language change: the interplay of internal, external and extra-linguistic factors*. Berlin: Mouton de Gruyter.

Falle, P., 1734. *An account of the Island of Jersey*, 2nd ed. London: John Newton

Fennell, D., 1981. Can a shrinking linguistic minority be saved? Lessons from the Irish experience. In E. Haugen, J. D. McClure and D. S. Thomson (eds), *Minority languages today*. Edinburgh: Edinburgh University Press, 32–9.

Ferguson, C. A., 1959. Diglossia. *Word* **15**, 325–40.

Fishman, J. A., 1972. Language maintenance and language shift as a field of inquiry: revisited. In A. S. Dil (ed.), *Language in sociocultural change: essays by Joshua A. Fishman*. Stanford: Stanford University Press, 76–134.

Fishman, J. A., 1983. Modeling rationales in corpus planning. In J. Cobarrubias and J. A. Fishman (eds), *Progress in language planning*. Berlin, New York and Amsterdam: Mouton de Gruyter, 107–18.

Fishman, J. A., 1991. *Reversing language shift* (Multilingual Matters 76). Clevedon, Philadelphia and Adelaide: Multilingual Matters.

Fleury, J. F. B., 1886. *Essai sur le patois normand de la Hague*. Paris: Maisonneuve et Leclerc.

Gadet, F., 1989. *Le français ordinaire*. Paris: Armand Colin.

Gadet, F., 1992. *Le français populaire*. Paris: Presses Universitaires de France.

Gal, S., 1989. Lexical innovation and loss: the use and value of restricted Hungarian. In N. C. Dorian (ed.), *Investigating obsolescence*. Cambridge: Cambridge University Press.

Gardner, R., 1982. Language attitudes and language learning. In E. Ryan and H. Giles (eds), *Attitudes towards language variation*. London: Arnold, 132–47.

Garzon, S., 1992. The process of language death in a Mayan community in Southern Mexico. *International Journal of the Sociology of Language* **93**, 53–66.

Giles, H., Bourhis, R. Y. and Taylor, D. M., 1977. Towards a theory of language in ethnic group relations. In H. Giles (ed.), *Language, ethnicity and intergroup relations*. London: Academic Press, 307–48.

Gorman, T. P., 1973. Language allocation and language planning in a developing nation. In J. Rubin and R. Shuy (eds), *Language planning: current issues and research*. Washington, D.C.: Georgetown University Press.

Gorter, D., 1981. Some recent developments in official language planning in Friesland. In E. Haugen, J. D. McClure and D. S. Thomson (eds), *Minority languages today*. Edinburgh: Edinburgh University Press, 177–81.

Grenoble, L. A. and Whaley, L. W., 1998. Toward a typology of language endangerment. In L. A. Grenoble and L. J. Whaley (eds), *Endangered languages: current issues and future prospects*. Cambridge: Cambridge University Press, 22–54.

Grevisse, M., 1988. *Le bon usage*, 12th ed. Paris and Gembloux: Duculot.

Guerlin de Guer, C., 1899. *Essai de dialectologie normande. La palatalisation des groupes initiaux gl, fl, kl, pl, bl étudiée dans îles parlers de 300 communautés du département du Calvados.* Paris: E. Bouillon.

Guillot, C., 1975. *Les îles anglo-normandes.* Paris: Presses Universitaires de France.

Hamers, J. F. and Blanc, M. H. A., 1989. *Bilingualism and bilinguality.* Cambridge: Cambridge University Press.

Hamp, E. P., 1989. On signs of health and death. In N. C. Dorian (ed.), *Language obsolescence.* Cambridge: Cambridge University Press, 197–210.

Harley, B., Cummins, J., Swain, M. and Allen, P., 1990. The nature of language proficiency. In B. Harley, P. Allen, J. Cummins and M. Swain (eds), *The development of second language proficiency.* Cambridge: Cambridge University Press, 7–25.

Haugen, E., 1959. Planning for a standard language in modern Norway. *Anthropological Linguistics* 1/3, 8–21.

Haugen, E., 1966. Dialect, language, nation. *American Anthropologist* 68, 922–35.

Hewitt, S., 1977. The degree of acceptability of modern literary Breton to native Breton speakers. Unpublished Diploma of Linguistics Thesis, University of Cambridge.

Hill, J. H., 1978. Language death, language contact and language evolution. In S. A. Wurm and W. McCormack (eds), *Approaches to language.* The Hague: Mouton, 45–78.

Hindley, R., 1990. *The death of Irish.* London: Routledge.

Hoenigswald, H. M., 1989. Language obsolescence and language history: matters of linearity, levelling, loss and the like. In N. C. Dorian (ed.), *Investigating obsolescence.* Cambridge: Cambridge University Press, 347–54.

Holm, J. A., 1988. *Pidgins and creoles.* Volume 1. Cambridge: Cambridge University Press.

Hornberger, N. H., 1989. Bilingual education and indigenous languages in the light of language planning. *International Journal of the Sociology of Language* 77, 5–9.

Hornberger, N. H. and King, K. A., 1996. Language revitalization in the Andes: can schools reverse language shift? *Journal of Multilingual and Multicultural Development* 17/6, 427–41.

Hovdhaugen, E., 1992. Language contact in the Pacific: Samoan influence on Tokelauan. In E. Håkon Jahr (ed.), *Language contact: theoretical and empirical studies.* Berlin and New York: Mouton de Gruyter, 53–69.

Hublart, C., 1979. Le français de Jersey. Unpublished thesis, Université de l'Etat à Mons.

Huëlin, L., Vibert, B. and Lucas, M. (eds), 2000. *Mille ditons en Jèrriais.* Jersey: Don Balleine.

Huëlin, L. and Nichols R. (eds), 2000. *Les preunmié mille mots.* Jersey: Societé Jersiaise.

Huffines, M. L., 1989. Case usage among the Pennsylvanian German sectarians and nonsectarians. In N. C. Dorian (ed.), *Investigating obsolescence.* Cambridge: Cambridge University Press, 211–26.

Huffines, M. L., 1991. Pennsylvania German: convergence and change as strategies of discourse. In H. W. Seliger and R. M. Vago (eds), *First language attrition.* Cambridge: Cambridge University Press, 125–37.

Hugo, V. M., 1883. *L'archipel de la Manche,* 2nd ed. Paris: Calmann Lévy.

Inglis, H., 1844. *The Channel Islands,* 4th ed. London: Whittaker.

Jacobs, D., 1997. Alliance and betrayal in the Dutch orthography debate. *Language Problems and Language Planning* 21/2, 103–18.

Jacobs, K. A., 1998. A chronology of Mohawk language instruction at Kahnasà:ke. In L. A. Grenoble and L. J. Whaley (eds), *Endangered languages: current issues and future prospects.* Cambridge: Cambridge University Press, 117–23.

Jones, B. L., 1981. Welsh: linguistic conservation and shifting bilingualism. In E. Haugen, J. McClure and D. Thomson (eds), *Minority languages today.* Edinburgh: Edinburgh University Press, 40–51.

Jones, G. W., 1993. *Agweddau ar ddysgu iaith.* Llandysul: Gwasg Gomer.

Jones, M. C., 1995. At what price language maintenance? Standardization in modern Breton. *French Studies* 49/4, 424–38.

Jones, M. C., 1996. The role of the speaker in language obsolescence: the case of Breton in Plougastel-Daoulas. *Journal of French Language Studies* 6/1, 45–73.

Jones, M. C., 1998a. *Language obsolescence and revitalization. Linguistic change in two sociolinguistically contrasting Welsh communities.* Oxford: Clarendon Press.

Jones, M. C., 1998b. Death of a language, birth of an identity: Brittany and the Bretons. *Language Problems and Language Planning* 22/2, 129–42.

Jones, M. C., 2000. The subjunctive in Guernsey Norman French. *Journal of French Language Studies* **10/2**, 177–203.

Jones, M. C. unpublished. A study of the Welsh of Aberystwyth. University of Wales Centre for Advanced Welsh and Celtic Studies, Aberystwyth.

Joret, C., 1883. *Des caractères et de l'extension du patois normand.* Paris: Vieweg.

Kibrik, A. E., 1991. The problem of endangered languages in the USSR. In E. M. Uhlenbeck and R. H. Robins (eds), *Endangered languages.* Oxford: Berg, 257–73.

King, K. A., 1999. Inspecting the unexpected: language status and corpus shifts as aspects of Quichua language revitalization. *Language Problems and Language Planning* **23/2**, 109–32.

Kloss, H., 1969. *Research possibilities on group bilingualism: a report.* Quebec: International Center for Research on Bilingualism.

Krauss, M., 1992. The world's languages in crisis. *Language* **68**, 4–10.

Kuter, L., 1989. Breton vs. French: language and the opposition of political, economic, social and cultural values. In N. C. Dorian (ed.), *Investigating obsolescence.* Cambridge: Cambridge University Press, 75–90.

Labov, W., 1966. *The social stratification of English in New York City.* Oxford: Blackwell.

Labov, W., 1985. *Sociolinguistic patterns.* Oxford: Blackwell.

Lambert, W. E., Hodgson, R. C., Gardner, R. C. and Fillenbaum, S., 1960. Evaluational reactions to spoken languages. *Journal of Abnormal and Social Psychology* **60/1**, 44–51.

Lebarbenchon, R. J., 1988. *La grève de Lecq. Litteratures et cultures populaires de Normandie. I: Guernsey et Jersey.* Cherbourg: Isoète.

Lechanteur, F., 1948. Le nouvel atlas linguistique de la France: l'enquête en Basse Normandie. *Le Français Moderne* **16**, 109–22.

Lechanteur, F., 1949. Le normand dans les îles anglo-normandes. *Le Français Moderne* **17**, 211–18.

Lechanteur, F., 1968. Quelques traits essentiels des parlers de la Basse-Normandie et plus particulièrement du département de la Manche. *Studier i Modern Sprakvelenskap* **3**, 185–223.

Le Feuvre, G. F., 1976. *Histouaithes et gens d'Jèrri.* Jersey: Don Balleine.

Le Feuvre, G. F., 1979. Des vièrs mots Jèrriais. *Chroniques du Don Balleine* **1**, 12–13.

Le Feuvre, G. F., 1983. *Jèrri jadis.* Jersey: Don Balleine.

Le Gros, A., 1883. The dialects of the Channel Islands. *Channel Gems* **1/1**, 18–25.

Le Hérissier, R. G., n.d. *The development of the government of Jersey, 1771–1972.* Jersey: States of Jersey.

Leith, D. A., 1983. *A social history of English.* London: Routledge.

Le Maistre, F., 1947. The Jersey language in its present state. The passing of a Norman heritage. Paper read before the Jersey Society in London, 8 July 1947. London: Jersey Society.

Le Maistre, F., 1966. *Dictionnaire Jersiais–Français.* Jersey: Don Balleine.

Le Maistre, F., 1979a. *The Jersey language.* (Booklet to accompany Cassette 2.) Jersey: Don Balleine.

Le Maistre, F., 1979b. *The Jersey Language.* (Booklet to accompany Cassette 3.) Jersey: Don Balleine.

Le Maistre, F., 1981. Lé Jèrriais – chiéthe vielle langue que j'laîssons couôrre! *Chroniques du Don Balleine* **4**, 91–4.

Le Maistre, F., 1993. *The Jersey language.* (Booklet to accompany Cassette 1.) Jersey: Don Balleine.

Lemprière, R., 1974. *History of the Channel Islands.* London: Robert Hale.

Le Pelley, J., 1975. I am Guernsey – me! *Review of the Guernsey Society* **21**, 17–19.

Lepelley, R., 1999. *La Normandie dialectale. Petite encyclopédie des langages et mots régionaux de la province de Normandie et des îles anglo-normandes.* Université de Caen: Office Universitaire d'Etudes Normandes.

L'Estourbeillon de la Garnache, Comte R. de, 1886. *Les familles françaises à Jersey pendant la Révolution.* Nantes: Forest et Grimaud.

Lewis, G., 1983. Implementation of language planning in the Soviet Union. In J. Cobarrubias and J. A. Fishman (eds), *Progress in language planning.* Berlin, New York and Amsterdam: Mouton, 309–26.

Liddicoat, A. J., 1990. Some structural features of language obsolescence in the dialect of Jersey. *Language Sciences* **12/2–3**, 197–208.

Lodge, R. A., 1993. *French: from dialect to standard.* London and New York: Routledge.

McDonald, M., 1989. *We are not French!* London and New York: Routledge.

McMahon, A. M. S., 1994. *Understanding language change.* Cambridge: Cambridge University Press.

Ma, R. and Herasimchuk, E., 1975. The linguistic dimensions of a bilingual neighborhood. In J. A. Fishman, R. L. Cooper, R. Ma et al. (eds), *Bilingualism in the barrio.* Bloomington: Indiana University Press, 347–64.

Mackinnon, K., 1977. *Language, education and social processes in a Gaelic community.* London: Routledge and Kegan Paul.

Mackinnon, K., 1982. Scottish opinion on Gaelic. *Social Sciences Reports Series* **14**.

Macnamara, J., 1971. Successes and failures in the movement for the restoration of Irish. In B. H. Jernudd and J. Rubin (eds), *Can language be planned?.* Honolulu: University Press of Hawaii, 65–94.

Maguire, G., 1991. *Our own language.* Clevedon: Multilingual Matters.

Mason, I., 1980. L'usage des temps narratifs en jersiaise et val de sairais. *Parlers et Traditions Populaires de Normandie* **47–8**, 99–106.

Matisoff, J. A., 1991. Endangered languages of mainland Southeast Asia. In E. M. Uhlenbeck and R. H. Robins (eds), *Endangered languages.* Oxford: Berg, 189–228.

Mertz, E., 1989. Sociolinguistic creativity: Cape Breton Gaelic's linguistic 'tip'. In N. C. Dorian (ed.), *Investigating obsolescence.* Cambridge: Cambridge University Press, 103–16.

Miller, J. and Brown, K., 1982. Aspects of Scottish English syntax. *English World-Wide* **3**, 3–17.

Milroy, L., 1980. *Language and social networks.* Oxford: Blackwell.

Milroy, L., 1987. *Observing and analysing natural language.* Oxford: Blackwell.

Mithun, M., 1992. The substratum in grammar and discourse. In E. Håkon Jahr (ed.), *Language contact: theoretical and empirical studies.* Berlin and New York: Mouton de Gruyter, 103–15.

Mougeon, R. and Beniak, E., 1989. Language contraction and linguistic change: the case of Welland French. In N. C. Dorian (ed.), *Investigating obsolescence.* Cambridge: Cambridge University Press, 287–312.

Mougeon, R. and Beniak, E., 1991. *Linguistic consequences of language contact and restriction. The case of French in Ontario, Canada.* Oxford: Clarendon Press.

N. N., 1849. Les îles de la Manche, Jersey et Guernsey en 1848 et 1849. *Revue des Deux Mondes* **4**, 937–67.

Nahir, M., 1984. Language planning goals: a classification. *Language Problems and Language Planning* **8/3**, 294–327.

Nyati-Ramahobo, L., 1998. Language planning in Botswana. *Language Problems and Language Planning* **22/1**, 48–62.

Ó Baoill, D. P., 1988. Language planning in Ireland: the standardization of Irish. *International Journal of the Sociology of Language* **70**, 109–26.

Ó Riagáin, P., 1988. Bilingualism in Ireland 1973–1983: an overview of national sociolinguistic surveys. *International Journal of the Sociology of Language* **70**, 29–51.

Oftedal, M., 1956. *The Gaelic of Leurbost, Isle of Lewis.* Oslo: H. Aschehoug (W. Nygaard).

Olshtain, E. and Barzilay, M., 1991. Lexical retrieval difficulties in adult language attrition. In H. W. Seliger and R. M. Vago (eds), *First language attrition.* Cambridge: Cambridge University Press, 139–50.

Payton, P., 1996. Which Cornish? Ideology and language revival in post-war Cornwall. In M. Nic Craith (ed.), *Watching one's tongue: aspects of Romance and Celtic languages* (Liverpool Studies in European Regional Cultures 5). Liverpool: Liverpool University Press, 111–35.

Petyt, K. M., 1980. *The study of dialect.* London: André Deutsch.

Petyt, K. M., 1985. *Dialect and accent in industrial West Yorkshire.* Amsterdam: John Benjamins.

Pool, J., 1979. Language planning and identity planning. *International Journal of the Sociology of Language* **20**, 5–21.

Price, G., 1984. French in the Channel Islands. In G. Price, *The languages of Britain.* London: Arnold, 207–16.

Price, G., 1993. *L. S. R. Byrne and E. L. Churchill's A Comprehensive French Grammar.* Oxford: Blackwell.

Puga, M., 1996. Language planning and policy in Galicia. In M. Nic Craith (ed.), *Watching one's tongue: aspects of Romance and Celtic languages.* (Liverpool Studies in European Regional Cultures 5). Liverpool: Liverpool University Press, 59–67.

Rabin, C., 1971. Spelling reform – Israel 1968. In B. H. Jernudd and J. Rubin (eds), *Can language be planned?.* Honolulu: University Press of Hawaii, 95–121.

Rabin, C., 1983. The sociology of normativism in Israeli Hebrew. *International Journal of the Sociology of Language* **41**, 41–56.

Ramisch, H., 1989. *The variation of English in Guernsey, Channel Islands.* Frankfurt: Peter Lang.

Richards, J. B., 1989. Language planning in Guatemala. *International Journal of the Sociology of Language* **77**, 93–115.

Rouchdy, A., 1989. 'Persistence' or 'tip' in Egyptian Nubian. In N. C. Dorian (ed.), *Investigating obsolescence.* Cambridge: Cambridge University Press, 91–102.

Rubin, J., 1983. Evaluating status planning: what has the past decade accomplished? In J. Cobarrubias and J. A. Fishman (eds), *Progress in language planning.* Berlin, New York and Amsterdam: Mouton de Gruyter, 329–43.

Sasse, H.-J., 1992a. Theory of language death. In M. Brenzinger (ed.), *Language death. Factual and theoretical explorations with special reference to East Africa.* Berlin and New York: Mouton de Gruyter, 7–30.

Sasse, H.-J., 1992b. Language decay and contact-induced change: similarities and differences. In M. Brenzinger (ed.), *Language death. Factual and theoretical explorations with special reference to East Africa.* Berlin and New York: Mouton de Gruyter, 59–80

Sauvageot, A., 1962. *Français écrit, français parlé.* Paris: Hachette.

Sauvageot, A., 1972. *Analyse du français parlé.* Paris: Hachette.

Schlieben-Lange, B., 1977. The language situation in Southern France. *International Journal of the Sociology of Language* **12**, 101–7.

Schlyter, B. N., 1998. New language laws in Uzbekistan. *Language Problems and Language Planning* **22/2**, 143–81.

Schmidt, A., 1985. *Young people's Dyirbal.* Cambridge: Cambridge University Press.

Schmidt, A., 1991. Language attrition in Boumaa Fijian and Dyirbal. In H. W. Seliger and R. M. Vago (eds), *First language attrition.* Cambridge: Cambridge University Press, 113–24.

Scott Warren, A., 1999. *Lé neu c'mîn.* Jersey: Don Balleine.

Seliger, H., 1991. Language attrition, reduced redundancy, and creativity. In H. W. Seliger and R. M. Vago (eds), *First language attrition.* Cambridge: Cambridge University Press, 227–40.

Seliger, H. W. and Vago, R. M., 1991. The study of first language attrition: an overview. In H. W. Seliger and R. M. Vago (eds), *First language attrition.* Cambridge: Cambridge University Press, 3–15.

Seren-Rosso, M. L., 1990. Les langues de Jersey passées et présentes. *Language International* **2**, 37.

Sharwood Smith, M. and Van Buren, P., 1991. First language attrition and the parameter setting model. In H. W. Seliger and R. M. Vago (eds), *First language attrition.* Cambridge: Cambridge University Press, 17–30.

Shorrocks, G., 1981. A grammar of the dialect of Farnworth and district (Greater Manchester County, formerly Lancashire). Unpublished PhD thesis, University of Sheffield. (Cited in Ramisch 1989: 126.)

Shuken, C., 1984. Highland and Island English. In P. Trudgill (ed.), *Language in the British Isles.* Cambridge: Cambridge University Press, 152–66.

Silvá-Corvalán, C., 1991. Spanish language attrition in a contact situation with English. In H. W. Seliger and R. M. Vago (eds), *First language attrition.* Cambridge: Cambridge University Press, 151–71.

Sjögren, A., 1964. *Les parlers bas-normands de l'île de Guernesey. I: lexique français–guernesiais.* Paris: Klincksieck.

Société Jersiaise: Section de la Langue, 1995. *Annual Report, 1995.*

Spence, N. C. W., 1957a. Jèrriais and the dialects of the Norman mainland. *Bulletin de la Société Jersiaise* **17**, 81–90.

Spence, N. C. W., 1957b. L'assibilation de l'r intervocalique dans les parlers jersiais. *Revue de Linguistique Romane* **21**, 270–88.

Spence, N. C. W., 1960. *Glossary of Jersey French.* Oxford: Blackwell.

Spence, N. C. W., 1984. Channel Island French. In P. Trudgill (ed.), *Language in the British Isles.* Cambridge: Cambridge University Press, 345–51.

Spence, N. C. W., 1985. Phonologie descriptive des parlers jersiais: I. Les voyelles. *Revue de Linguistique Romane* **49**, 151–65.

Spence, N. C. W., 1987. Phonologie descriptive des parlers jersiais: II. Les consonnes. *Revue de Linguistique Romane* **51**, 119–33.

Spence, N. C. W., 1988. R aboutissement de latérale + consonne en jersiais. *Revue de Linguistique Romane* **52**, 365–70.

Spence, N. C. W., 1990. Sporadic changes in Jersey French. In J. N. Green and W. Ayres-Bennett (eds), *Variation and change in French*. London: Routledge, 210–25.

Spence, N. C. W., 1993. *A brief history of Jèrriais*. Jersey: Don Balleine.

Spencer, C., 1986. The survival of language. Unpublished research project, Trent Polytechnic.

Spolsky, B., 1989. Maori bilingual education and language revitalization. *Journal of Multilingual and Multicultural Development* **10/2**, 89–106.

Spolsky, B. and Boomer, L., 1983. The modernization of Navajo. In J. Cobarrubias and J. A. Fishman (eds), *Progress in language planning*. Berlin, New York and Amsterdam: Mouton de Gruyter, 235–52.

Stead, J., 1809. *A picture of Jersey*. London: Longman.

Stowell, B., 1996. The Manx language today. In M. Nic Craith (ed.), *Watching one's tongue: aspects of Romance and Celtic languages* (Liverpool Studies in European Regional Cultures 5). Liverpool: Liverpool University Press, 201–24.

Syvret, M. and Stevens, J., 1998. *Balleine's history of Jersey*. West Sussex: Phillimore.

Tapley, J., 1998. *Jersey Norman French is fun*. Jersey: Don Balleine.

Thomas, A. R., 1984. Welsh English. In P. Trudgill (ed.), *Language in the British Isles*. Cambridge: Cambridge University Press, 178–94.

Thomason, S. G., 1997. On mechanisms of interference. In S. Eliasson and E. Håkon Jahr (eds), *Language and its ecology: essays in memory of Einar Haugen*. Berlin and New York: Mouton de Gruyter, 181–207.

Thomason, S. G. and Kaufman, T., 1988. *Language contact, creolization and genetic linguistics*. Berkeley, Los Angeles and London: University of California Press.

Thomson, D. S., 1979. Gaelic: its range of uses. In A. J. Aitken and T. McArthur (eds), *Languages of Scotland* (Association for Scottish Literary Studies Occasional Paper Number 4). Edinburgh: W. and R. Chambers, 14–25.

Timm, L. A., 1980. Bilingualism, diglossia and language shift in Brittany. *International Journal of the Sociology of Language* **25**, 29–41.

Tomlinson, H., 1981. Le Guernésiais – étude grammaticale et lexicale du parler normand de l'île de Guernesey. Unpublished PhD thesis, University of Edinburgh.

Tosco, M., 1992. Dahalo: an endangered language. In M. Brenzinger (ed.), *Language death. Factual and theoretical explorations with special reference to East Africa*. Berlin and New York: Mouton de Gruyter, 137–55.

Trudgill P., 1974. *The social differentiation of English in Norwich*. Cambridge: Cambridge University Press.

Trudgill, P., 1983. Language contact, language shift and identity. In P. Trudgill (ed.), *On dialect. Social and geographical perspectives*. Oxford: Blackwell, 127–40.

Trudgill, P., 1986. *Dialects in contact*. Oxford: Blackwell.

Trudgill, P., 1992. Dialect typology and social structure. In E. Håkon Jahr (ed.), *Language contact: theoretical and empirical studies*. Berlin and New York: Mouton de Gruyter, 195–211.

Tuaillon, G., 1974. Review of Marie-Rose Simoni-Aurembou *Atlas linguistique et ethnographique de l'Ile-de-France et de l'Orléanais*. Volume I. Paris: CNRS 1973. *Revue de Linguistique Romane* **38**, 575–6.

UPN (Université Populaire Normande du Coutançais), 1995. *Essai de grammaire de la langue normande*. Périers: Garlan.

Uttley, J., 1966. *The story of the Channel Islands*. London: Faber and Faber.

Vakhtin, N., 1998. Copper Island Aleut: a case of language resurrection. In L. A. Grenoble and L. J. Whaley (eds), *Endangered languages: current issues and future prospects*. Cambridge: Cambridge University Press, 317–27.

Vincent, N., 1982. The development of the auxiliaries *habere* and *essere* in Romance. In N. Vincent and M. Harris (eds), *Studies in the Romance verb*. London and Canberra: Croom Helm, 71–96.

Watson, S., 1989. Scottish and Irish Gaelic: the giant's bed-fellows. In N. C. Dorian (ed.), *Investigating obsolescence*. Cambridge: Cambridge University Press, 41–59.

Weinreich, U., 1953. *Languages in contact: findings and problems*. New York: Linguistic Circle of New York. (Reprinted 1963, The Hague: Mouton.)

Williams, G., 1992. *Sociolinguistics: a sociological critique*. London: Routledge.

Winter, W., 1992. Borrowing and non-borrowing in Walapai. In E. Håkon Jahr (ed.), *Language contact: theoretical and empirical studies*. Berlin and New York: Mouton de Gruyter, 213–28.

Wolf, L., 1993. *Le français régional d'Alsace*. Paris: Klincksieck.

Zepeda, O. and Hill, J. H., 1991. The condition of native American languages in the United States. In E. M. Uhlenbeck and R. H. Robins (eds), *Endangered languages*. Oxford: Berg, 135–55.

GENERAL INDEX

adjectives
  English 102, 106–7, 111, 113, 157
  français populaire 106
  Jèrriais 101, 102, 103, 105–7, 105 n6, 108,
    111–14, 120, 157
  Norman 22, 111, 157
  Regional French of Jersey 157
adverbs
  français populaire 106
  French 160
  Mainland Norman 160
  Regional French of Jersey 161–1
affirmation
  Guernsey English 171
  Jèrriais 100, 104–5, 171
  Jersey English 171
Alderney 7, 19, 19 n3, 190
'ambiguous change' 6, 107, 136
Anglicization 4, 8, 11, 12–17, 38, 50, 56, 59,
  61, 167
article, definite
  Guernsey English 170–1, 190 n6
  Jèrriais 101, 106 n7, 147–8, 170
  Jersey English 170–1
  Mainland Norman 20
  Picard 20
L'Assemblîée d'Jèrriais 73–4, 77, 94
assibilation of intervocalic [r] 26 n11, 27 n16,
  29, 33–4, 103, 120, 129–31, 135
attitudes 4, 15, 23 n7, 41, 49, 59 n11, 62–7,
  68, 69, 81, 85, 183
auxiliaries
  English 110
  French 109, 109 n10, 110
  Jèrriais 101, 109–10, 109 n10
  Latin 110
  Mainland Norman 110
  Regional French of Jersey 158

borrowings 1, 80–2, 104 n5, 139, 148, 154,
  184
  from Celtic 82, 150
  from English 23, 30, 81–2, 83 n15, 84,
    103, 118–22, 127–8, 142, 143, 144, 145,
    146, 147, 148, 149–50, 149 n14, 152–3,
    154, 166, 170, 178, 182
  from French 22, 81–2, 84, 103, 104, 111,
    118, 142, 145, 146, 148, 149–50, 152–3,
    157 n2, 173 n9, 175, 176 n14, 176–8, 179
  from Germanic 81

from Italian 81
from Jèrriais 164, 173, 173 n9
from Latin 81
from Norse 7 n3
from the Regional French of Jersey
  173 n9
from Samoan 81
from Turkish 120

calques
  in Jèrriais 82, 82 n14, 83, 84, 103, 104,
    122–7, 128, 144, 147, 161–2
  in Jersey English 168, 170, 171
  in the Regional French of Jersey 158,
    161–3, 165, 166
  in Welsh 126
Census of Jersey
  1989 5, 16, 16 n24, 38–9, 45, 48, 50 n4,
    50 n5, 51, 61 n12, 132 n24, 185
  1996 7 n1, 15–16
Congrès des Parlers Normands et Jèrriais 75,
  77, 79, 80

'danger of death' question 98
dialect mixing 40, 48, 103, 128–36, 140, 155
Dictionnaire Jersiais–Français (DJF) 27, 43,
  53, 54, 73, 76, 78, 87, 98 n2, 100, 101,
  104, 121, 131, 138, 141, 143, 144, 145,
  146, 147, 148, 154, 162, 164, 165,
  165 n5, 166, 175, 176, 179
diglossia 65 n18, 94, 156, 183, 187
diphthongization 18, 19, 23, 26 n12, 28,
  30–3, 35, 36, 103, 129, 131–5, 149,
  149 n4
domains, linguistic 6, 15, 16, 22, 43, 57, 58,
  59, 65, 65 n18, 68, 71, 72, 74, 75, 77, 79,
  80, 81, 82, 83, 84, 85, 89, 90, 95, 119,
  121, 139, 140–55, 145 n9, 178, 183, 188
Don Balleine Trust 75–7, 78, 79
donor-language 83
  English 140, 147, 149, 152–3, 178
  French 82, 140, 149, 152–3, 178

education *see also* schools 12, 64, 66, 68, 71,
  77–9, 89, 93, 94, 96, 138, 149, 154 n17,
  167, 185, 187, 188, 189
  evening classes 60, 77–8, 91, 138, 187
Eisteddfod 77, 94
extension of meaning 127–8, 146, 153

INDEX OF AUTHORS

Sjögren, Albert 36
Spence, Nicol C. W. 4, 7 n3, 19, 22, 23, 24, 24n9, 27, 28, 29, 30, 30 n17, 31, 33, 34, 34 n21, 34 n22, 34 n25, 35–6, 36–7, 38, 40, 41, 42, 43, 76, 81 n13, 118, 118 n18, 119, 129, 130, 131, 132 n25, 132 n26, 135, 155, 157, 165
Spencer, Caroline 78
Spolsky, Bernard 70, 72, 73, 73 n4, 85, 87, 188
Stead, John 10
Stevens, Joan 9, 10, 12, 15
Stowell, Brian 69 n20, 96 n23, 187, 187 n2
Swain, Merril 186
Syvret, Marguerite 9, 10, 12, 15

Tapley, Joan 76
Taylor, Donald M. 182
Thomas, Alan R. 189 n5
Thomason, Sarah G. 2, 107, 136, 184
Thomson, Derrick S. 149
Timm, Lenora A. 143

Tomlinson, Harry 169
Tosco, Mauro 108 n8
Trudgill, Peter 62, 97 n1, 98, 135, 136
Tuaillon, Gaston 190

Uttley, John 12

Vago, Robert M. 128
Vakhtin, Nikolai 2
Van Buren, Paul 136–7, 184
Vibert, Brian 77
Vincent, Nigel 110

Watson, Seosamh 62
Weinreich, Uriel 156
Whaley, Lindsay W. 2, 63, 64, 68
Williams, Glyn 46
Winter, Werner 57 n9, 83
Wolf, Lothar 189

Zepeda, Ofelia 64 n15, 95

INDEX OF LANGUAGES AND DIALECTS